Postcard History Series

Carroll and Haralson Counties

in Vintage Postcards

WEST GEORGIA REGIONAL LIBRARY SYSTEM
Neva Lomason Memorial Library

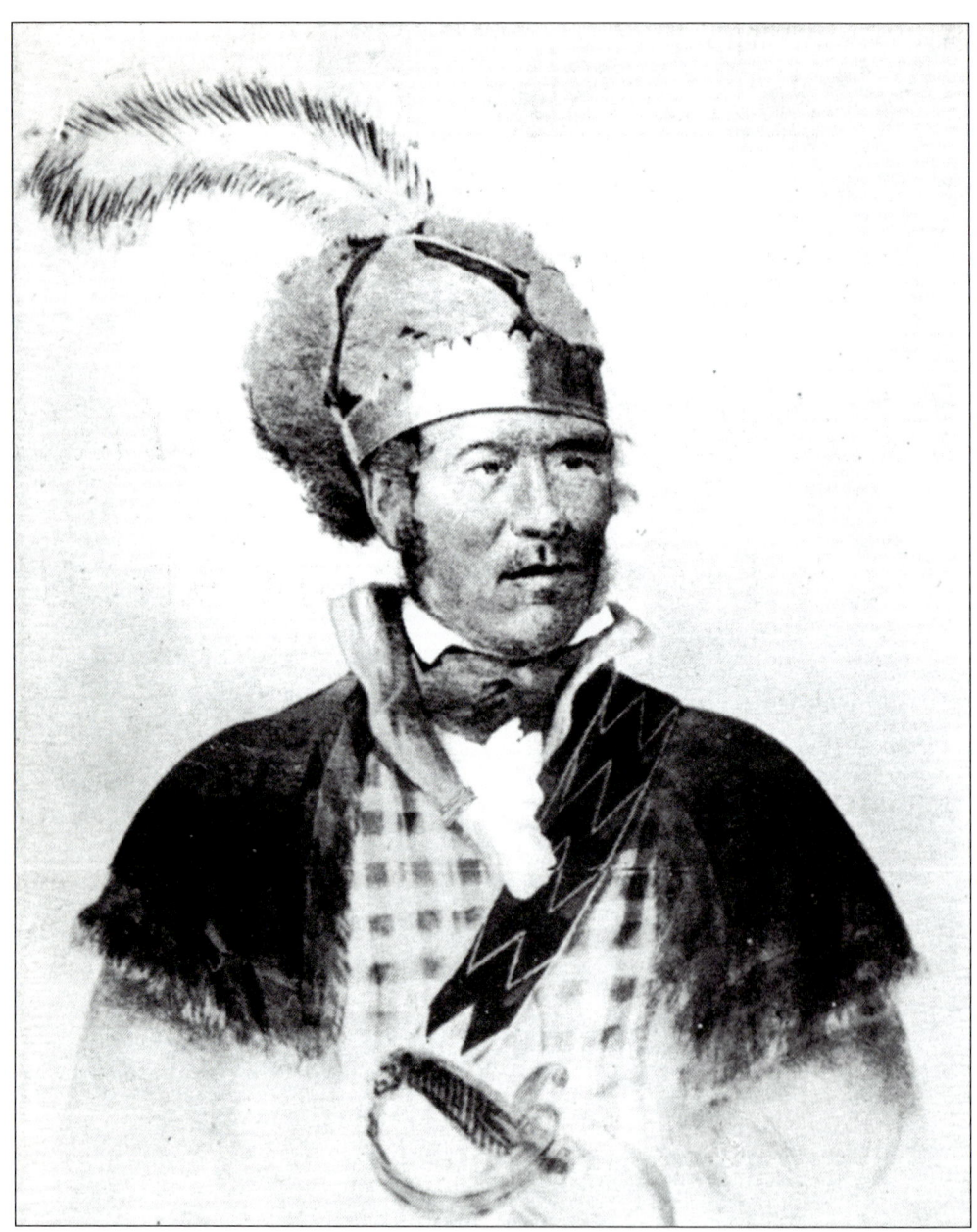

Chief William McIntosh, featured in this 1910 postcard image by Newman Hungerford, was one of the most important figures to shape Georgia's history. His mother was a full-blooded Creek, and his father was of the Scottish McIntosh clan. Chief McIntosh was made a brigadier general for his heroism in the Creek Indian War serving under Gen. Andrew Jackson, and he was the signer of all treaties between the Creeks and American government between 1805 and 1825. These treaties were to include some 20 million acres of land for Georgia. Chief McIntosh was murdered at his home, Lochchau Talau, on May 1, 1825, by a group of hostile Creeks who were upset with his signing of the latest treaty, which included the lands to become Carroll and Haralson Counties. The area of his home and subsequent murder is now known as the McIntosh Reserve and is located near Whitesburg in Carroll County.

Postcard History Series

Carroll and Haralson Counties
in Vintage Postcards

Dr. David N. Wiggins

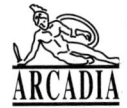

Copyright © 2004 by Dr. David N. Wiggins
ISBN 0-7385-1714-3

Published by Arcadia Publishing
Charleston SC, Chicago IL, Portsmouth NH, San Francisco CA

Printed in Great Britain

Library of Congress Catalog Card Number: 2004110905

For all general information contact Arcadia Publishing at:
Telephone 843-853-2070
Fax 843-853-0044
E-mail sales@arcadiapublishing.com
For customer service and orders:
Toll-Free 1-888-313-2665

Visit us on the internet at http://www.arcadiapublishing.com

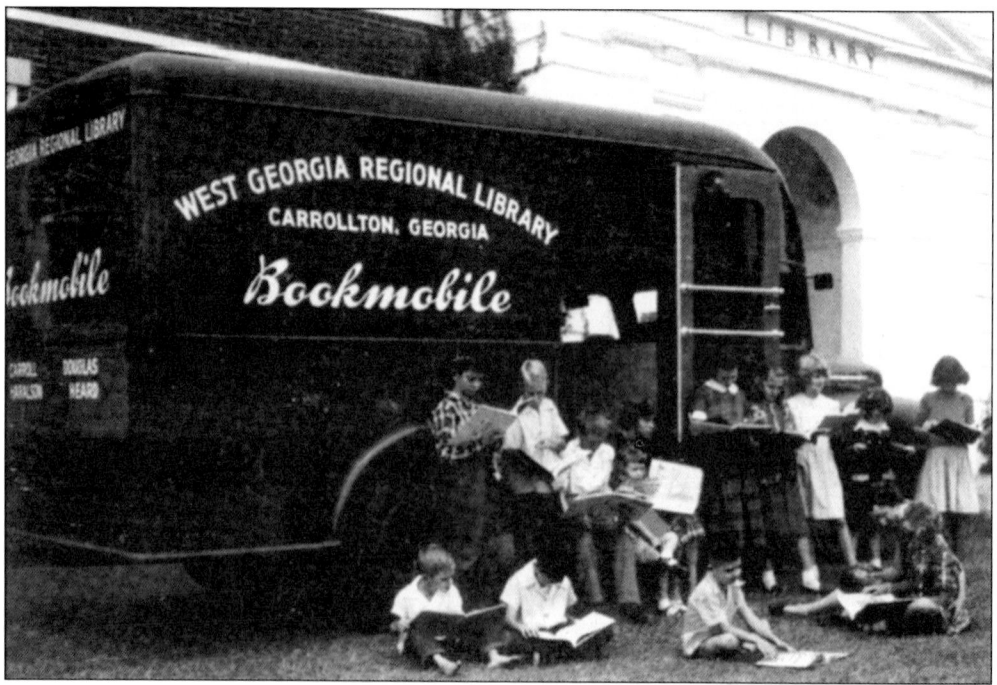

"Carroll, Douglas, Haralson, and Heard Counties are served by the West Georgia Regional Library and its famous bookmobile, with annual circulation figures above 260,000 through schools and public library service." This c. 1950s card features children in front of the bookmobile in front of the old Sanford Library at West Georgia College. The regional library, started by Miss Edith Foster, began in the basement of this building in 1944. (Courtesy of the City of Whitesburg.)

Contents

Acknowledgments   6

Introduction   7

Carroll County

1.   Bowdon   9

2.   Carrollton   25

3.   Roopville   77

4.   Temple   81

5.   Villa Rica   87

6.   Whitesburg   93

Haralson County

7.   Bremen   97

8.   Buchanan   105

9.   Tallapoosa   107

Index   127

Acknowledgments

The great majority of images for the book are from postcards owned by the author; however, the book would not be possible without the support of others who collect cards and those who helped with captions. All involved have the same desire, to preserve and share our heritage, and to all those who helped I wish to extend my sincerest thanks. Gary Doster, the preeminent collector of vintage Georgia cards, has over the years become an inspiration, a mentor, and a dear friend. He has published eight books on vintage postcards in Georgia, and his willingness to share his images is legendary. Jim and Judy Rowell are the epitome of local historians—their families have long lived in the area, and their assistance, resources, and friendship will always be remembered and appreciated by the author and his family. I also offer a special thanks to my wife, Sara, for her support and patience.

A special thanks is extended to other contributors: Chief Jimmy Bearden, John Beckvermitt, Violette Denney, Norma Gray, Susan Patton Hamersky, Imogene Carnes Harris, Ruth Holder, Doyce Lee, Carol Barnes McWhorter, Michael Miller, Betty Jo Parsons, the John Pate family, Alan Pearce, Sam Pyle, the Spivey Collection, Mignon Wessinger, Classical Photography, Haralson County Historical Society, and the City of Whitesburg. Special thanks to Arcadia Publishing and in particular, Katie White and Laura New, for all their help in making this project a reality.

INTRODUCTION

Carroll and Haralson Counties in Vintage Postcards mainly features images from the early 20th century. Many of these images have not been previously published in any modern work. These cards represent the author's intensive love affair of local history and his passion for collecting postcards. The book includes images of street scenes, railroad scenes, public buildings, schools, churches, local businesses, college views, advertisement cards, and real photo cards of individuals. There are many images that one would love to include if this were a pure history work; however, postcard images are generally what the photographer or artist thought could make a profit, or they were images of particular interest to the maker. The creation of relatively cheap postcard cameras in the early 1910s allowed for an explosion of personal photo cards. Certainly, this book will not show every card available for the area, as no such thing as a complete collection exists. It is the author's desire that the images presented will give the viewer a better understanding of local postcards and their importance to the preservation of the area's visual history.

Postcards tell stories. Visually they show us the way things were. Occasionally, information on the back of the card gives light to mystery, romance, and humor of an area, an era, or of a personal exchange. Those who have collected cards for any length of time understand that many historical images of early 1900s life remain only because of the popularity of postcards of that time. With no radio or television, and with very little photography used in newspapers, the real shared images of the time came in the form of postcards. Postcards were so popular that the United States post office for the fiscal year ending in June 1908, showed over 677 million postcards mailed in the country that year—amazing for a population of 88 million! They were inexpensive and offered the average person local views, as well as those of exotic places, people, and things. It is no wonder that postcard clubs sprang up all over the world and as a result have saved images for posterity. Although some postcards were mass-produced, many personal family cards would only consist of one or two prints. The penny postcard no longer exists today, and rare vintage postcards can run in the hundreds of dollars to collectors. With this in mind, the author wishes to share his and like-minded individuals' collections of postcard images of Carroll and Haralson Counties.

The area of land to become Carroll County was created from Creek Indian lands that were originally sold to the State of Georgia by Chief William McIntosh, who was subsequently murdered by fellow Creeks for this act. An additional treaty and supplementary article with the Creek Nation were signed in 1826, paving the way for the state's acquisition of lands in western

Georgia. Carroll County land boundaries were established June 9, 1825, by an act of the Georgia General Assembly. However, the naming of the county did not occur until Governor Troup, McIntosh's cousin, signed an act on December 11, 1826. The county was named for Charles Carroll of Maryland, who was the last surviving delegate to have signed the Declaration of Independence. In 1827, a land lot near Sand Hill became known as "Old Carrollton." In 1829 the legislature designated Carrollton as the county seat, and the town was thus incorporated.

Haralson County was created from Carroll and Polk Counties on January 26, 1856, by an act of the Georgia General Assembly. Originally the business of establishing the county seat was done in Tallapoosa, then a part of Carroll County, but the county seat was then designated to be Buchanan. The chapter of incorporation was granted for Buchanan on December 22, 1857. Haralson County was named for Georgia statesman and general Hugh A. Haralson, of Troup County, who died in 1854.

The counties of Carroll and Haralson have a long-standing geographic relationship. However, family, business, and ideology have made them long-standing partners, as well. It is quite natural and fitting that the two areas be included in this endeavor. It is the author's sincerest hope that the images and the stories these postcards tell will be enjoyed by the viewer and promote interest in the hobby, thereby saving images for future generations. My apologies to the areas of the counties that are not featured, such as Mt. Zion and Waco; to date, the author has been unable to find postcards of these areas. Any mistakes or omissions are not intentional and the author's objective was to publish an accurate and factual account of the postcards presented within the work. Queries, suggestions, or corrections concerning the work should be directed to the author.

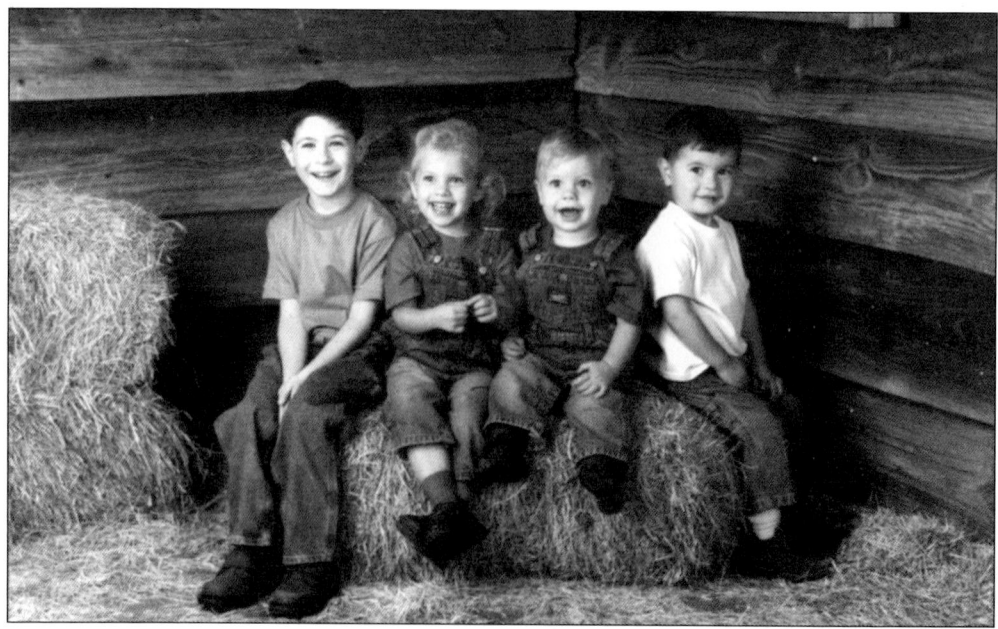

This book is dedicated to the author's four grandchildren, all born and raised in Carroll County. This is a modern postal card sent at Christmas 2003 featuring four of Santa's elves: (from left to right) John Knight Pate, Karis Quinn Askin, Ethan Errol Askin, and Asher Knight Pate. (Courtesy of Classical Photography.)

One
BOWDON

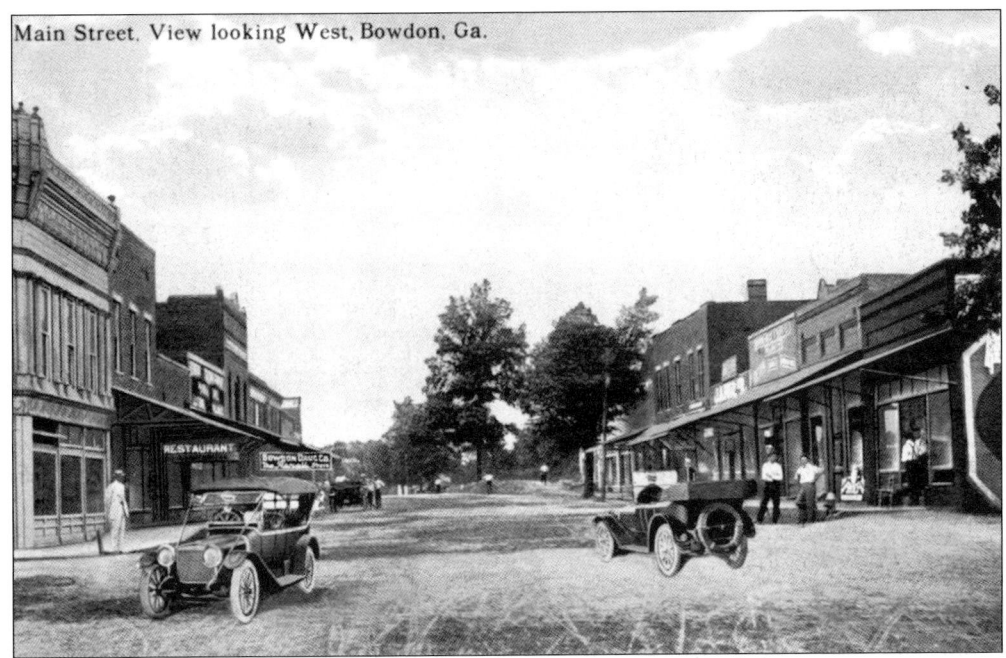

In 1848, citizens honored Alabama Congressman Franklin Welch Bowdon, who assisted the town in acquiring a post office, by naming their town for him. This postcard, published by Bowdon Drug Co., features an early view of Main Street looking west in downtown Bowdon. On the left can be seen the Bowdon Bank, a restaurant sign, and the Bowdon Drug Co. The cars are artistically drawn into the real image of downtown to enhance the card.

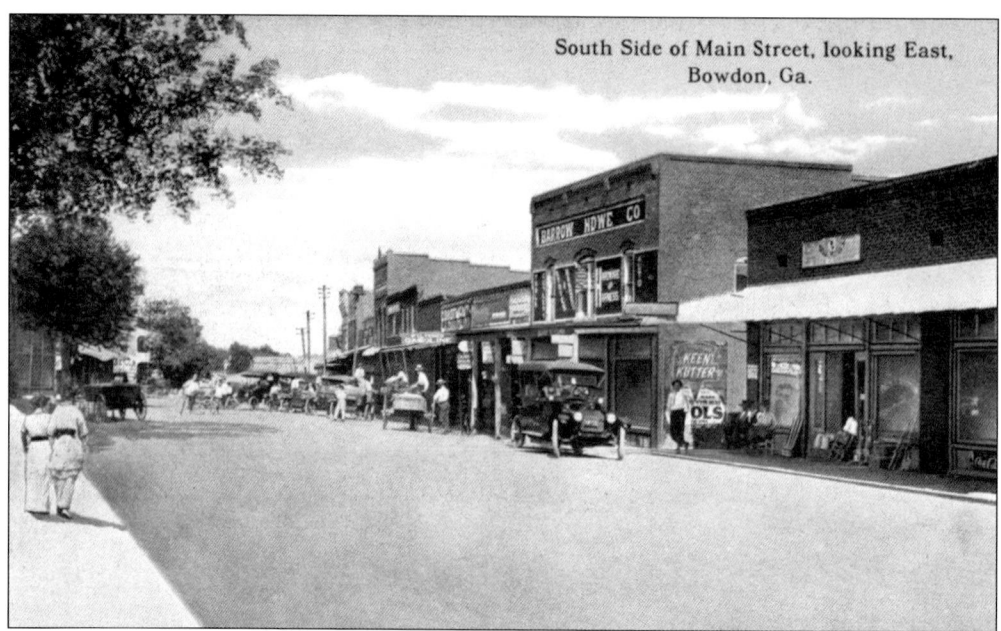

Published by Bowdon Drug Co., "The Rexall Store," this postcard features the south side of Main Street looking eastward. On the right side of the card can be seen the Beck and Adamson Store and the Barrow Hardware Store. Signs include advertisements for tools, cutlery, stoves, ranges, hardware, harness, wagons, and automobiles. Bicycles, wagons, and vintage autos can be seen in this card.

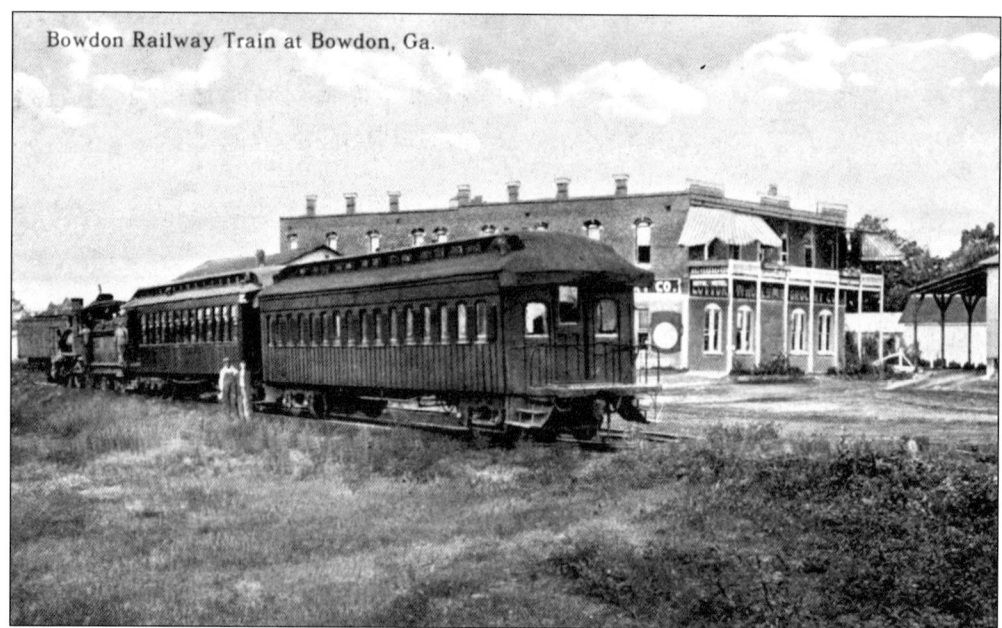

Postmarked in July 1932 and published by Bowdon Drug Co., this image is of the Bowdon railway train. Behind the train is the Lovvorn Wholesale Grocery Company and the Royal Hotel. The message on the back reads, "I am having a swell time down here. We are having lots of fun and the greatest eats ever. Hope I don't put on any extra lbs. Pearl."

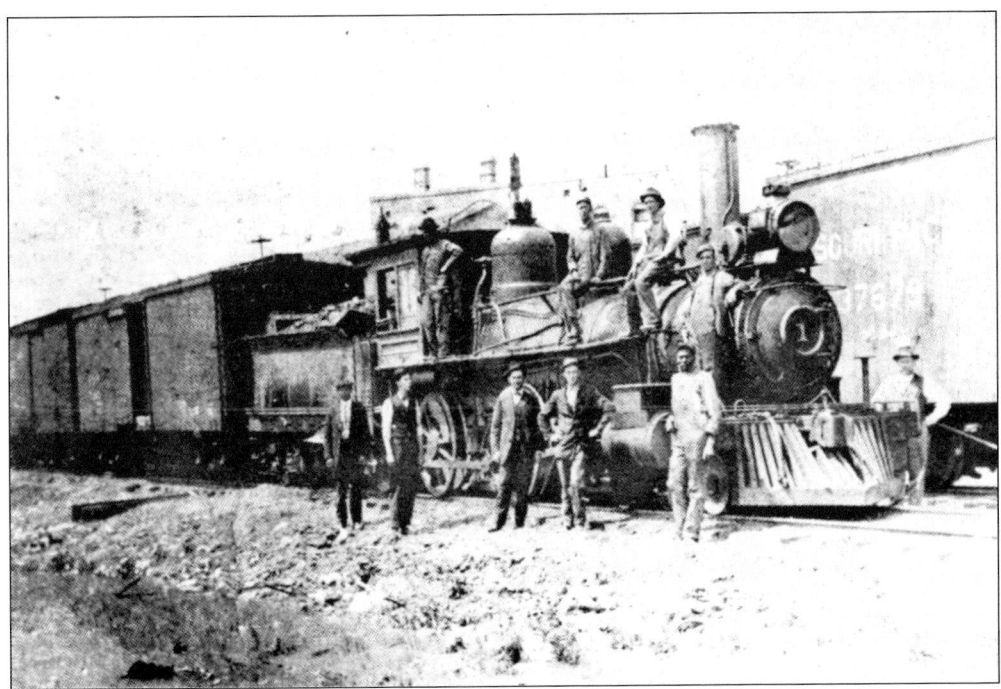

Dr. J.L. Lovvorn and other Bowdon citizens organized the Bowdon Railroad in the early 1900s. Bought in 1941 by Mr. Will Roop, it was disbanded about 1962. This view shows Engine #1 on the tracks in Bowdon. The roof of the Royal Hotel in Bowdon can be seen in the background. The Bowdon Historical Society published this commemorative card.

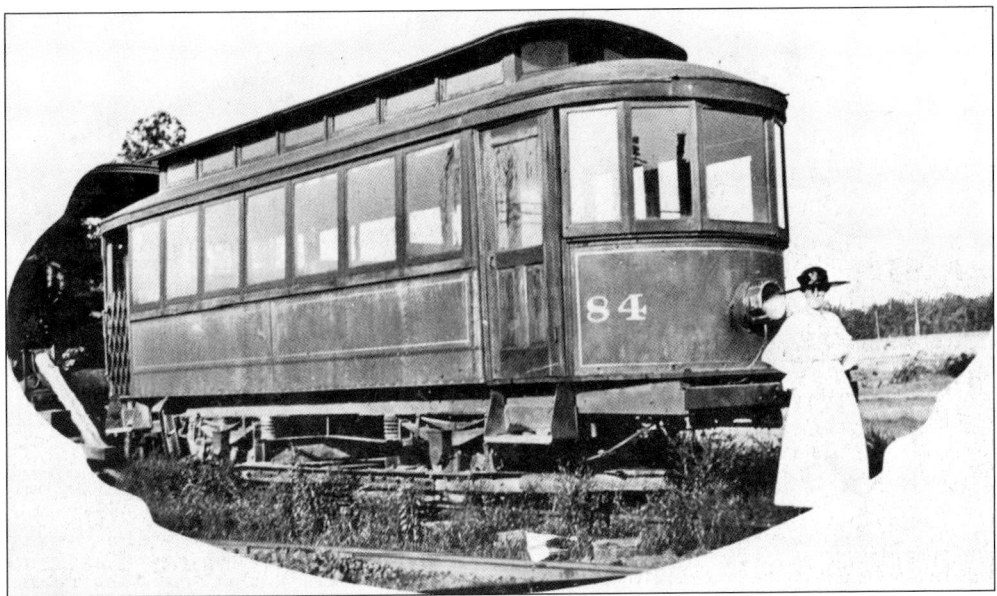

This photo card was taken by Oscar F. Jackson and given to his sister Myrtie Jackson of Carrollton in the summer of 1917. This trolley car was the only transportation from Carrollton to Bowdon by rail. Leaving Carrollton for Bowdon Junction, passengers would then transfer from the Central of Georgia Railroad to this trolley to Bowdon. (Courtesy of Judy and Jim Rowell.)

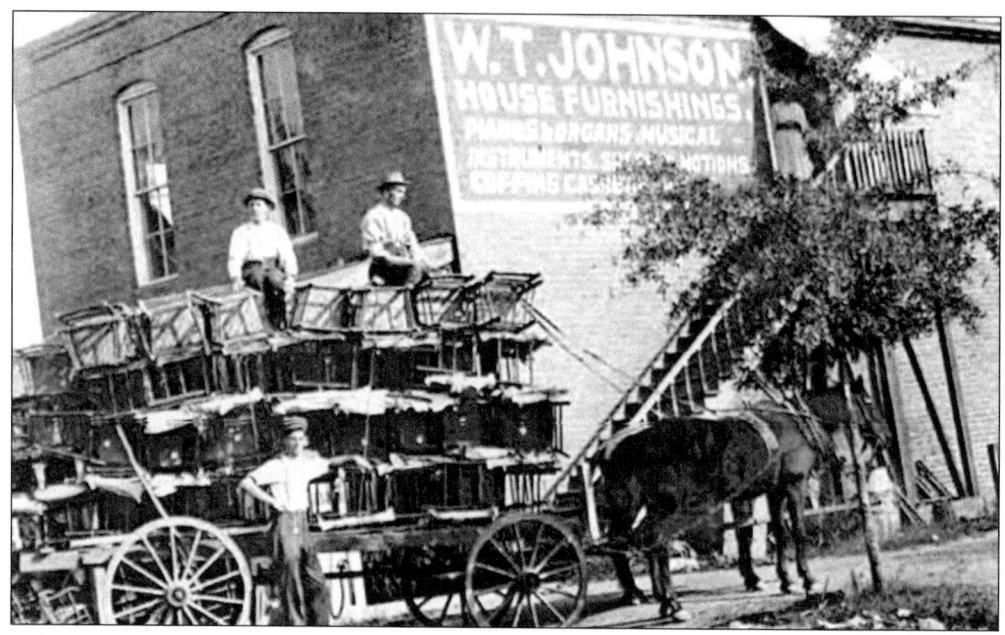

This photo from about 1903 shows the W.T. Johnson Store, which featured house furnishings, musical instruments, and coffins. Will T. Johnson Jr. is standing beside the loaded wagon of chairs. (Courtesy of Judy and Jim Rowell.)

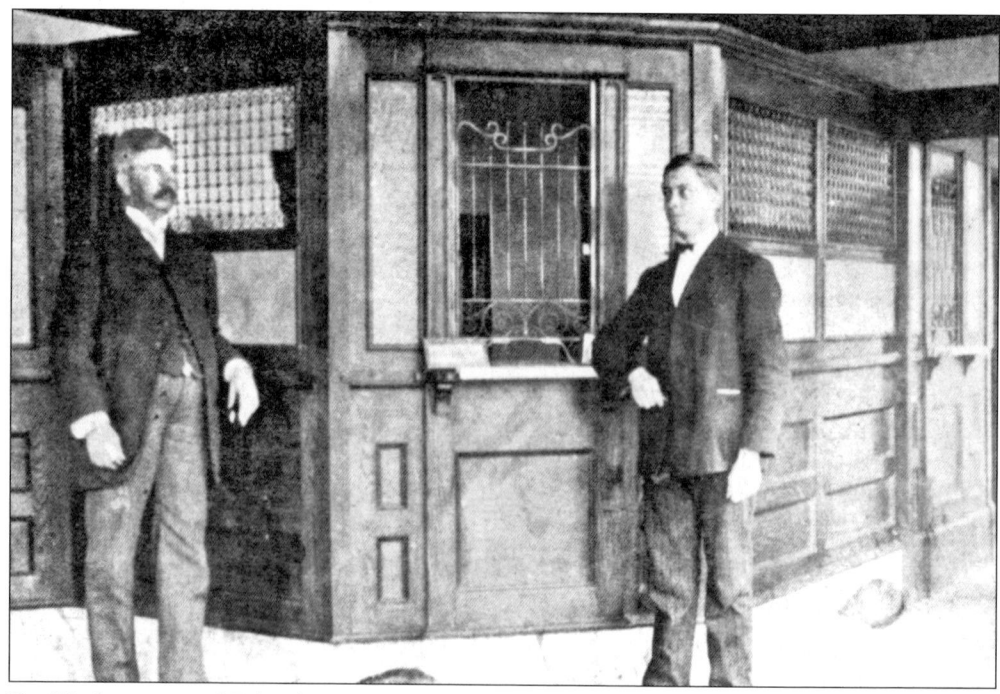

Dr. J.L. Lovvorn and E.A. Fleming are featured in this image of the interior view of the Bank of Bowdon, c. 1910. The bank was organized around 1900 by E.J. Dunn but was purchased by a group of leading citizens that included Dr. Lovvorn. E.A. Fleming was a cashier and later became president of the bank. (Courtesy of Judy and Jim Rowell.)

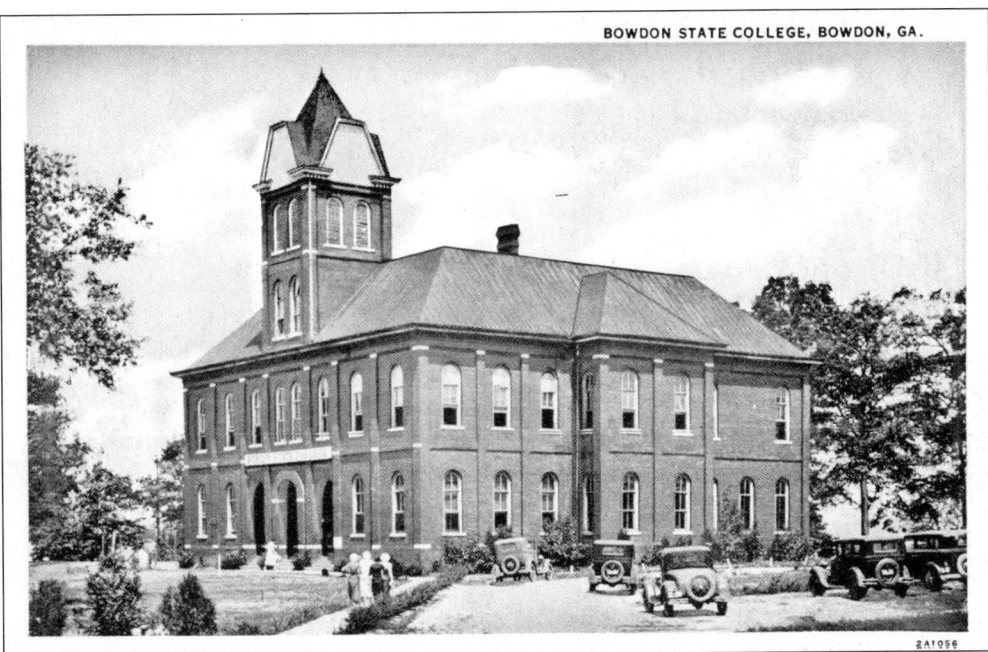

Bowdon Collegiate Institute was chartered by Charles A. McDaniel and John M. Richardson on December 22, 1857. The brick building seen in the postcard was completed in 1901 and continued as a college until 1936. It was used as a school until it was demolished around 1960. Bowdon Drug Co. published this postcard c. 1930.

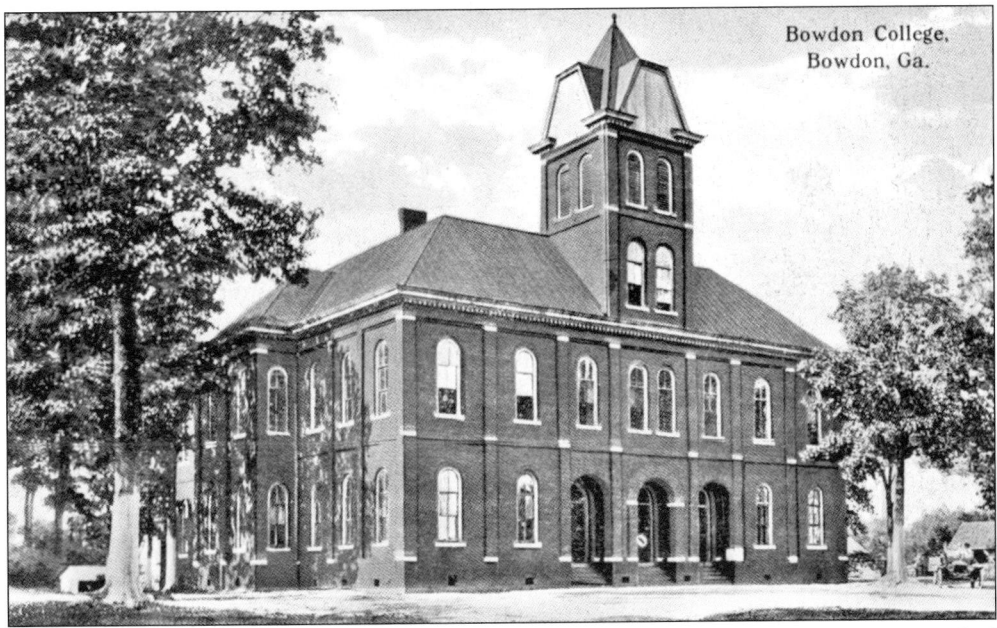

Published by the Bowdon Drug Co, a different view of Bowdon College is shown. Postmarked on December 23, 1915, and addressed to Mr. J.P. Wyatt of Ensley, Alabama, the message reads, "Hello, How are you all—we will not get away from Bowdon before Xmas. Clara." Perhaps this is a student note home to a loved one.

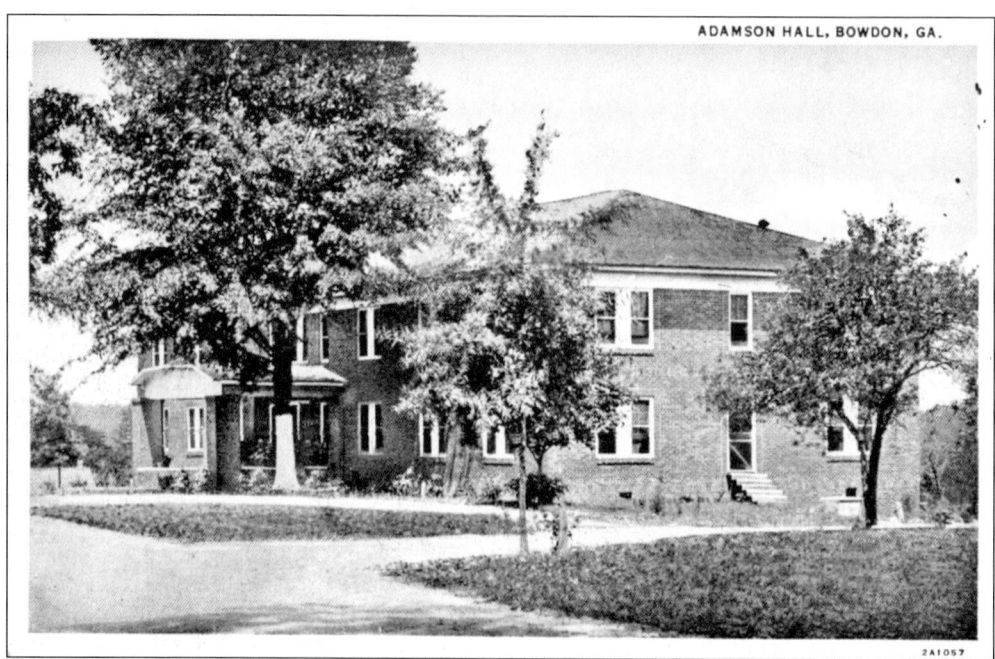

This postcard is a view of Adamson Hall, which was a female dormitory built in 1929 to accommodate up to 100 boarders. The cost of the building was $30,000. The hall was named for Judge William Charles Adamson, born in Bowdon and a graduate of Bowdon College. Judge Adamson went on to serve as a United States congressman for over 20 years. The card is postmarked November 26, 1939, Bowdon.

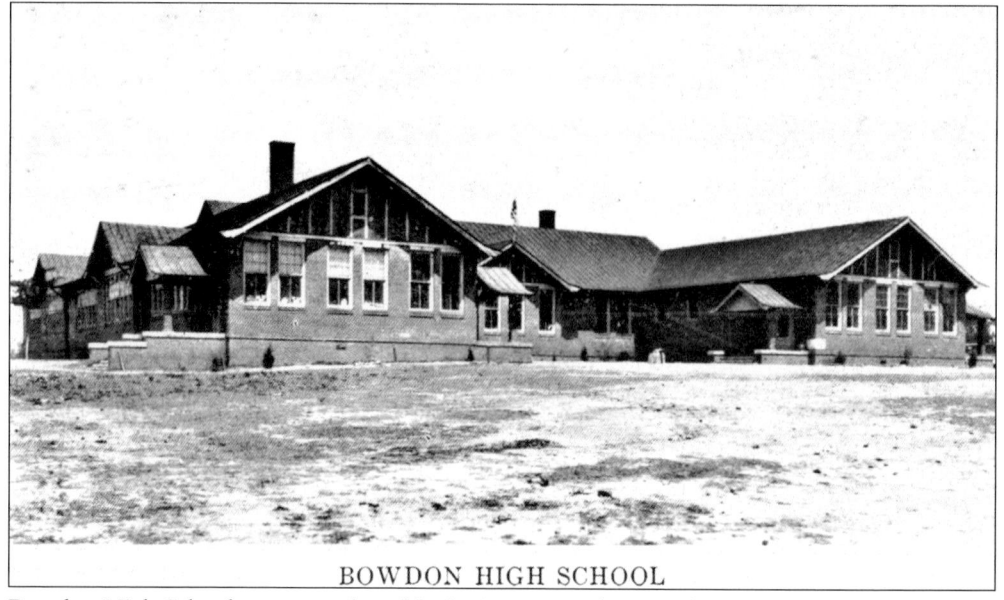

Bowdon High School was moved to this site in 1922 and was at first a junior high school with 300 pupils and 10 teachers. In 1926, the 10th grade was added, and in 1927, the 11th grade was added. Dr. G.W. Camp, president of Bowdon State Normal and Industrial College, became the first supervisor of the school. (Courtesy of Jim and Judy Rowell.)

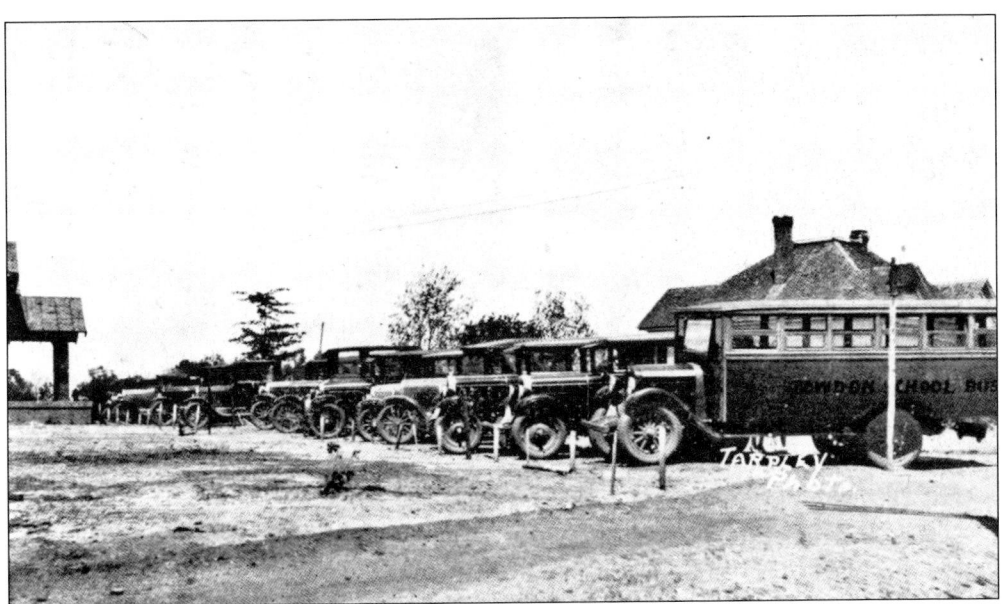

This image shows the transportation fleet at Bowdon High School in 1928. J.W. Tarpley, a local photographer who captured many of the early images of Bowdon, took the photo. He is credited for preserving much of the early visual history of the community. (Courtesy of Jim and Judy Rowell.)

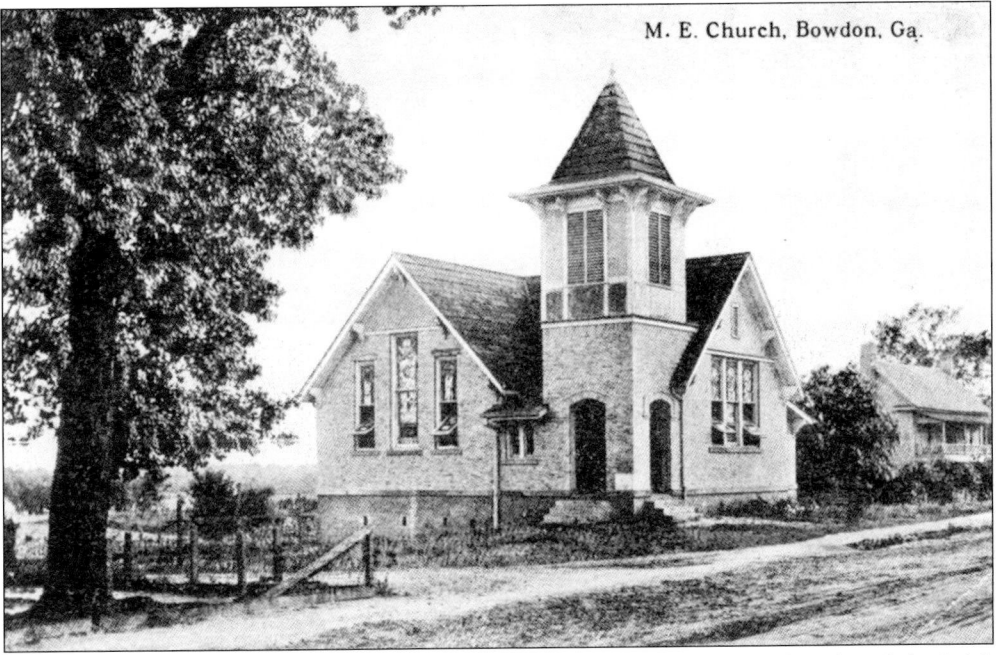

On January 2, 1913, a lot on the corner of College and McElroy was purchased, and the brick Methodist Episcopal Church of Bowdon was completed in February 1914. Rev. Newt T. Crumpton was the first minister, and services were held twice a month. The church served the community for 25 years until it was closed in 1939 after church unification. Bowdon Drug Co. published the card.

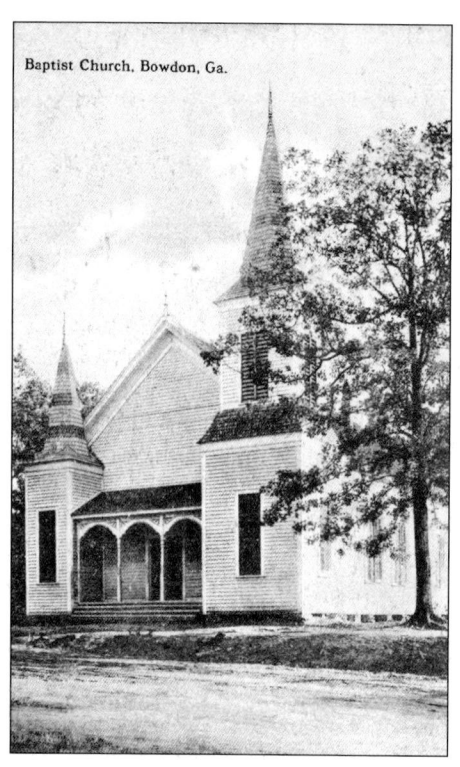

The Bowdon Baptist Church was first erected in Bowdon in 1859. The card shows the second wooden building, which was built in 1894. Published by Bowdon Drug Co. and postmarked on March 13, 1917, it reads, "Thanks for the card. How long ago has it been since you was here. I have been here for 22 years. That is a long time to live in one place. Pryor." (Courtesy of Gary Doster.)

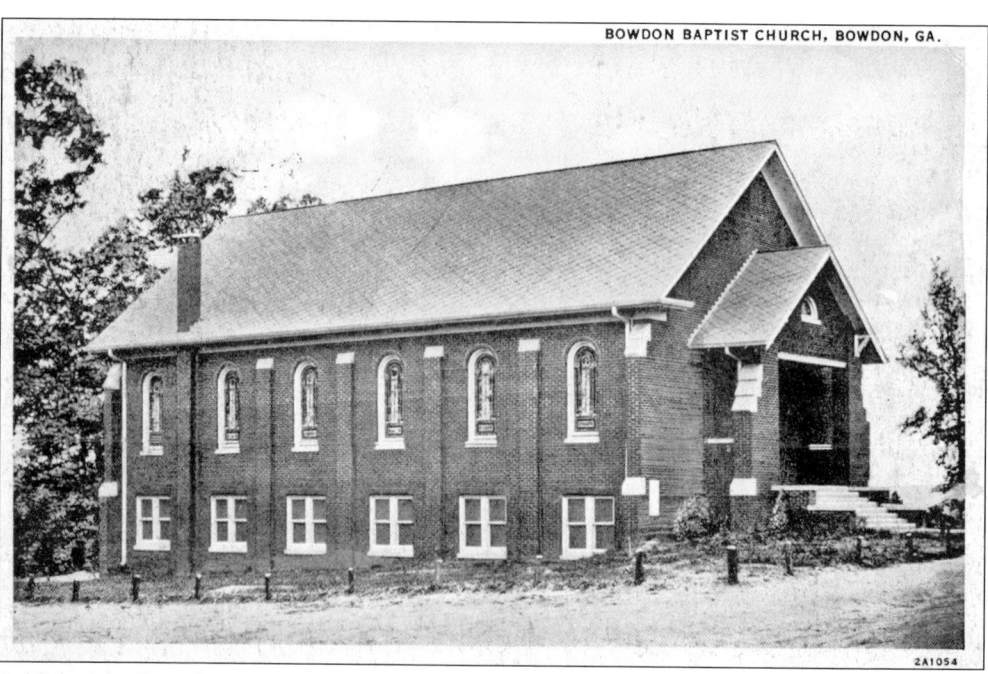

Published by Bowdon Drug Co., this image of the Bowdon Baptist Church shows the brick church building that was constructed in 1931. Postmarked in Bowdon in August 1938, the writer, Caroline, encourages her friend to "have a good time on your vacation and keep those men on the fence."

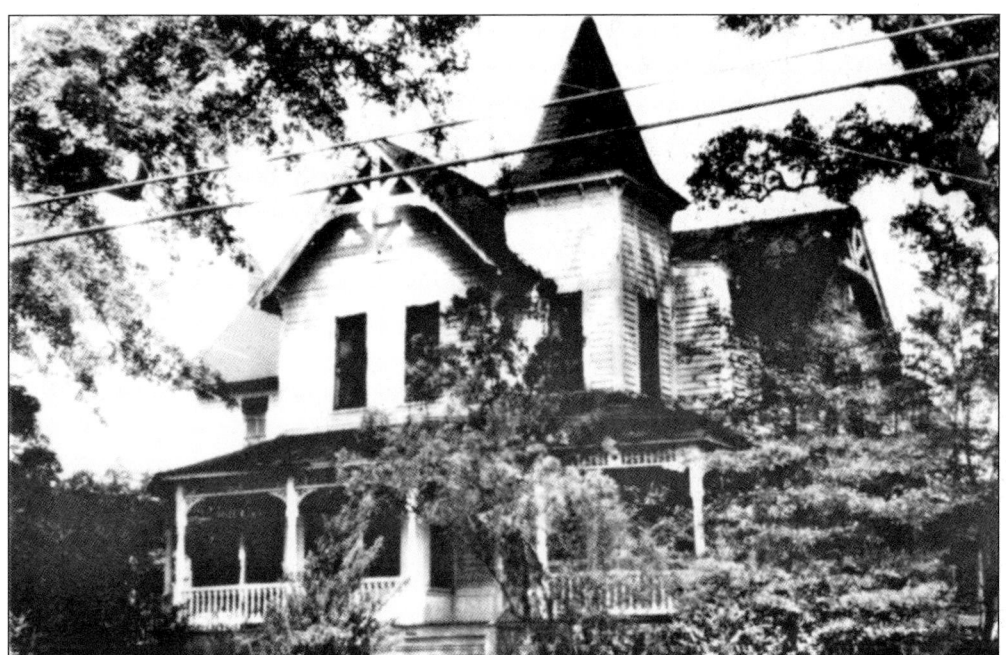

A commemorative card presented by the Bowdon Historical Society features the Bowdon Inn. On the back is written the following: "The Bowdon Inn was built by Dr. Robert Lovvorn. Queen Anne style architecture, it is presently owned by Diana and Jackie Jackson."

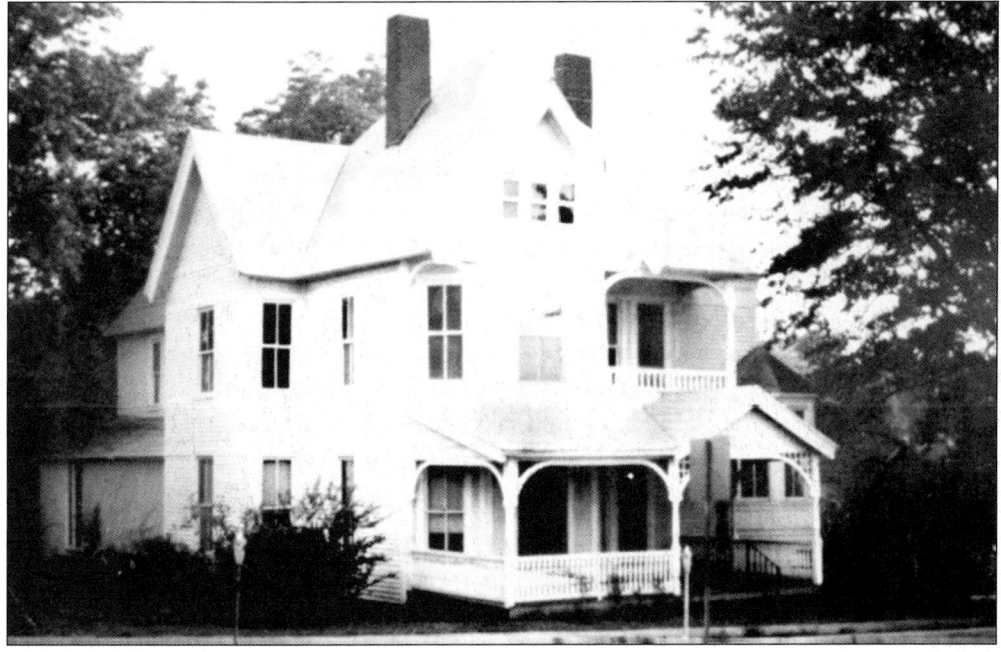

A commemorative card presented by the Bowdon Historical Society features the Lovvorn House and reads as follows: "The James L. Lovvorn house built in 1895–96 according to the plans supplied by George Baker of Knoxville, Tennessee. It is presently owned by the granddaughters of Dr. Lovvorn."

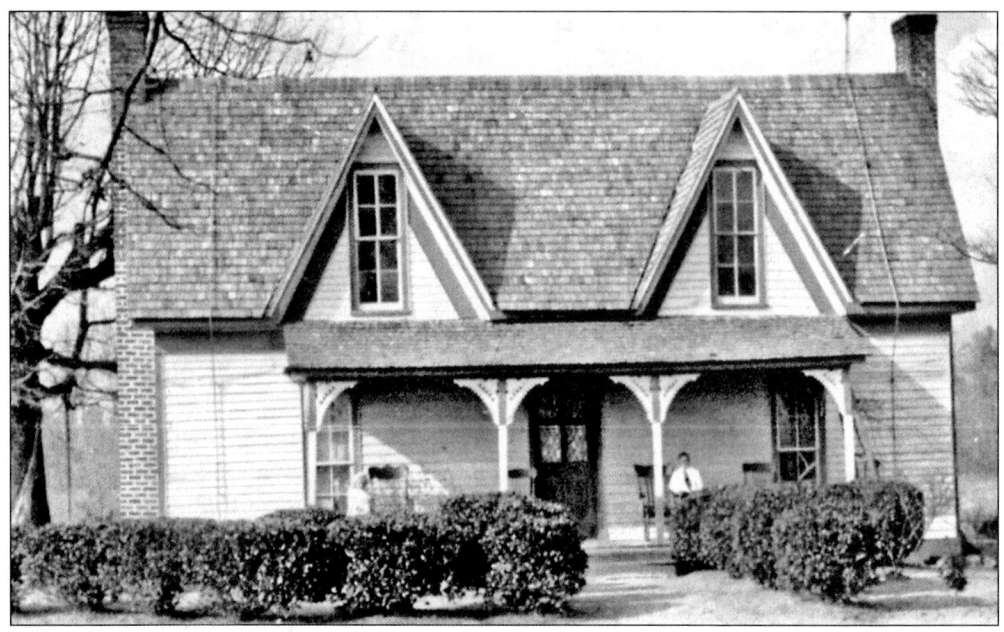

The Price home was located on Bowdon-Tyus Road just outside Bowdon. This was the homeplace for the Price families for many years. The last owners of the Price family were John Thomas Price and his wife, Ella Lee Tuggle. The home and land sold in the early 1960s, and the family moved to the Carrollton-Tyus Road. Later owners included the Wessinger family and Henry Butler. The house burned several years ago. (Courtesy of Alan Pearce.)

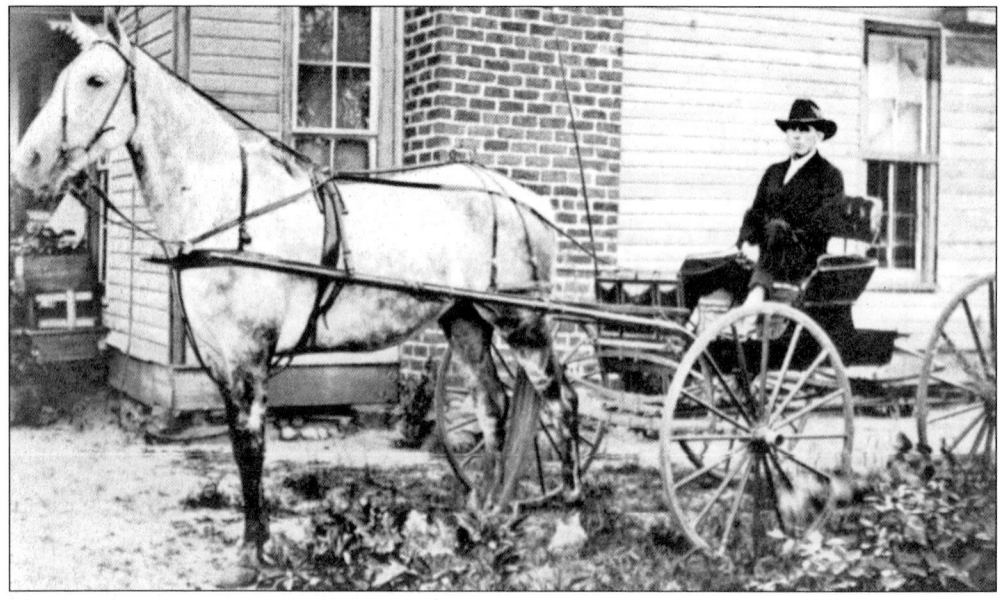

John Thomas Price sits in his horse and buggy outside the Price home on the Bowdon-Tyus Road. He was known to many as "Mr. Johnnie" and was a well-respected and liked member of the Bowdon community. He was a farmer and lifelong resident of Carroll County from his birth in August of 1894 until his death in 1973. He was the son of Winston Brazeal Price and Jerusha Ann Word. (Courtesy of Alan Pearce.)

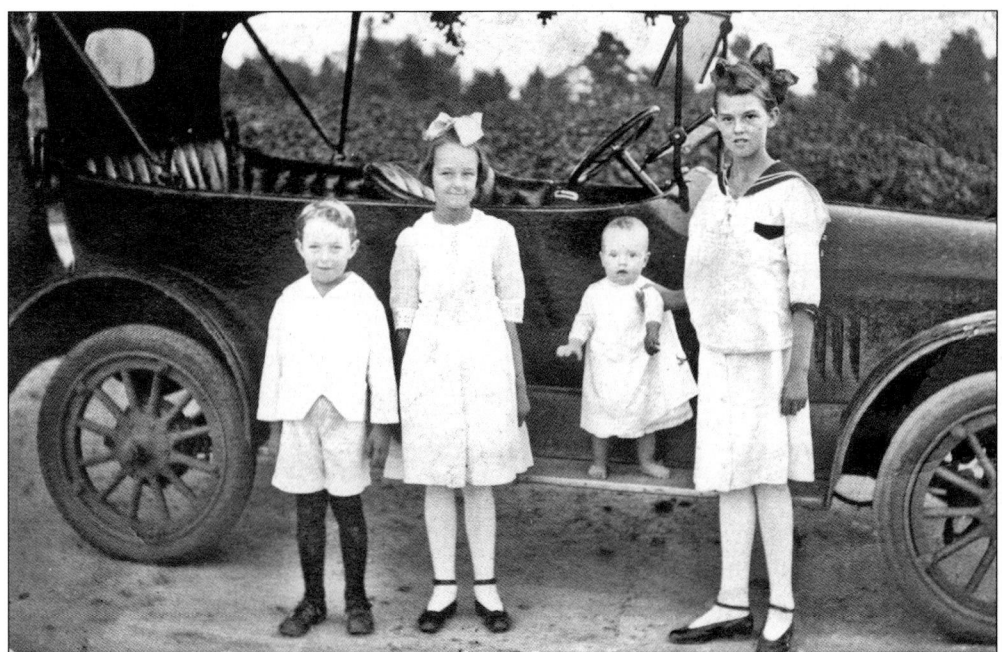

"Bee" and Annie Lee Jackson Copeland were proud of their new Dodge car in 1917. When the photographer came by, they lined their children up for the photo card using the car as a backdrop. The children, from left to right, are Millard, Reba (Lancaster), O.B., and Bessie (Nixon). (Courtesy of Judy and Jim Rowell.)

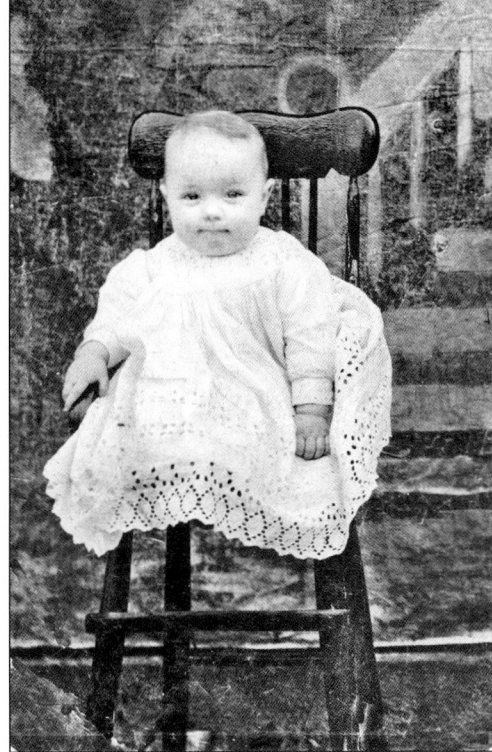

James Millard Copeland was born on July 2, 1911, the first son of J.B. and Annie Lee Jackson Copeland. In May of 1912, his mother mailed this card to her sister, Millie Jackson Lee. The card shows Millard in his white baby dress and his mother tells her sister, "Here's the boy . . . ." She goes on to relate that their father's "folks" had recently visited and attended a singing. (Courtesy of Judy and Jim Rowell.)

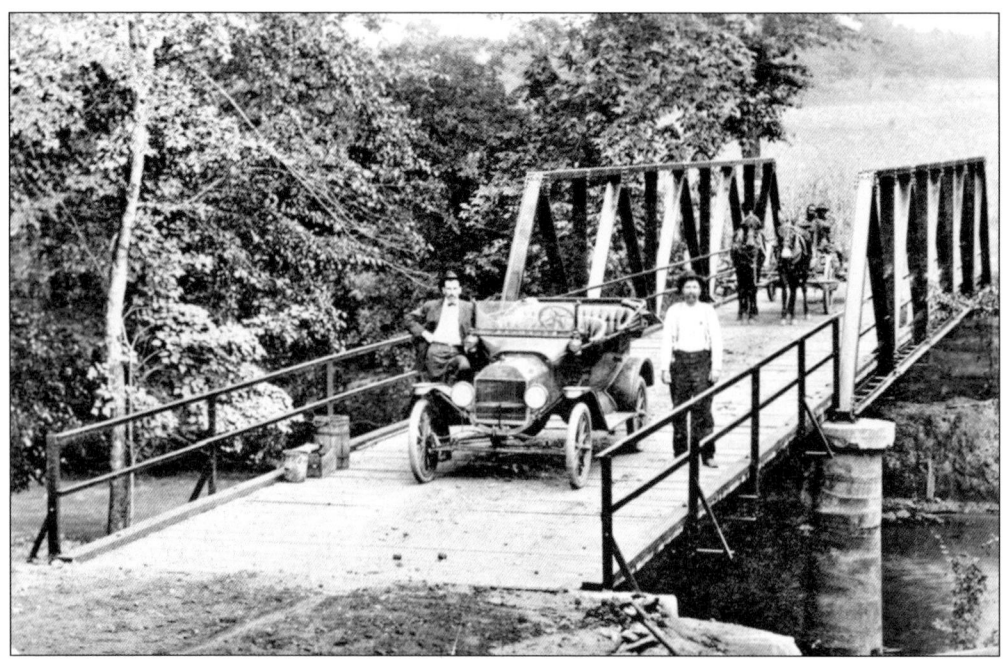

W.B. Rowell, a rural mail carrier for Bowdon, forded the Little Tallapoosa River until the bridge was built on the Bowdon-Tyus Road around 1914. On the day the bridge was opened, Henry Bonner, who lived just past the river and can be seen in the wagon, held his team so Rowell and the mail could be the first to cross the bridge. Note the construction materials located on the bridge. (Courtesy of Judy and Jim Rowell.)

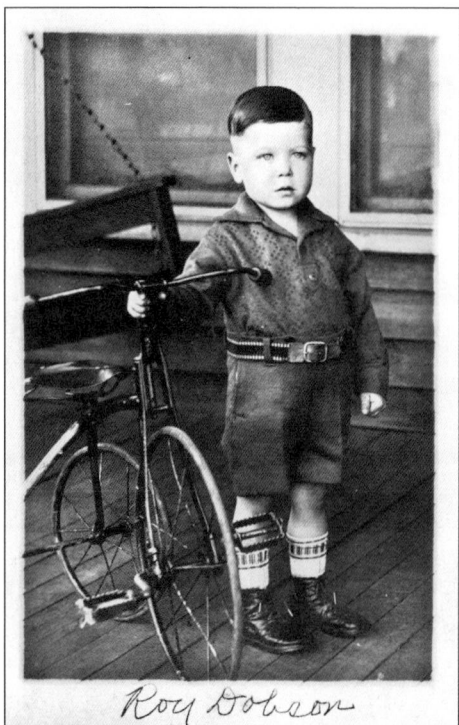

Roy Edward Dobson was the youngest child of George Washington Dobson and Adren Saxon Dobson of Bowdon. He is shown in his short pants and high top shoes with his tricycle in this 1920s postcard. Though it was unknown to him at the time of this photo, it was his destiny to become a B-17–bomber pilot in World War II. (Courtesy of Judy and Jim Rowell.)

This Tarpley photo shows the first airplane to come to Bowdon. It made a forced landing on February 21, 1920, in a cotton field on Tyus Road. The Canadian Curtis biplane drew a large crowd. After repairs were made, the plane took off with pilot C.W. Meyer and Bunt Hood as a passenger. When someone ran across the field in front of the plane, the pilot swerved and the wing hit a tree. No one was hurt. (Courtesy of Judy and Jim Rowell.)

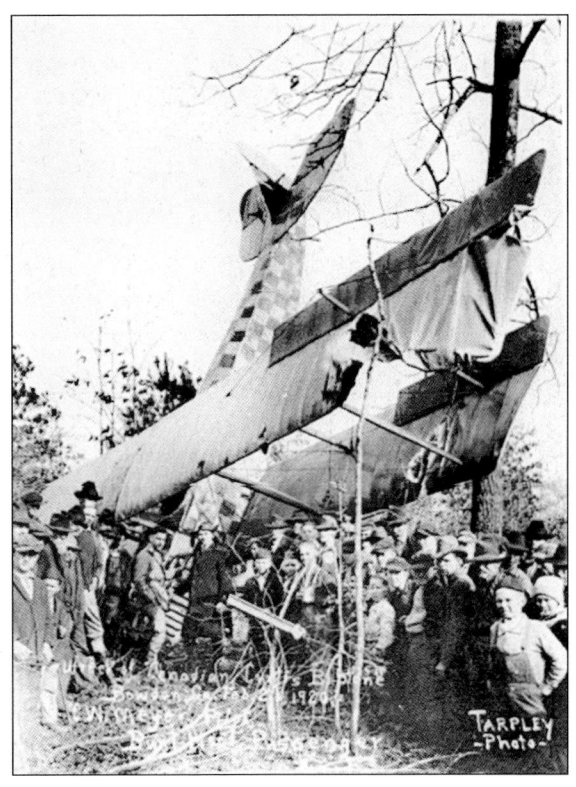

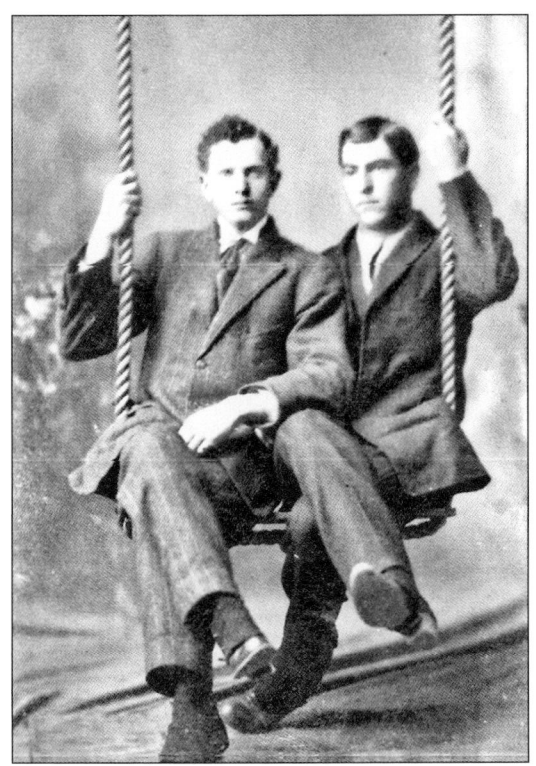

This photo card, taken prior to 1910, is of friends Ode Hinesley (left) and Charles Morrow Douglas (1886–1954). Charles and his three-year-old brother, Lang, were orphaned by the time he was four or five. Raised by their mother's sister, Elizabeth Morrow Strickland, Charles became a lifelong farmer and resident of Carroll County. (Courtesy of Mignon Wessinger.)

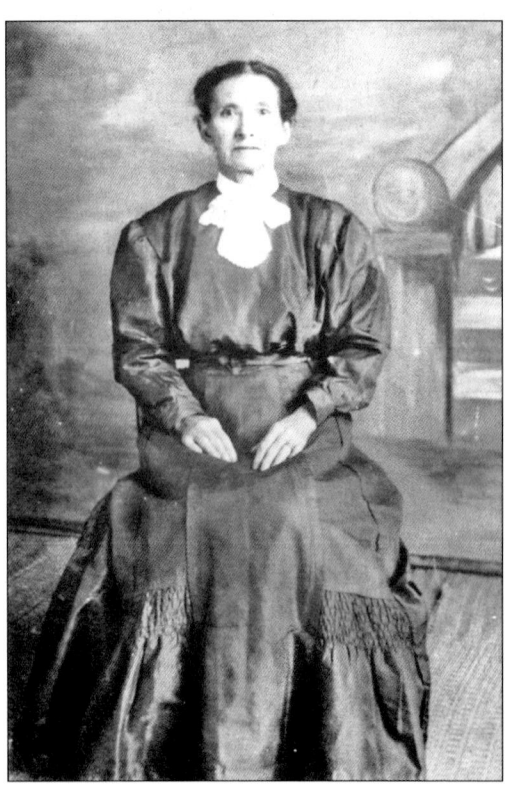

Neaty Ann Johnson (1847–1924), daughter of Samuel and Lucinda Burt Johnson, is listed with her parents in Bowdon in the 1850 census. Her first husband was James Walter Wessinger (1840–1893). He owned and operated a store and brick mill. In 1902, Neaty Ann married W.F. McElroy. This card was dated April 7, 1911. Family members said she enjoyed music, dancing, and an occasional toddy in the evening. (Courtesy of Mignon Wessinger.)

Brothers Alonzo "Lon" Woodrow Wessinger and Edgar Johnson Wessinger are featured in this photo card. Lon, who was a haberdasher by trade, was flamboyant and had a reputation as a "ladies' man." Ed reared his family of 10 in Tyus where he farmed and ran a store, just as his parents had done in Bowdon. One of Ed's sons, named Lon, later ran a grocery store on Maple Street in Carrollton. (Courtesy of Mignon Wessinger.)

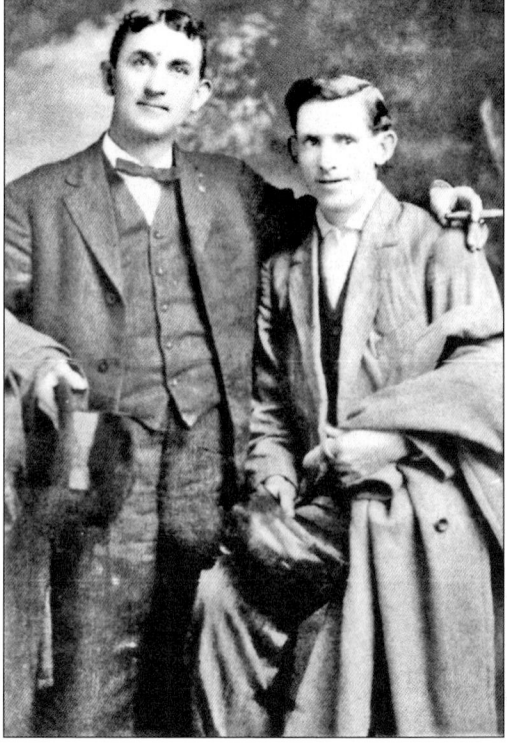

Frances Ann Price was eight months old in 1933 when this photo card was taken. Born on December 1, 1932, she lived her entire life in Carroll County until her death in March of 1990. She was the daughter of John Thomas Price and Ella Lee Tuggle of the Bowdon area. She married Elmer C. Pearce in 1958 and raised two sons, living most of her life in the Farmers High community. (Courtesy of Alan Pearce.)

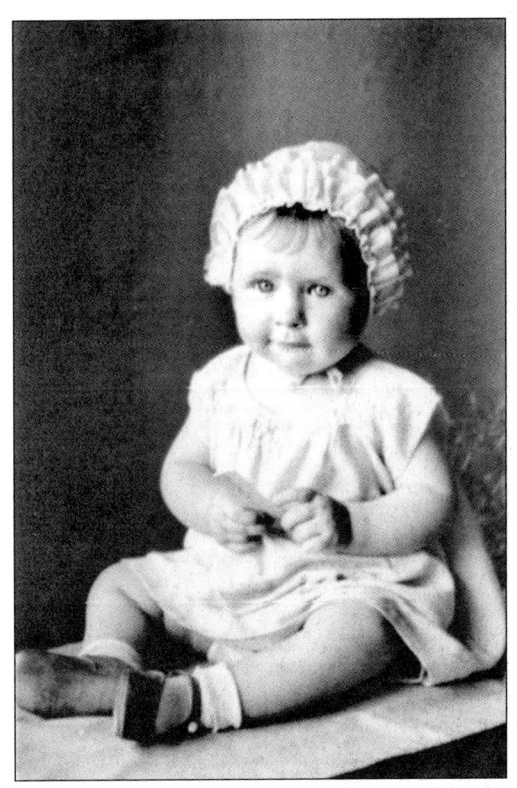

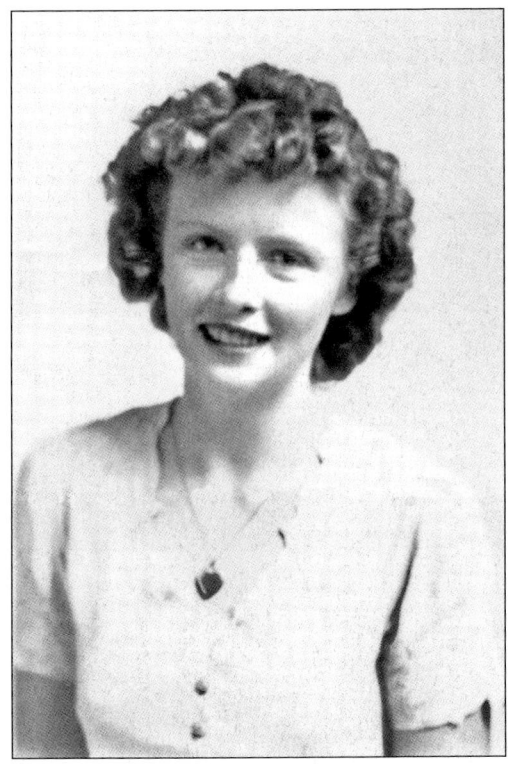

This photo card, dated c. 1949, shows a grown-up Frances Ann Price from the previous baby picture. She lived in the Bowdon area and attended Bowdon High School. A lifelong resident of Carroll County, she was a beautician and a mother, and she worked for many years at the Sewell Manufacturing Plant in Bowdon. (Courtesy of Alan Pearce.)

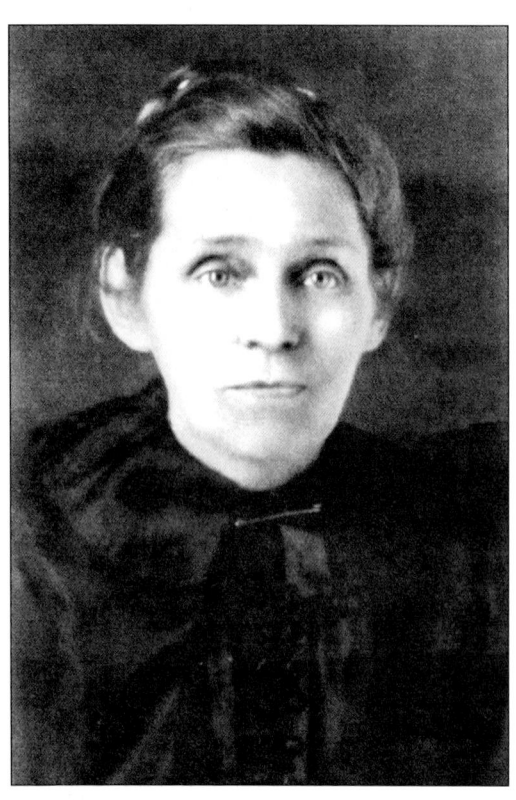

Mrs. Jerusha Ann Word Price lived in the Bowdon area and was a lifelong resident of Carroll County. Born on June 21, 1874, she passed away on July 17, 1955. She was married to Winston Brazeal Price and was the daughter of John Branch Word and Elizabeth Ann Alford. The photo is from the early 1900s. (Courtesy Alan Pearce.)

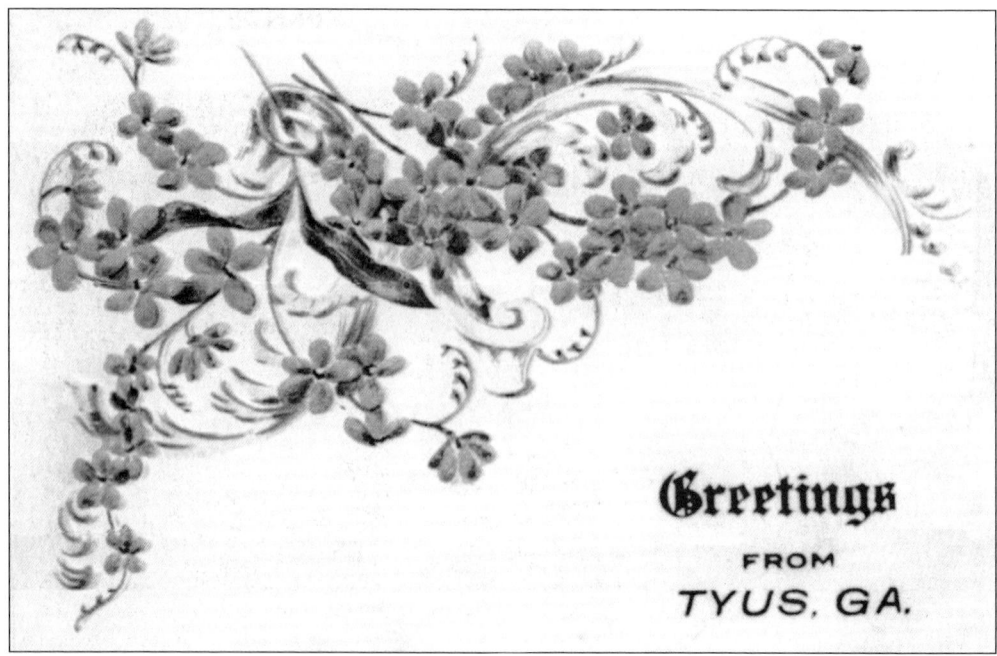

This vintage ornate postcard declares, "Greetings from Tyus, GA." Located near Bowdon, the community of Tyus had a post office in 1892. It is believed that Tyus got its name from a coin toss between Andrew Hallum and Jack Tyus; Jack won. (Courtesy of Norma Gray.)

Two
CARROLLTON

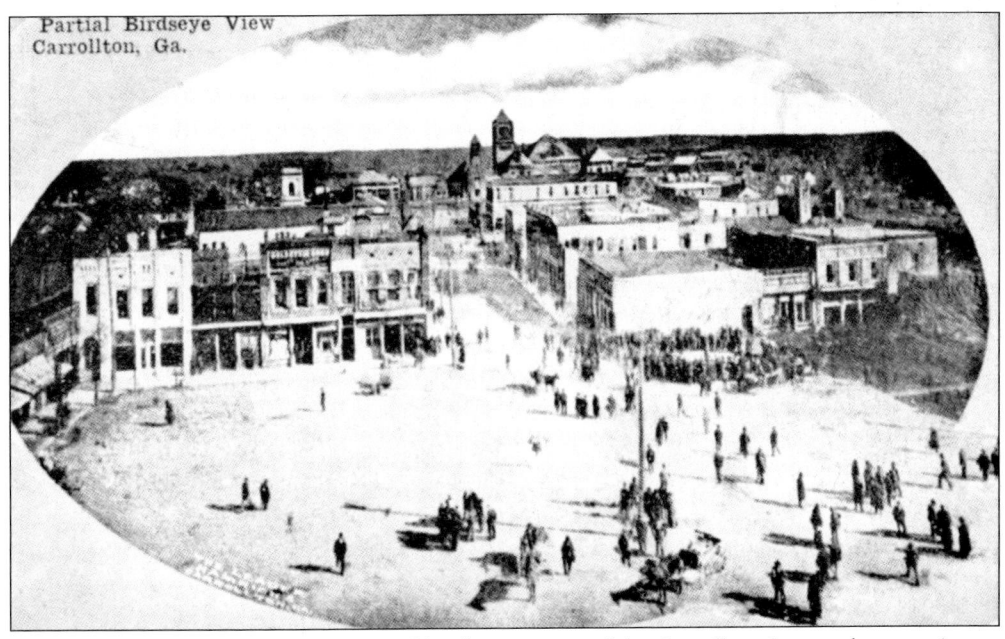

Postmarked March 22, 1912, this partial bird's-eye view of the Carrollton Square shows an image made during or prior to 1910, looking down Newnan Street. The M.E. Church tower can be seen in the left background, and the county courthouse and First Baptist Church towers can be seen in the center background. The card was published by Turner's 10¢ Store and was signed by Sam Gray and mailed from Clem, Georgia.

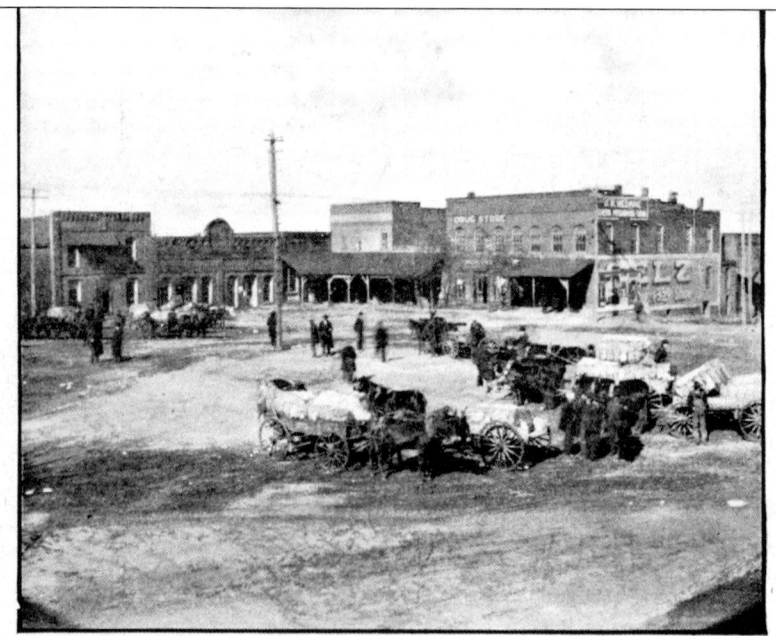
NORTHWEST CORNER PUBLIC SQUARE.

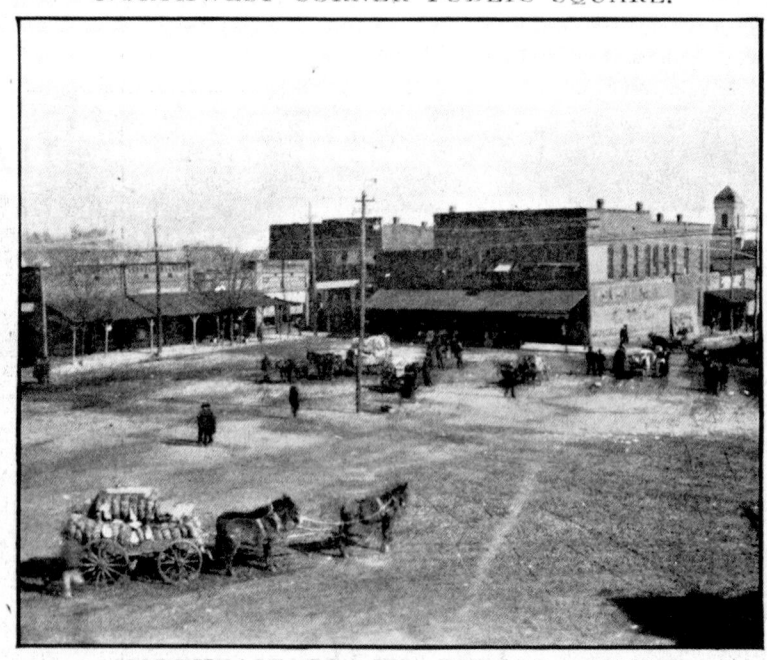
NORTHEAST CORNER PUBLIC SQUARE, CARROLLTON, GA.

A very active town square is seen in this card with two pre-1908 views of the northwest and northeast corners. The square, the commercial center for Carrollton for over 100 years, would later be named for William Charles Adamson and today is known as Adamson Square. Born in Bowdon, Judge Adamson served in the United States Congress for over 20 years and was one of Carrollton's leading citizens.

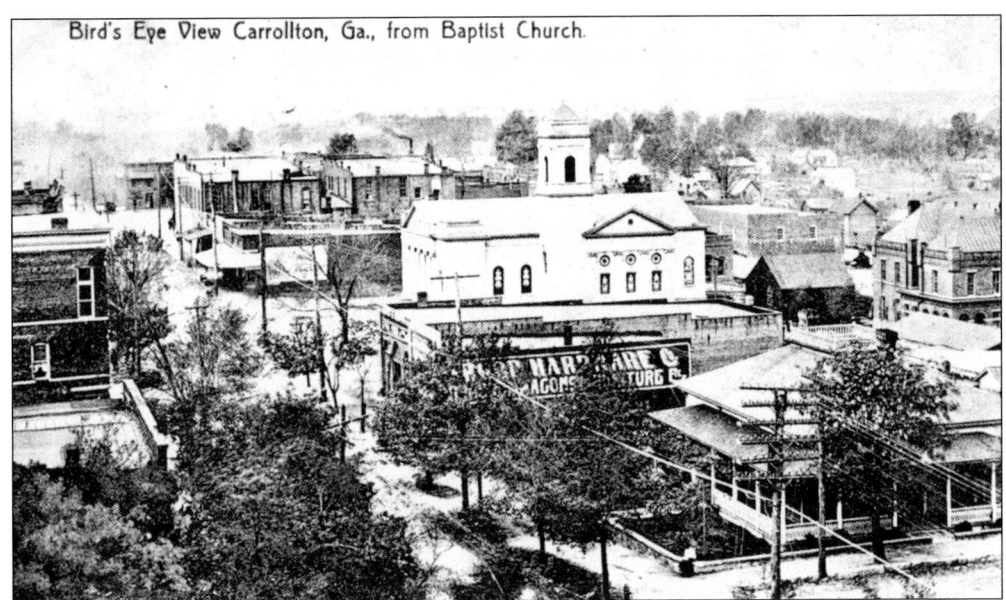

Looking down Newnan Street towards the town square, this postcard written by Myrtie Burnham was postmarked April 1911. The Roop Hardware Company and M.E. Church are prominent in the photo, and the Carrollton City Jail can be seen to the right. The view is from 1908 or earlier, as the modern four-story bank building on the square is not yet built. This view is taken from the tower of the First Baptist Church.

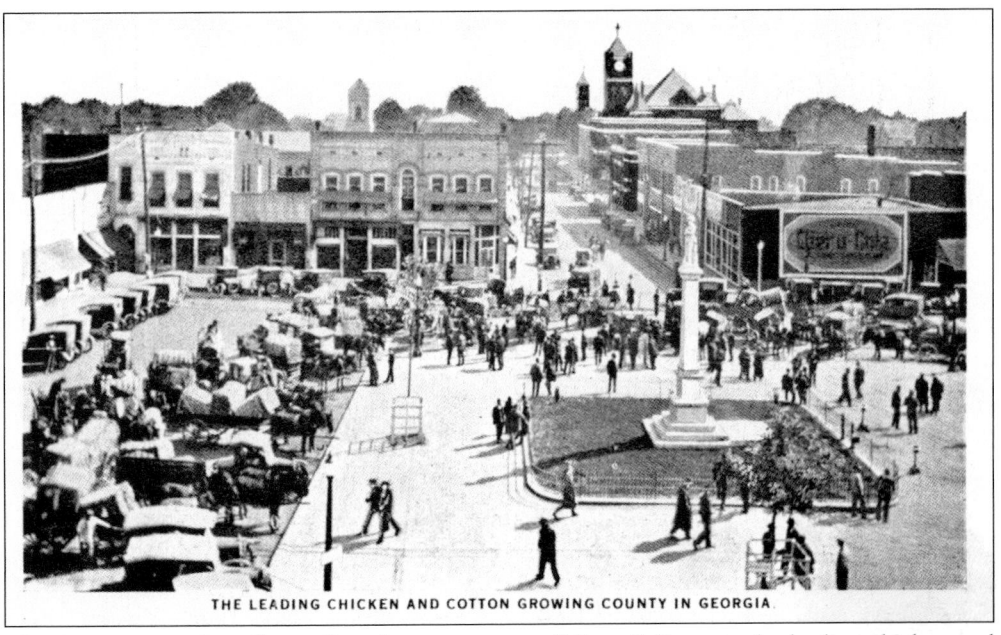

This is a scene at Carrollton, Georgia, county seat of Carroll County, the leading chicken and cotton-growing county in the state. In this postcard, mailed in June of 1933 to Oklahoma, the writer reveals a visit with the Merrells in Carrollton. Published by Fisher's 5–10 and 25¢ Store in Carrollton, the card features a very busy "cotton day" when farmers brought their products to the square for sale.

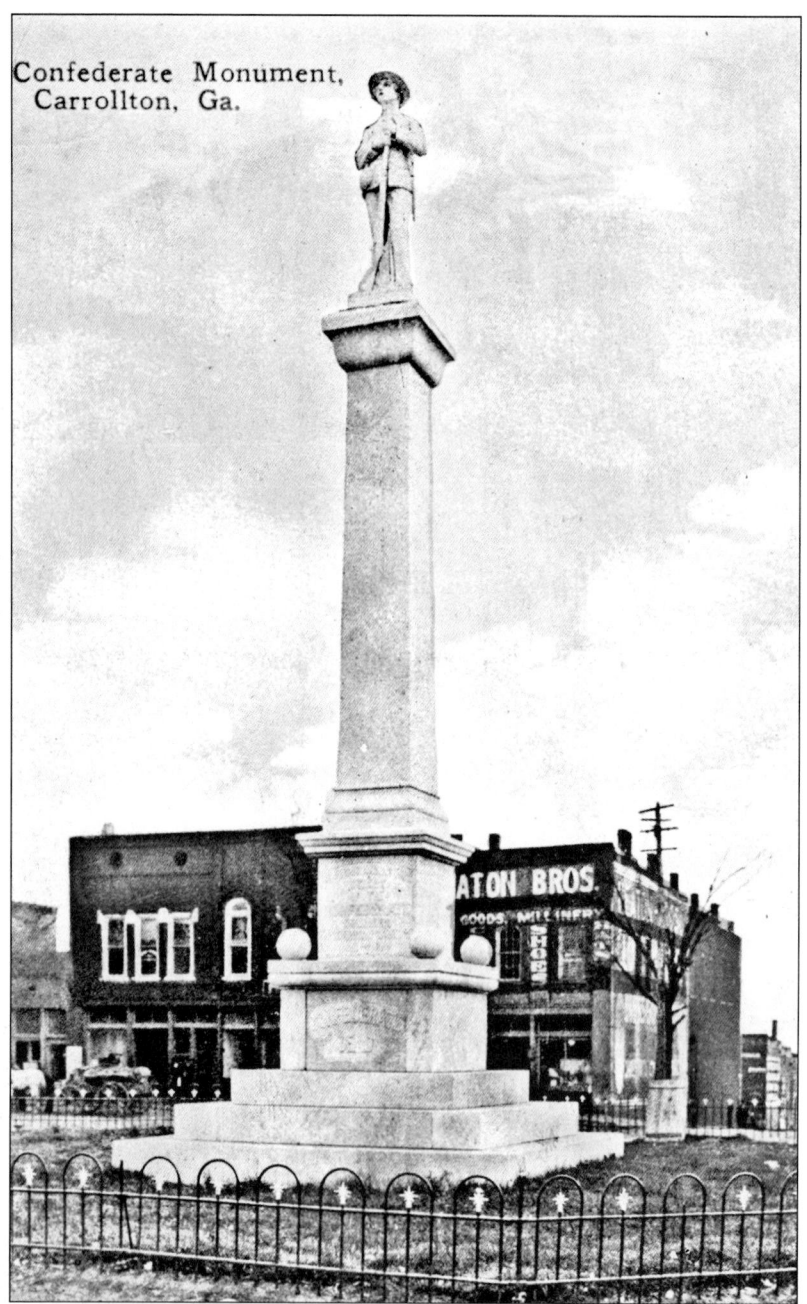

Carrollton's Confederate Monument was dedicated on May 28, 1910, in honor of the soldiers of Carroll County who served the Confederacy. Engraved on the back of the monument is the following: "Erected by the Annie Wheeler Chapter United Daughters of the Confederacy, April 26, 1910." The discrepancy in the dates occurs due to the dedication being postponed from the traditional Confederate holiday due to a contractor delay. Originally, there were four cannonballs on the monument that are now no longer there. Two of the cannonballs can be seen at the entranceway to the city cemetery. As the monument looks northward down Rome Street, the buildings seen in the background are in the southeast quadrant of the square.

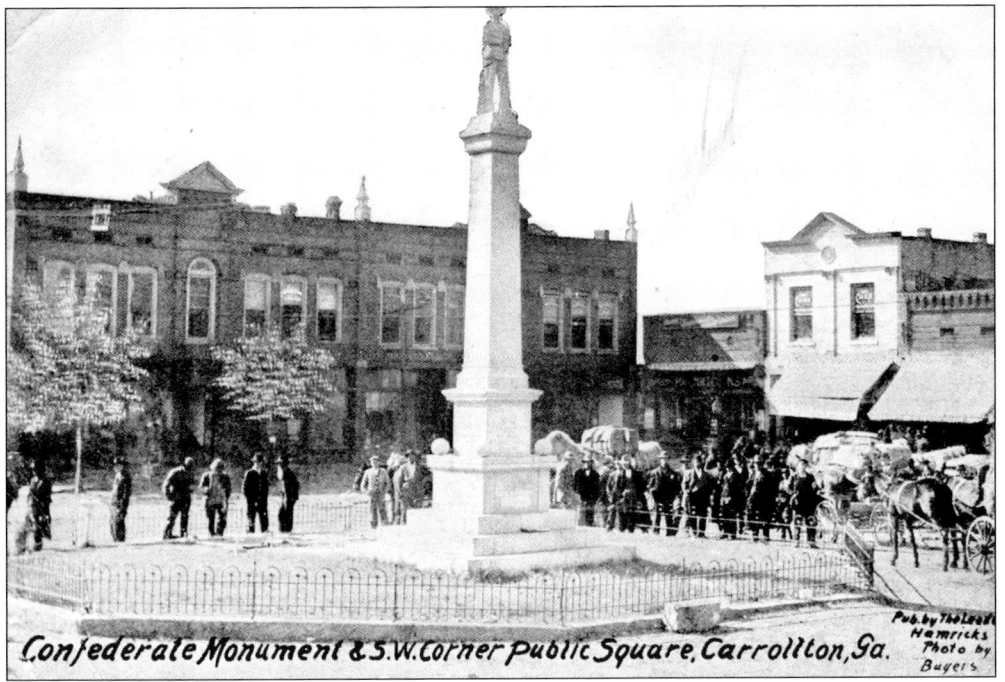

This card was published by The Leader, Hamricks, and photographed by Buyers, as is seen in the lower right-hand corner. It was printed c. 1912. The view is of the monument and the southwest corner of the square. G.M. Holmes's name can be seen on one of the store canopies. (Courtesy of Gary Doster.)

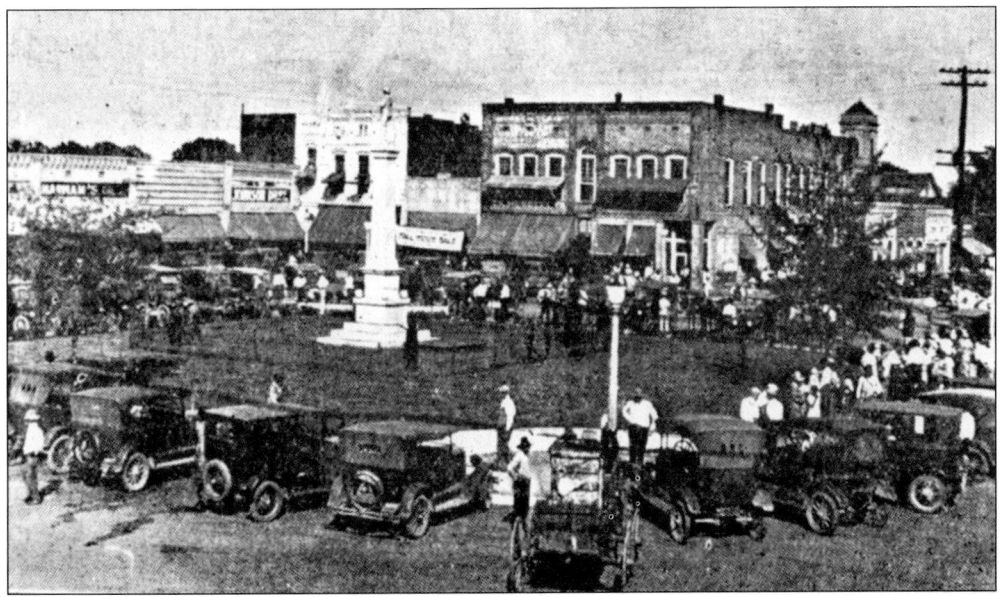

This 1928 view of the Confederate monument and busy downtown shows the northeast quadrant of the square. Harman's and Johnson's Drug Store are two of the stores in the background. Johnson's Drug Store was in business on the square for 117 years and closed in 1972. The M.E. Church tower can be seen in the far right.

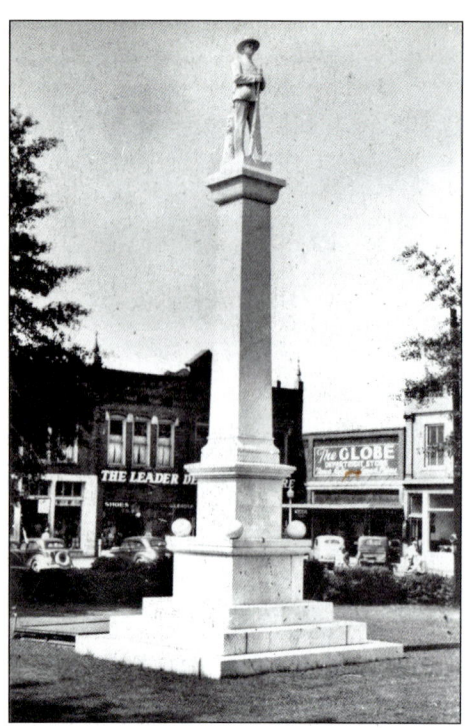

Another view, c. 1940, shows the Confederate monument in the center of the Adamson Square. Located behind the monument are buildings within the southwest quadrant that features (left) the Leader Department Store (1933–1993) and (right) the Globe Department Store (1940–1973).

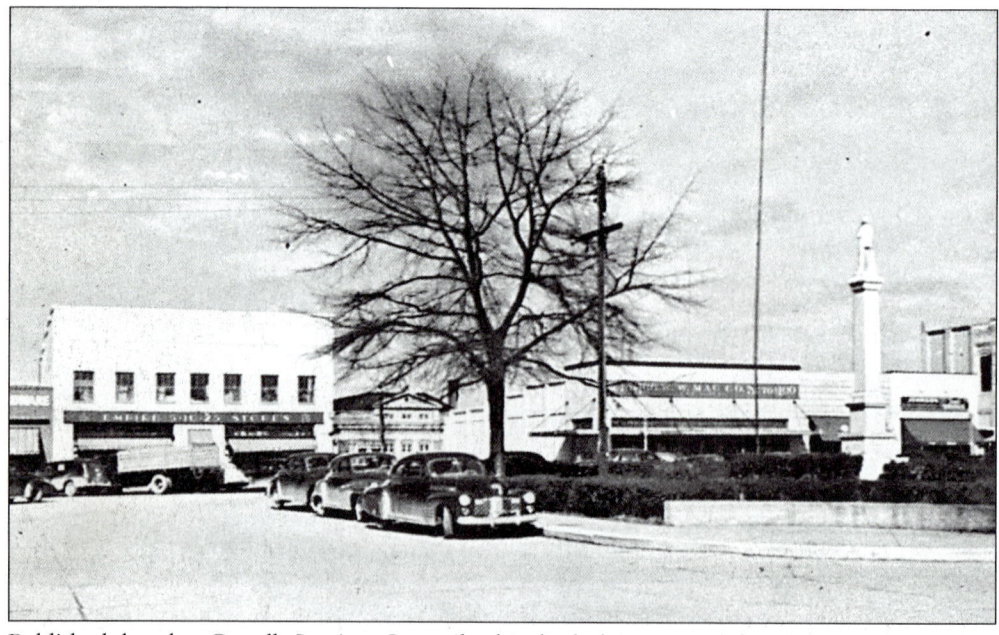

Published by the Carroll Service Council, this kodachrome card by J. Taylor features a promotional message on the back: "Street Scene and Business Section in Carrollton, Ga. Climate where you never have a sleepless night." The northwest and northeast quadrants of Adamson Square can be seen in the background. The monument was moved to the grounds of Tanner Memorial Hospital in 1958 and then to its present location at the courthouse in 1976. Prominent in the background are the Empire 5-10-25¢ Store, city hall, and W.W. Mac Co.

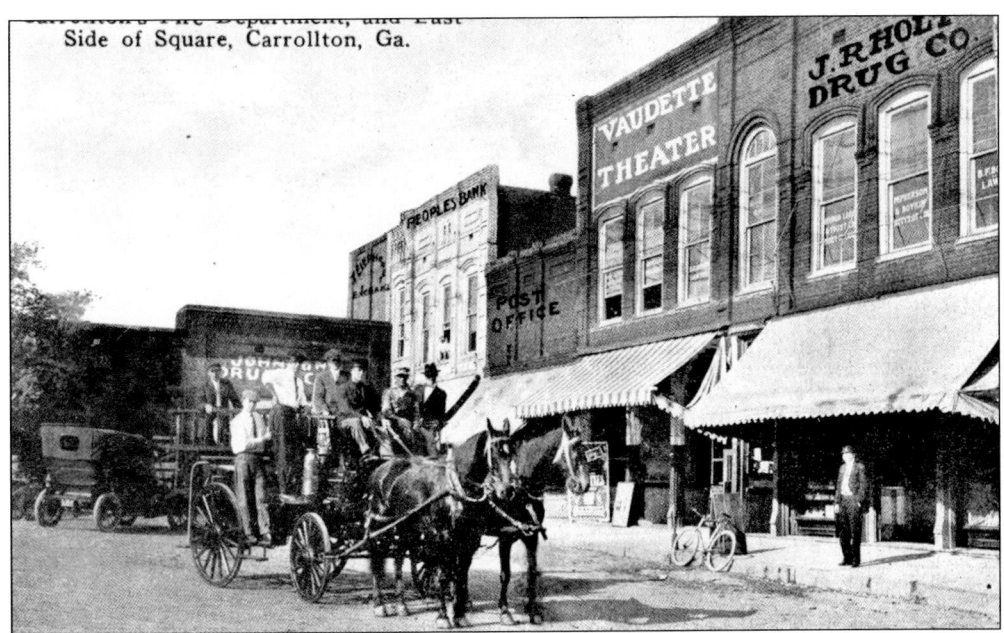

This rare c. 1908 image shows the horse-drawn fire engine in front of early stores in the northeast quadrant of the square. J.R. Holt Drug Co., the Vaudette Theatre, post office, People's Bank, Telephone Exchange, and Johnson Drug Company can all be seen. Lawyers and a loan office are advertised in the upstairs of the buildings. Note the two-horse-drawn engine, the firefighter's uniform, and the theater playbill. The horse-drawn fire engine was abandoned in 1916.

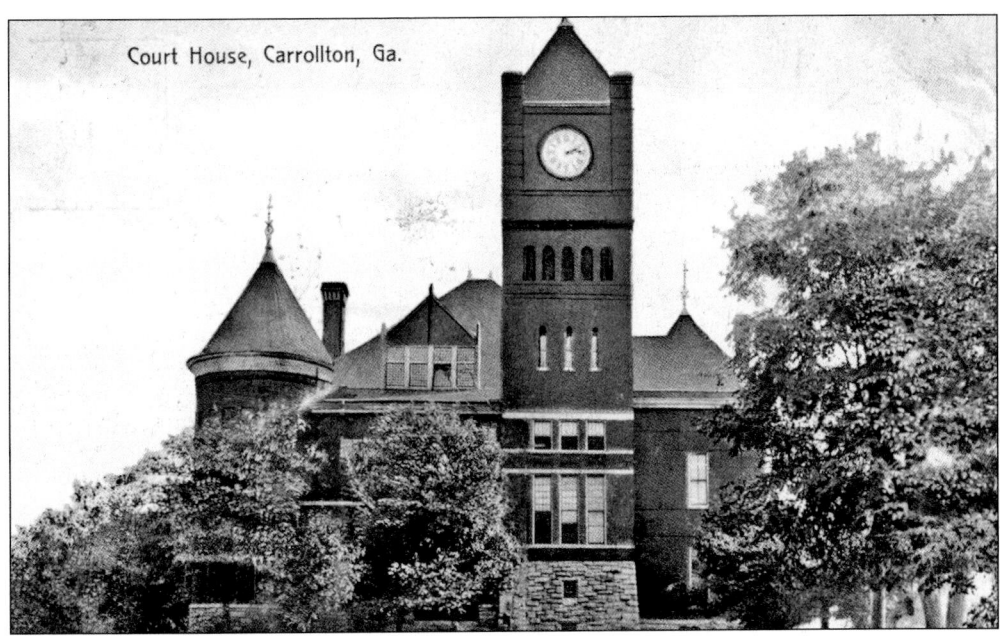

Mailed to Miss Glen North of Route 10 in Carrollton in 1909, this card was published by N.A. Horton of Carrollton and printed in Germany. This view is of the courthouse building on the corner of Dixie and Newnan Streets. The red brick courthouse built in 1893 replaced the courthouse that was located in the center of the square.

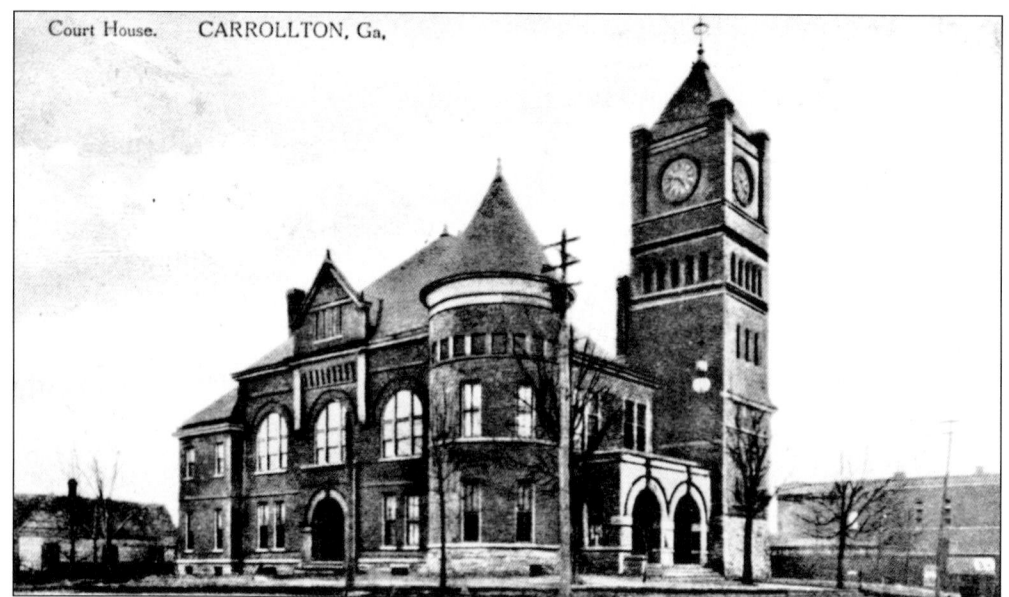

Postmarked March 28, 1913, and addressed to Miss E.L. Downs of Bowdon, this card features another view of the old Carrollton Courthouse The card was published by The Leader, Hamricks, of Carrollton. This postcard view was also used as the front illustration of the 1910 *Carroll County, Georgia Souvenir-Historical Edition,* proceeds from which helped pay for the Confederate monument.

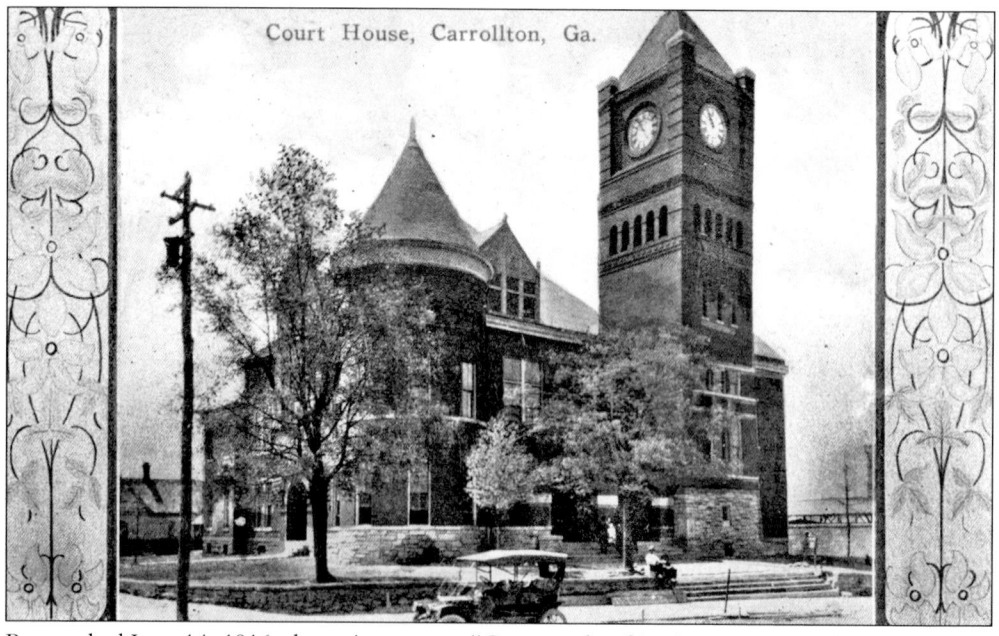

Postmarked June 14, 1916, the writer wrote, "Our temple of justice appears on the other side—quite a nice looking building." The two-story building featured a large clock tower that was used both as a clock and as a warning system for possible fires within the community. The courthouse burned in 1927, and the warning system featured at the courthouse was not successful in saving itself.

GOOD ROADS MACHINERY CO.,
Road Machinery, Tools and Supplies.
Repairs for all Road Machines.

KENNETT SQUARE, PA. *April 13th* 1903

My *S. J. Brown*
Carrollton Ga

Dear Sir :—
Your esteemed favor of the *9th* inst. is at hand with order for *one front wheel, one Steel Bar Seven middle sections blades two dozen end sections and 1 gross short bolts for points* for which you will please accept our thanks.
Will ship via *Freight*

Yours very truly, GOOD ROADS MACHINERY CO.,
Per *E. H. Richardson*

Postcards were used in many ways that included business, advertisements, and notifications. Addressed to S.J. Brown, ordinary of Carrollton, Georgia, this card was dated April 13, 1903, and confirms the order of supplies for the county's road equipment.

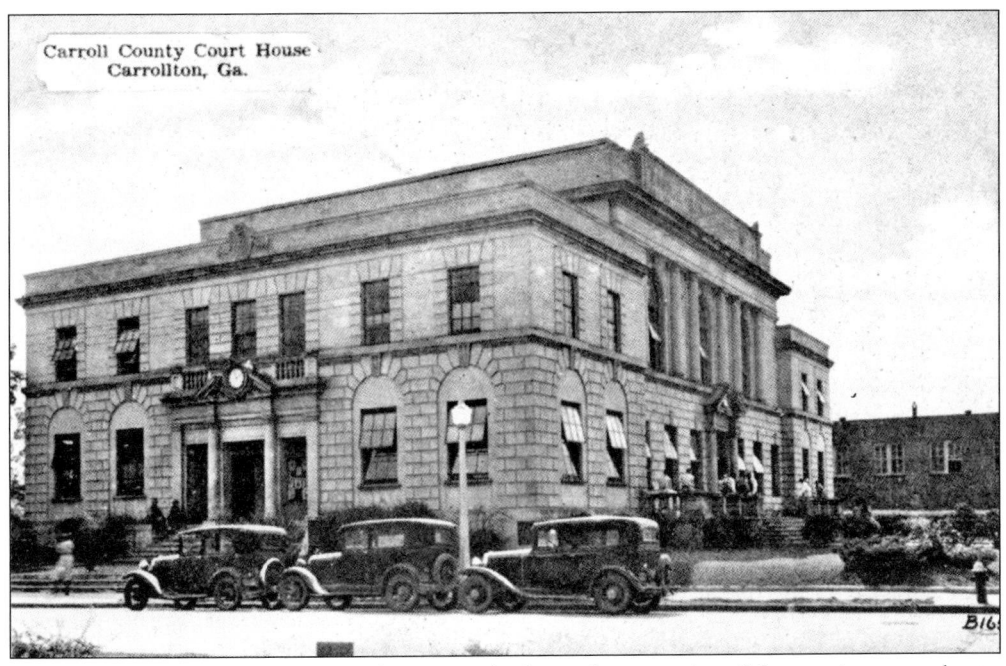

In 1928, the Carroll County Courthouse was built on the same site of the previous courthouse that had burned. Note the sitting porches and the fact that all the windows are open, for without air conditioning the courthouse was known for being a hot place for more than one reason. Dexter Press of Buford published the card.

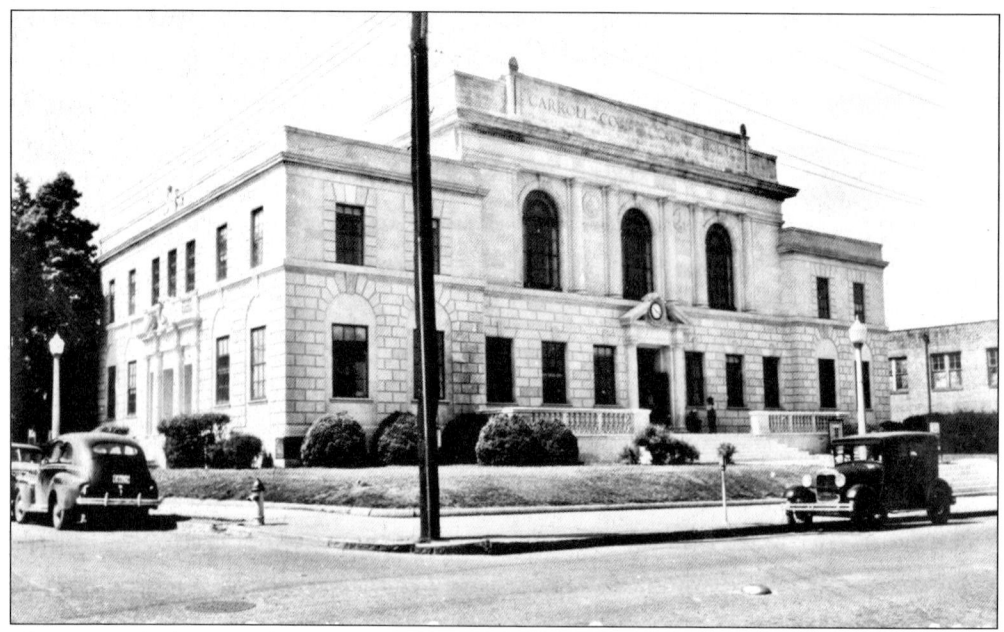

This is another view of the Carroll County Courthouse. The architectural style is Italian Renaissance Revival, and it was designed by William J.J. Chase. The current courthouse and added annex building are found here today. The Confederate monument is also now located on the courthouse lawn.

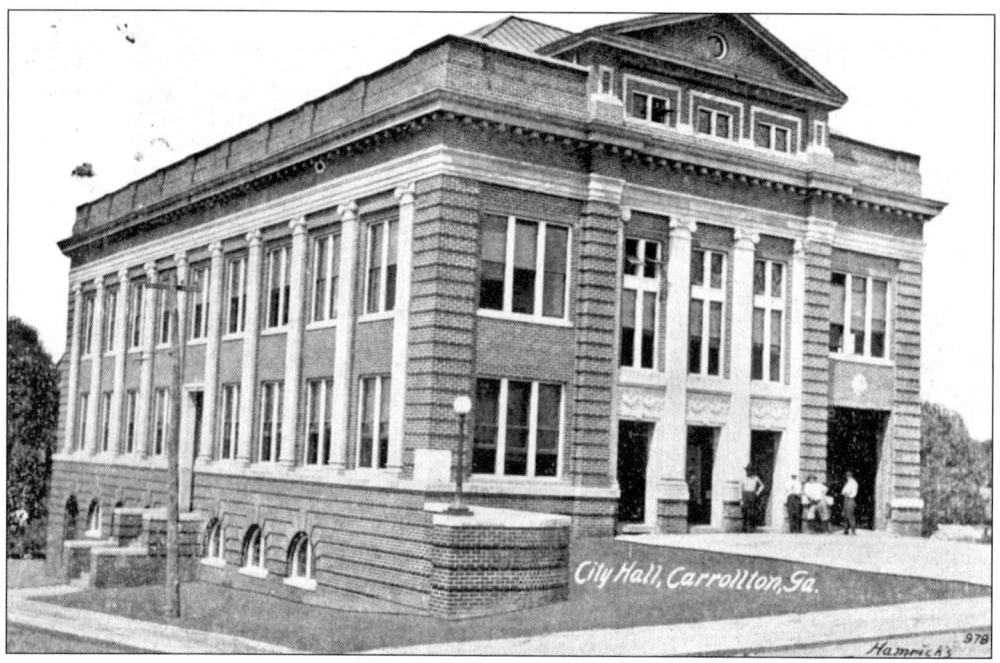

Published by Hamrick's of Carrollton and dated May 7, 1914, this real photo card shows an early view of the Carrollton City Hall. The large entrance where the men are standing housed the fire station. The card carries a simple message, "Best wishes to you all, T.A. Quinlan, Jr."

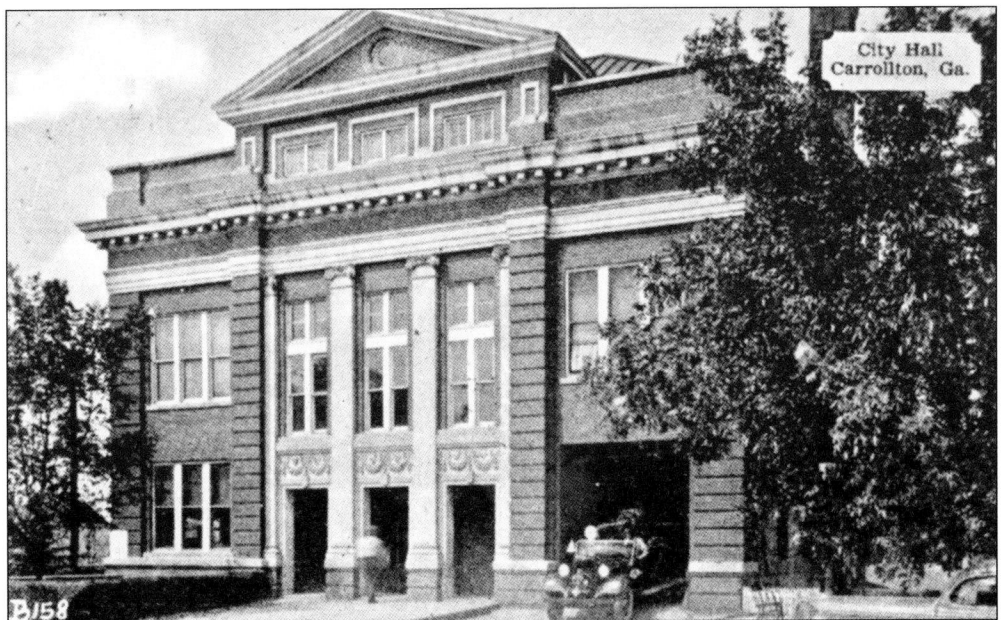

Another view of city hall is postmarked November 15, 1945, and was sent to Mrs. Kison from Mrs. Charlie McCray of Bowdon. It states, "Judy (my baby) will be a year old November 19. She is so sweet, looks like Charlie and has his ways. I'm so glad I have her, she is so much joy and comfort."

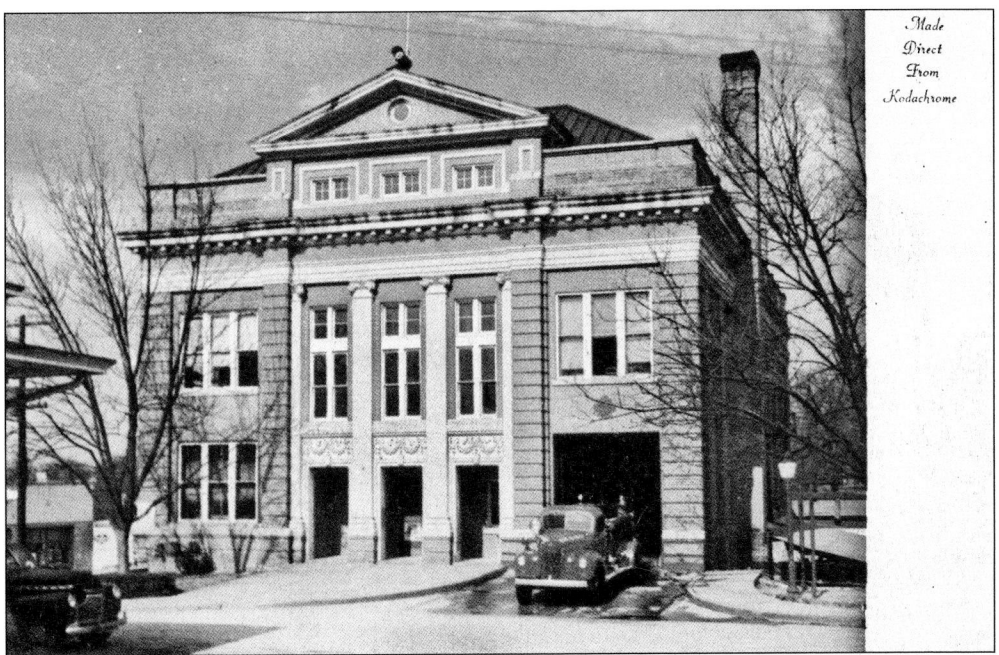

Published by the Carroll Service Council of Carrollton, this kodachrome card features a newer model fire truck, c. 1950. The photo was by J. Taylor and features the following message: "Carrollton City Hall, Carrollton, Ga., Climate where you never have a sleepless night."

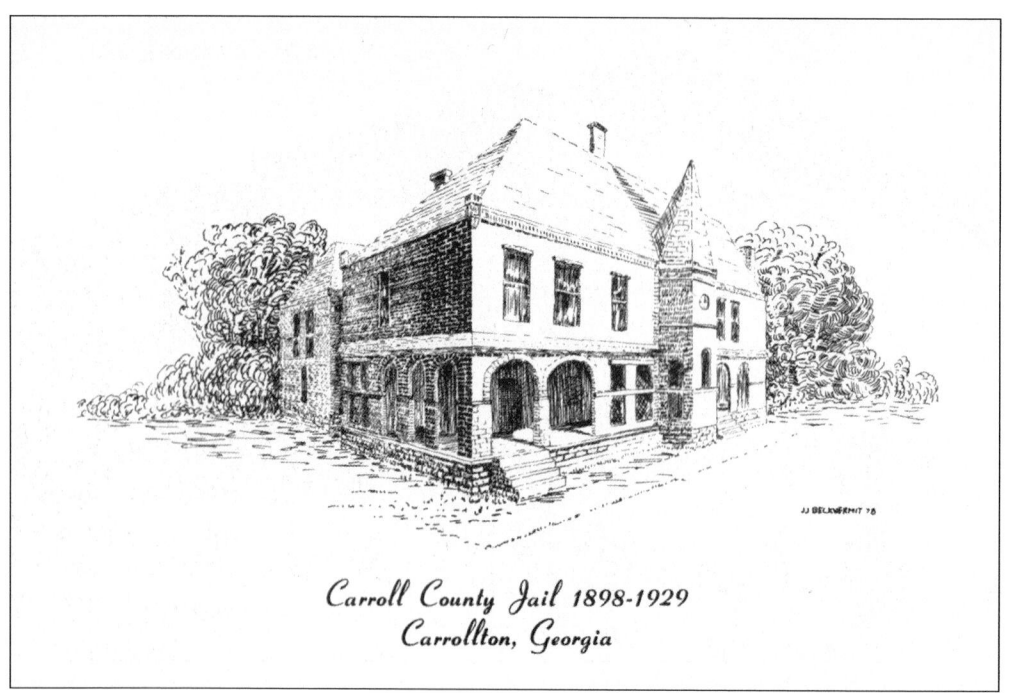

Carroll County Jail 1898-1929
Carrollton, Georgia

The Carroll County Jail, as featured in this image, was located in front of the city hall from 1898 to 1929. The pen and ink drawing was done by a local artist, John Beckvermitt, in 1978.

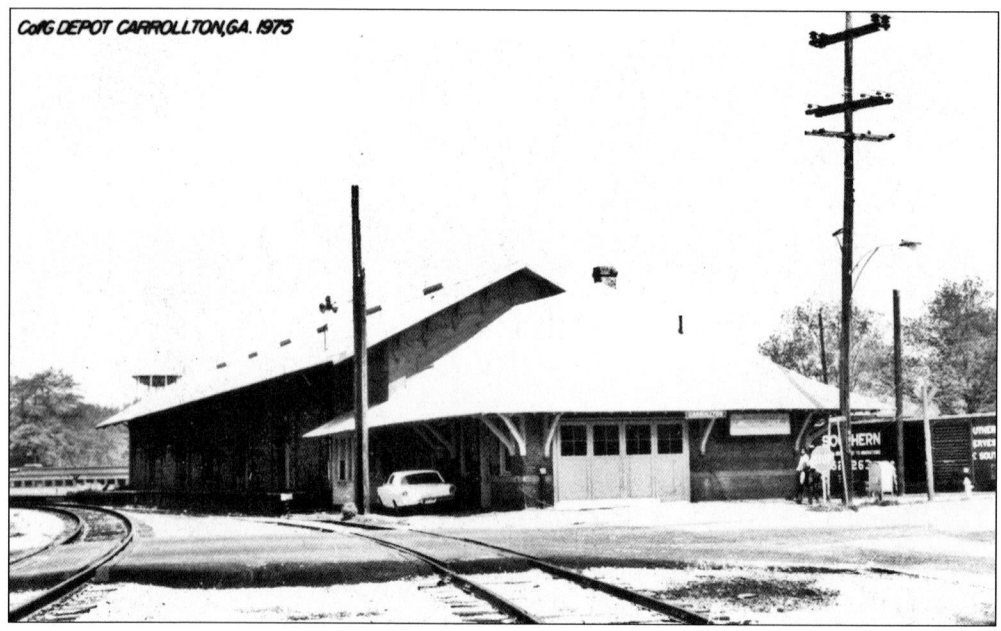

This is a view of a snow day at the Central of Georgia Depot in 1975. The SG&N (the Savannah-Griffin-North Alabama Railroad) was completed in 1874. In 1882, the Georgia Pacific (later named the Southern) came to Carrollton, and in 1888, the CR&C (the Chattanooga-Rome-and-Columbus Railroad) was completed. The depot became a major commercial area for cotton and cotton products from the local mills.

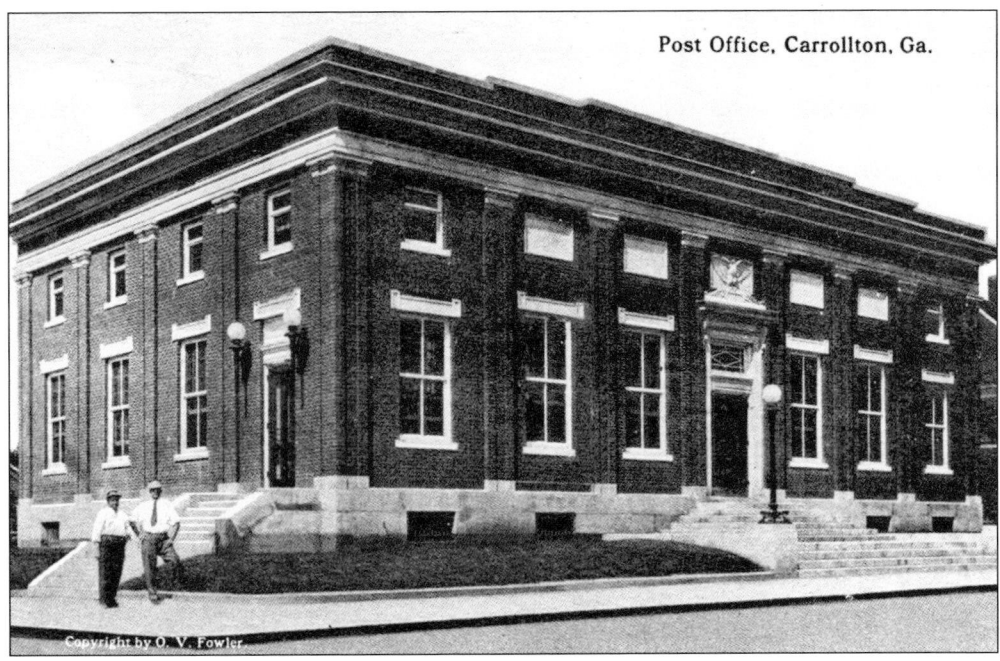

The United States Post Office, located on Newnan Street across from the Carroll County Courthouse, served the postal needs of Carrollton from 1913 to 1966. It then became the home of the Carroll County Board of Education and is presently a law office named Smith, Diment, and Conerly LLP. The photo is by O.V. Fowler and was taken on August 1, 1914.

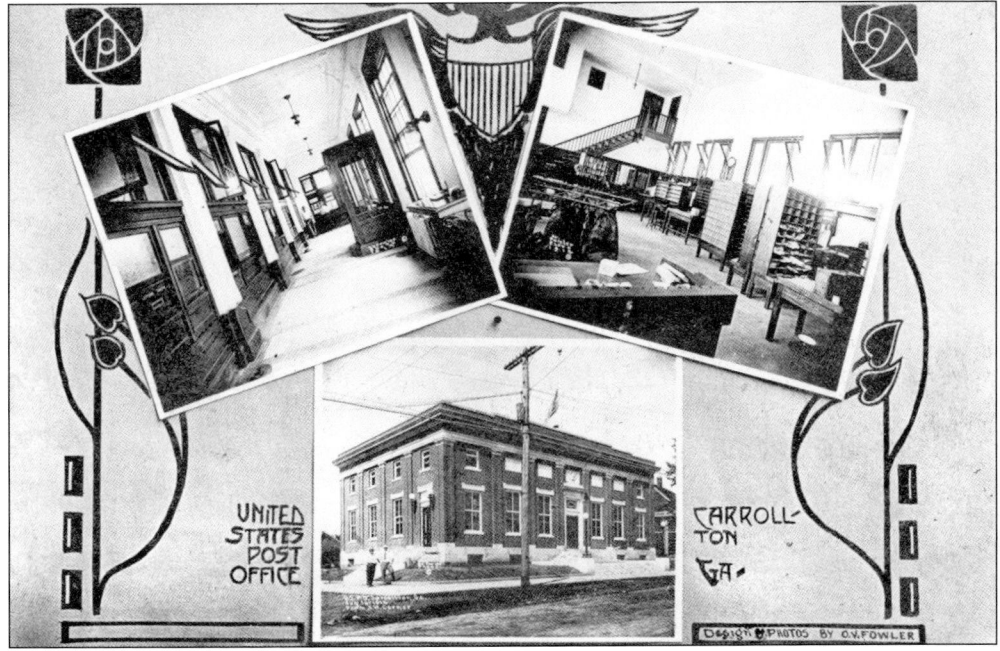

Designed and photographed by O.V. Fowler in August 1914, this is an ornate postcard of the post office, along with two scenes of the interior showing the lobby to the left and the mailroom to the right. (Courtesy of Chief Jimmy Bearden.)

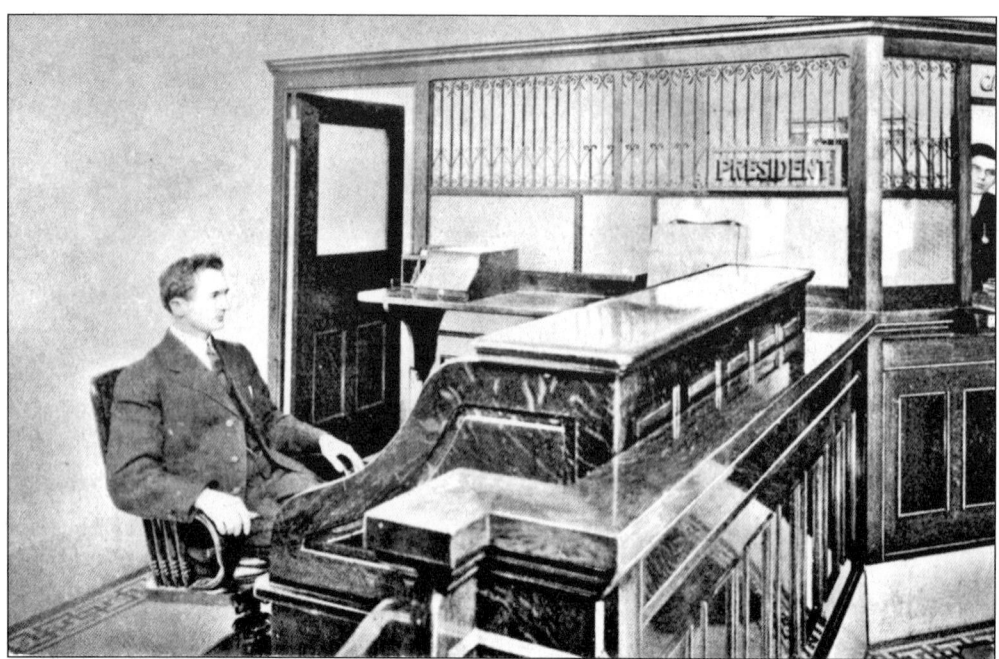

A rare bi-fold card is located above and on the opposite page. The two cards are connected to make a panoramic view of the interior of the People's Bank. It opened for business on December 1, 1909, and gave Carrollton four banks at that time. (Courtesy of Gary Doster.)

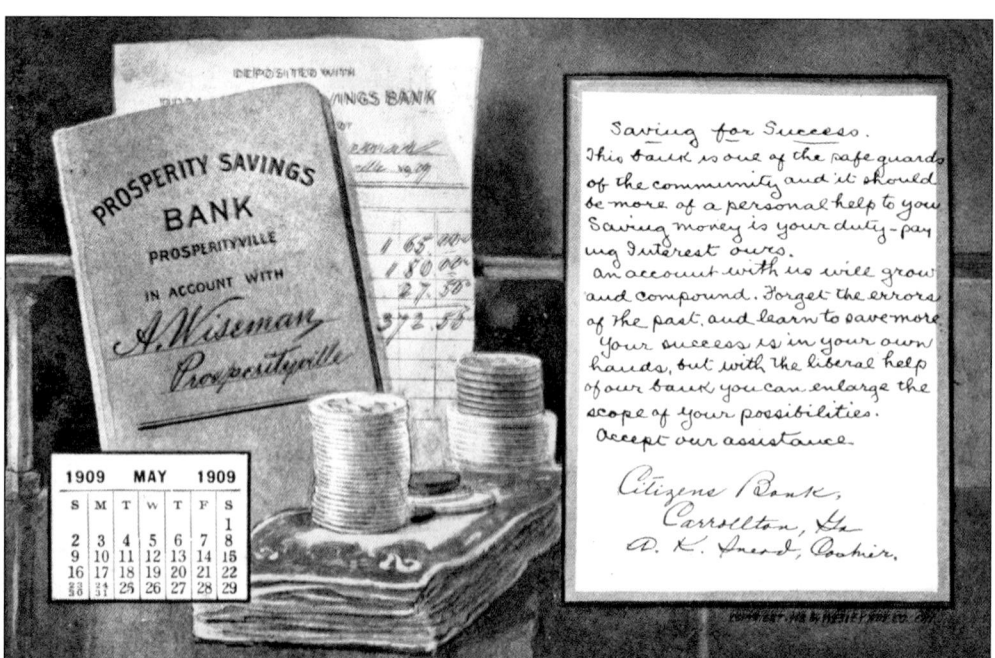

An advertisement card addressed to J.M. Neil of Route 10 in Carrollton is from the Citizens Bank of Carrollton. It features a calendar of May 1909 and a message from cashier A.K. Snead. Note the Prosperity Savings Book made out for A. Wiseman. The color card shows gold and silver coins as well as the popular $2 bill.

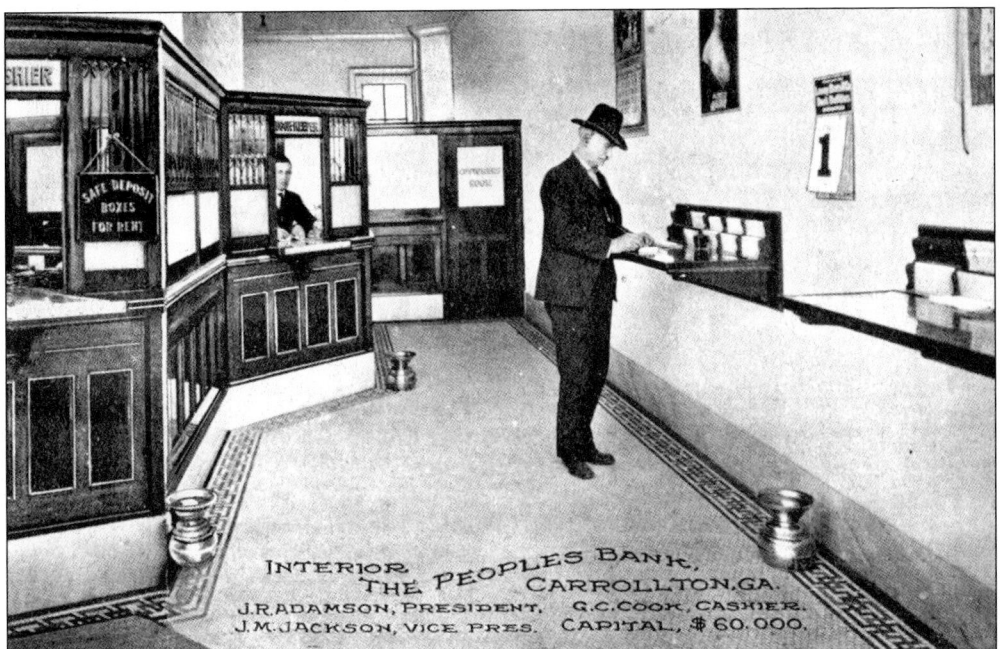

At the People's Bank, J.R. Adamson was president, John M. Jackson served as vice president, and G.C. Cook served as cashier. Note the spittoons on the floor. (Courtesy of Gary Doster.)

This embossed advertisement card from the Citizens Bank of Carrollton features the picture of a child that could someday be president. Citizens Bank of Carrollton was opened for business in 1906. J.C. Bass was president, and W.W. Heaton served as vice president. The card was postmarked on June 29, 1910, in Carrollton and was addressed to Mr. C.E. Jordan. (Courtesy of Gary Doster.)

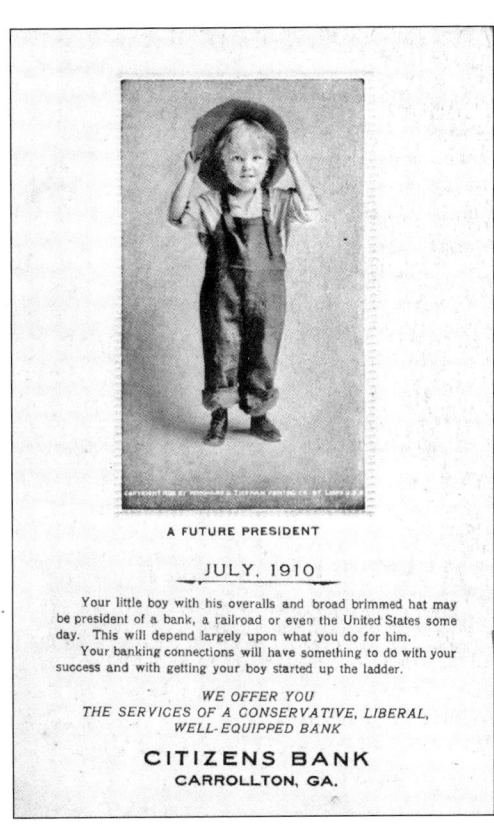

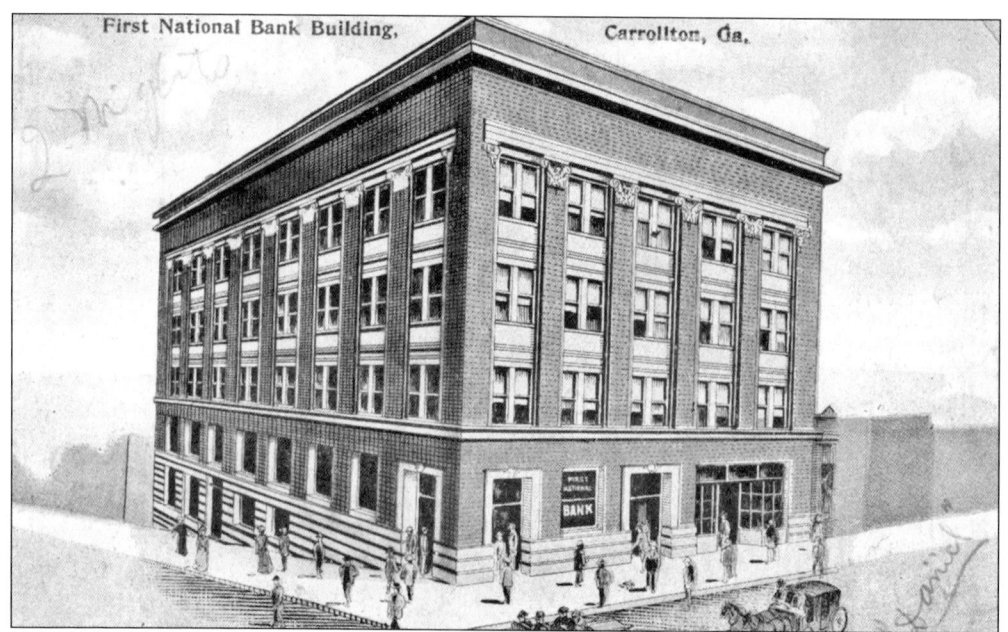

This postcard, mailed February 1910 and published by N.A. Horton of Carrollton, shows an artist's rendition of the First National Bank of Carrollton. Sanford Kingsberry, who built a store on the site and became Carrollton's first merchant, originally owned the lot. A hotel was later erected on the Kingsberry Corner, but it was destroyed by fire in 1870.

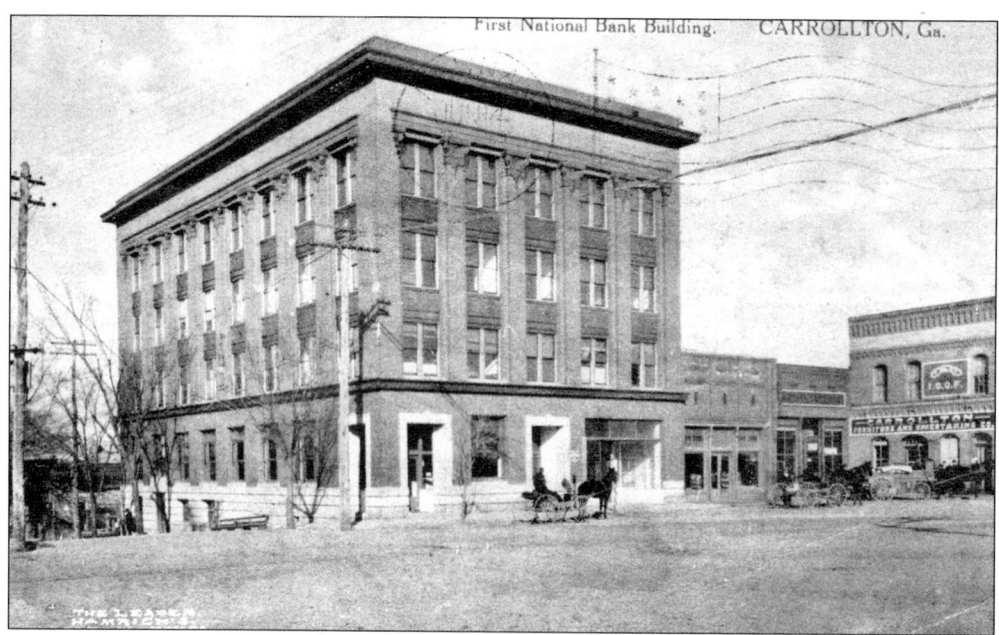

A real photo card of the First National Bank, postmarked June 1910 and addressed to Miss Alzie Holmes, says, "We are enjoying life. Grandad is alright. Auntie." The card was published by The Leader, Hamricks, of Carrollton. The Carrollton Furniture and Undertaking Company can be seen on the right and an IOOF (Independent Order of Odd Fellows) can be seen on a second-story window of the same building.

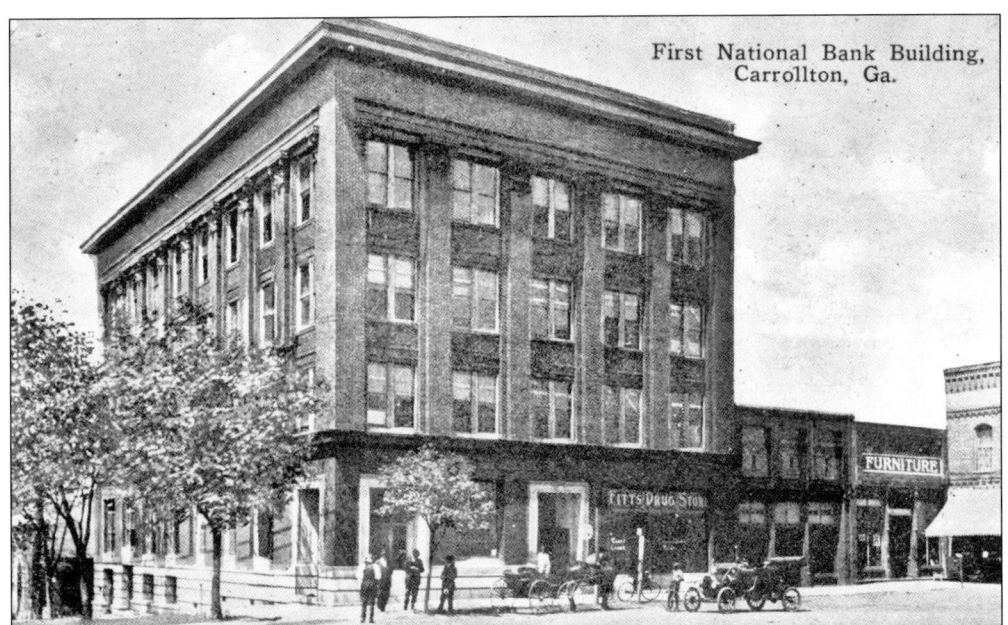

Postmarked May 1913, this card featuring various modes of transportation shows the First National Bank building. In the lower right-hand corner of the building is the Fitts Drug Store. Also of note is a furniture store in the corner. Originally the Merchants and Planters Bank, chartered in 1888, the bank was nationalized in 1900. The building is believed to have opened in 1908.

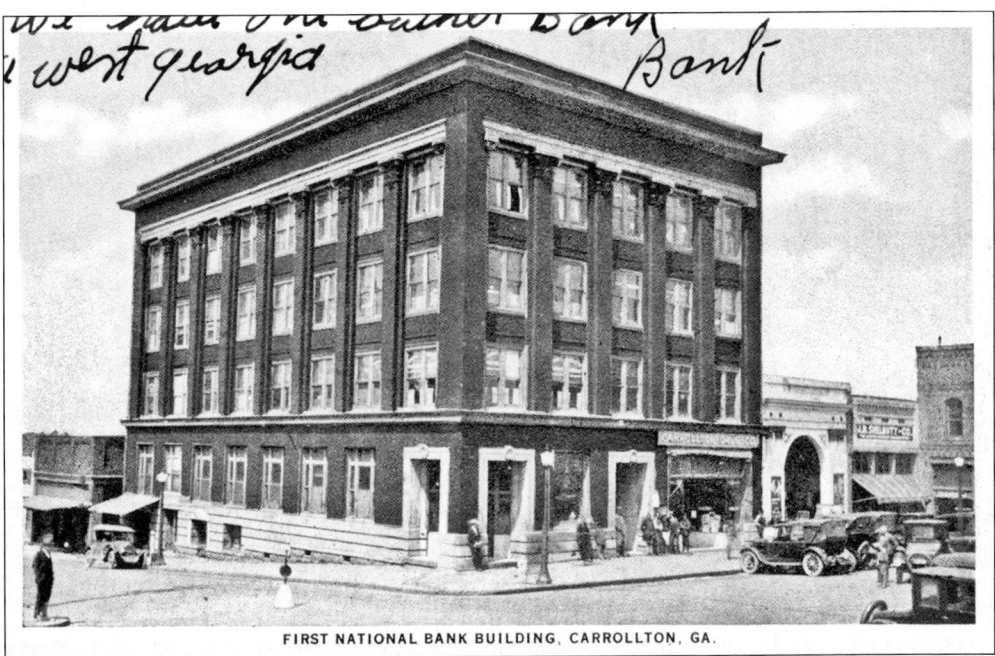

This card of the First National was published by Fisher 5–10 and 25¢ Store in Carrollton in the 1920s. For many years, the building was the tallest building in Carroll County. By the time of this card, only automobiles are seen on the street. A Carrollton Drug Co. sign is now seen where Fitts Drug Store was located, and a J.B. Shellnut Co. sign can be seen on the corner building.

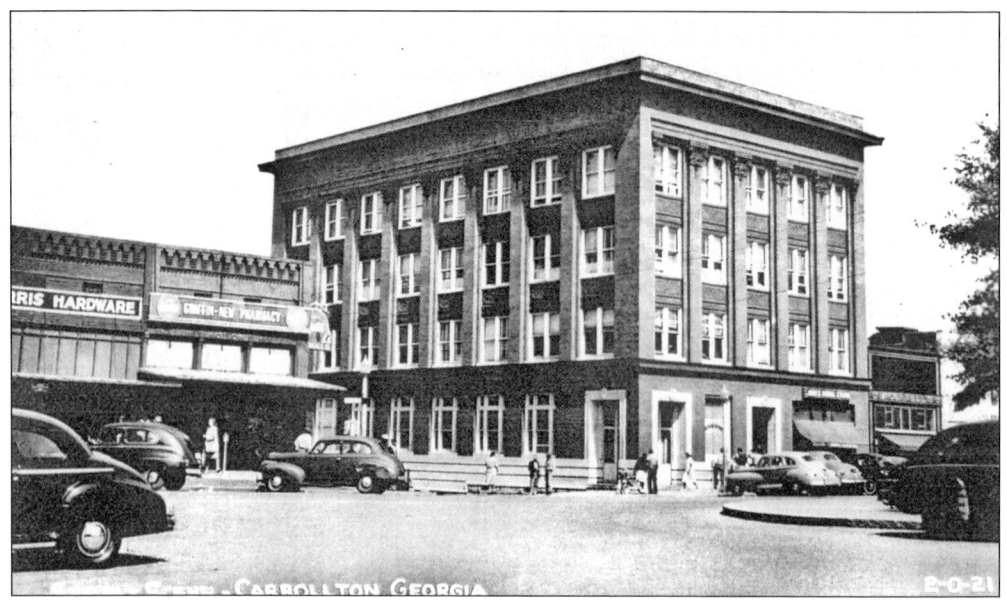

The First National Bank continued until 1931 when it merged with the People's Bank and reopened in a four-story building in 1932. The People's Bank was in operation until 1986. The top two floors of the bank building were removed several years ago, and the Colonial Bank is the current occupant. Located in the southwest quadrant of the square is Harris Hardware (1940–1947) and Griffin's Pharmacy (1940s–early 1960s)

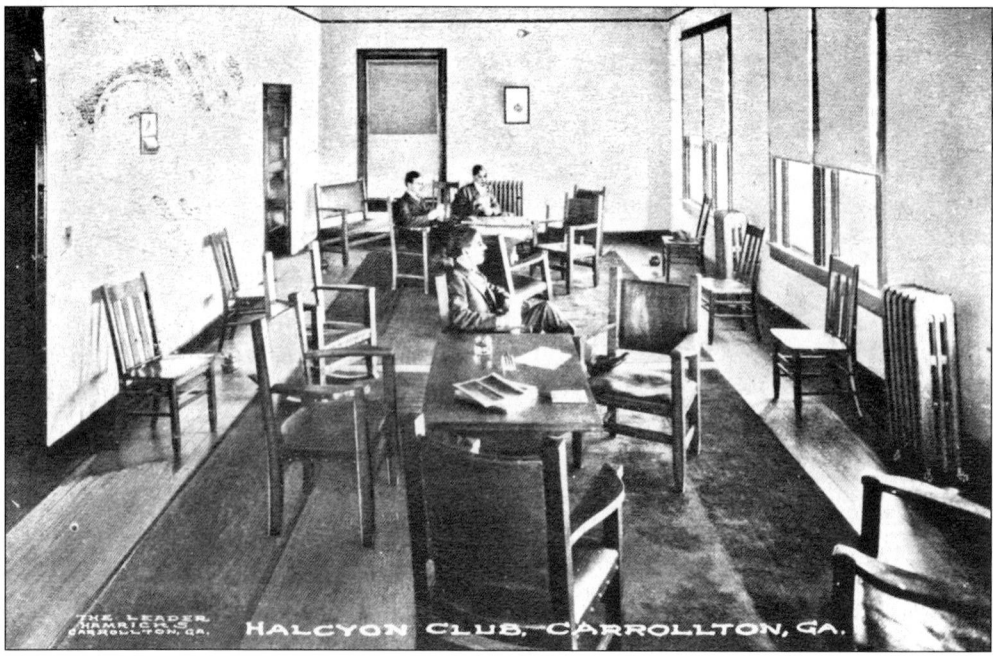

In the upper floors of many of the downtown buildings was space that was rented by various clubs and civic organizations. This card shows the interior of the Halcyon Club that was located above the First National Bank. The club had several furnished rooms and a ballroom. Postmarked April 22, 1913, the card was published by The Leader, Hamricks, of Carrollton.

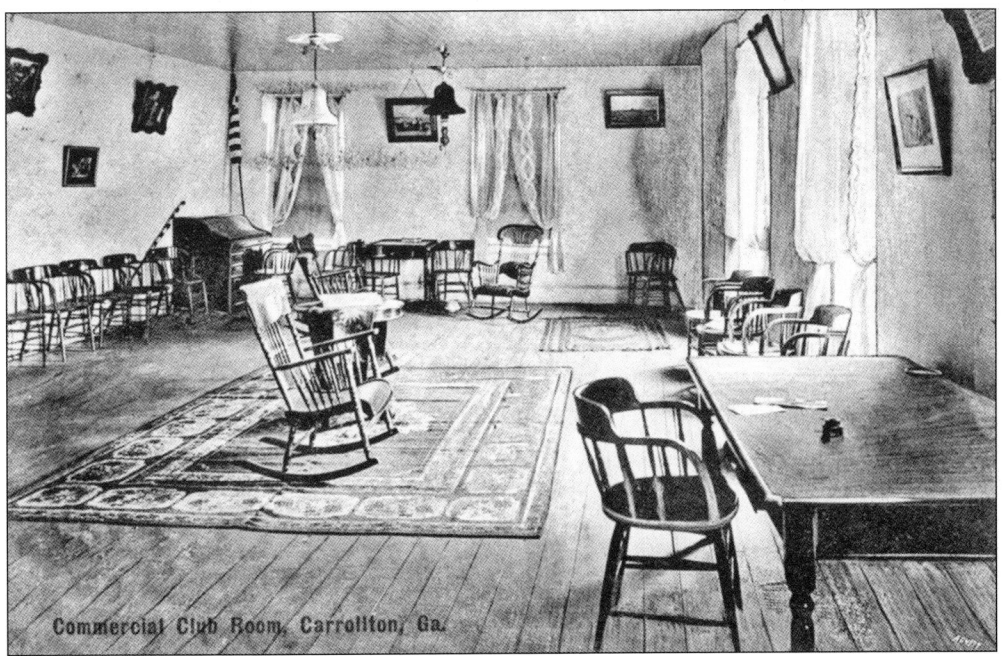

Written to Miss Alice Trimble of Carrollton and postmarked January 1909, this card features a view of the Commercial Club Room in Carrollton. (Courtesy of Gary Doster.)

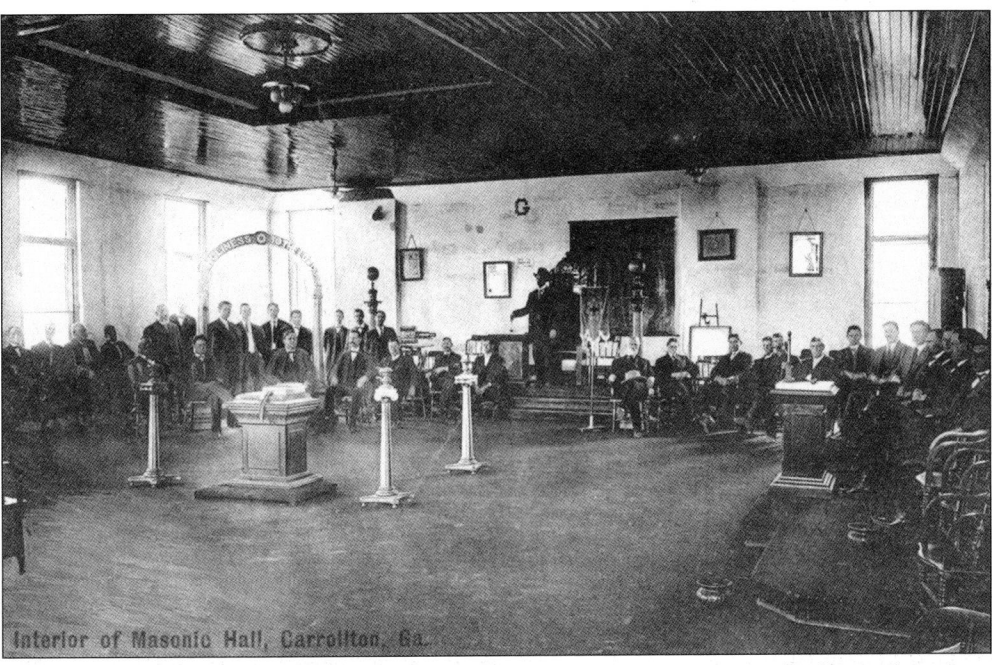

Postmarked January 1908 in Roopville, this card was addressed to J.M. Neill of Carrollton from C.A. Neill. The card was published by the Holt & Cates Co. of Newnan and features a rare view of the interior of the Masonic Hall in Carrollton. Note the many features, including the ornate arch that reads, "Holiness to the Lord," the decorative ceiling fixture, Masonic artifacts, and the spittoons on the floor.

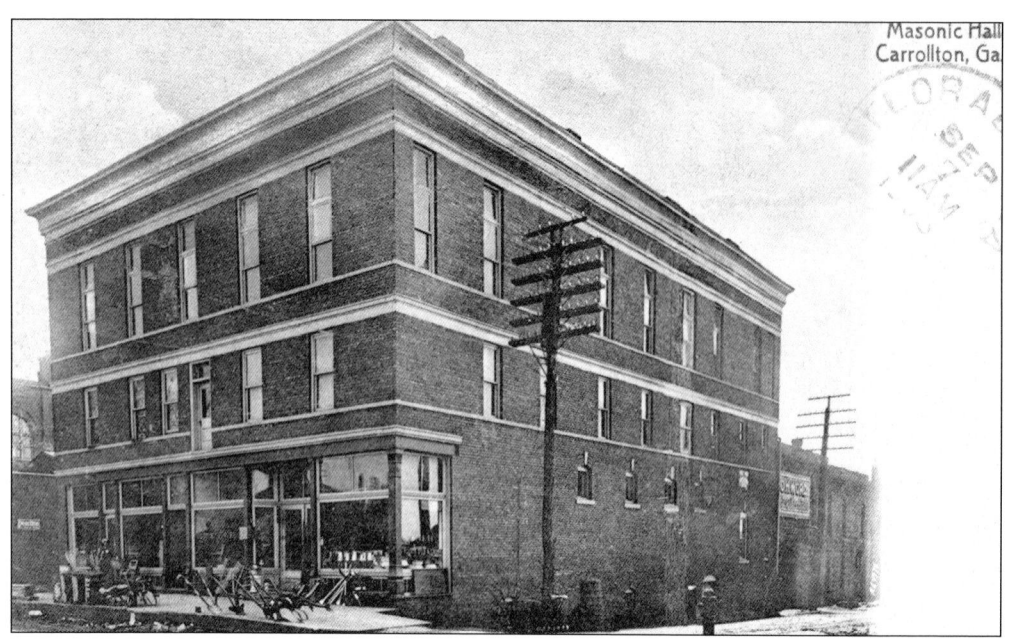

Chartered in 1848, the Masons first met in a two-story wood structure in the southwest quadrant of the square. Later, they met at the Carroll Masonic Institute, the Kramer House, the Mandeville Building, and the Masonic Building. Postmarked September 7, 1908, this building was on Newnan Street and was known as the Masonic Building. H.O. Roop's store was on the first floor. The sign on the wall behind the building shows the name O.H. Word.

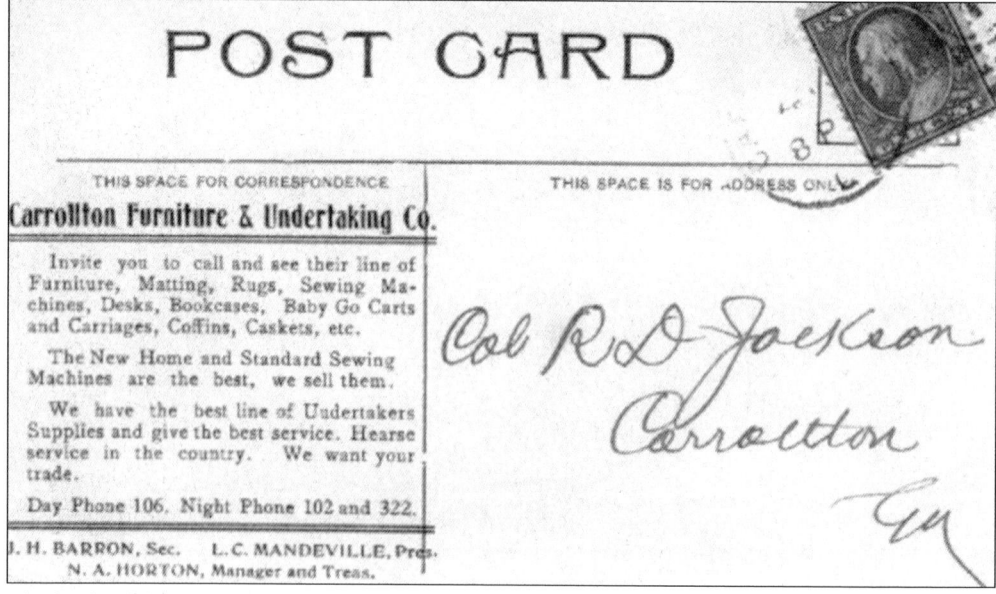

The back of this Dixie Street postcard features an advertisement for the Carrollton Furniture and Undertaking Company. The company featured a great variety of items for sale, as well as hearse service for the country. The card is addressed to Col. R.D. Jackson of Carrollton. In 1892, N.A. Horton, manager and treasurer of this business, founded Horton's Bookstore, Georgia's oldest bookstore and Carrollton's oldest business still in existence. (Courtesy of Gary Doster.)

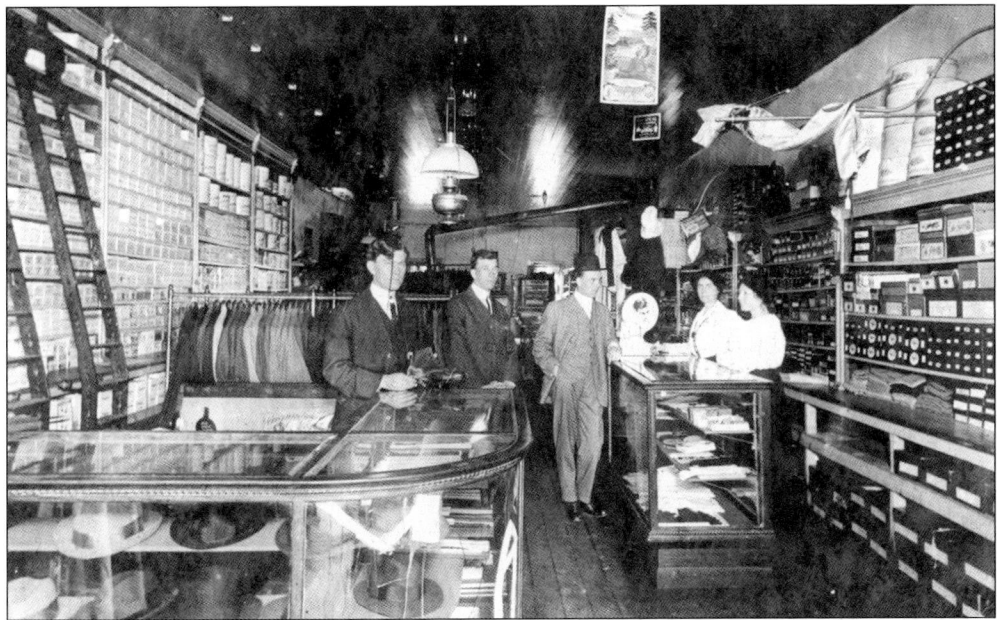

This photo card is believed to be an interior view of A.J. Baskin Co. on the square in the early 1900s. They began business in 1900 as the firm Summers & Baskin, became Baskin & Baskin in 1903, and then became A.J. Baskin Co. in 1909. The store dealt in dry goods, notions, clothing, shoes, hats, and millinery. (Courtesy of Gary Doster.)

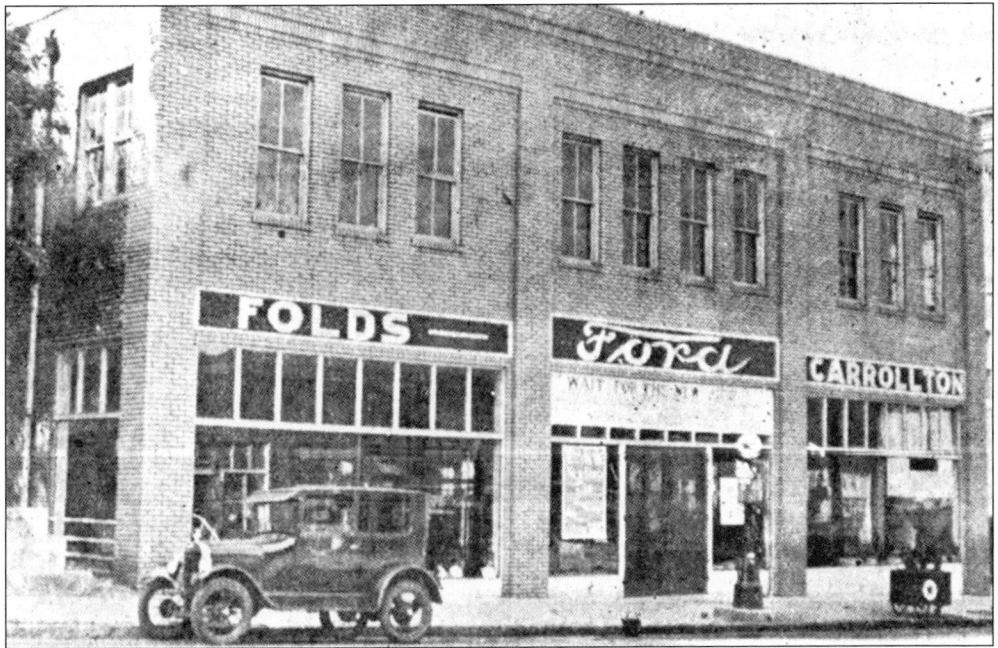

This is a 1928 real photo of the Folds Motor Company on Newnan Street. The dealership began in 1913. The building was constructed in 1920 and later housed Chalkley Motors, but the building now no longer exists. The current courthouse annex and monument area stands on the site where it was located.

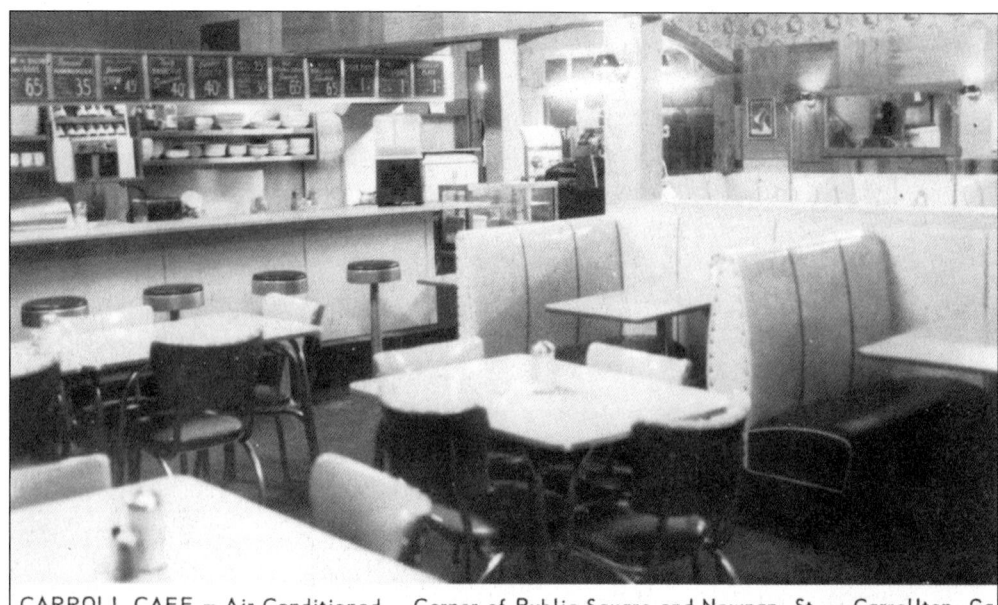

CARROLL CAFE – Air Conditioned – Corner of Public Square and Newnan, St. – Carrollton, Ga.

An interior view of the Carroll Café is featured here. The back of the card indicates, "Carroll Café—Air Conditioned—Quality Food—Western Steaks—Chicken—Garden Fresh Vegetables, Corner of Newnan St., Rt. 27 and Public Square, Carrollton." Signs above the counter list a barbecue sandwich or brunswick stew for 40¢.

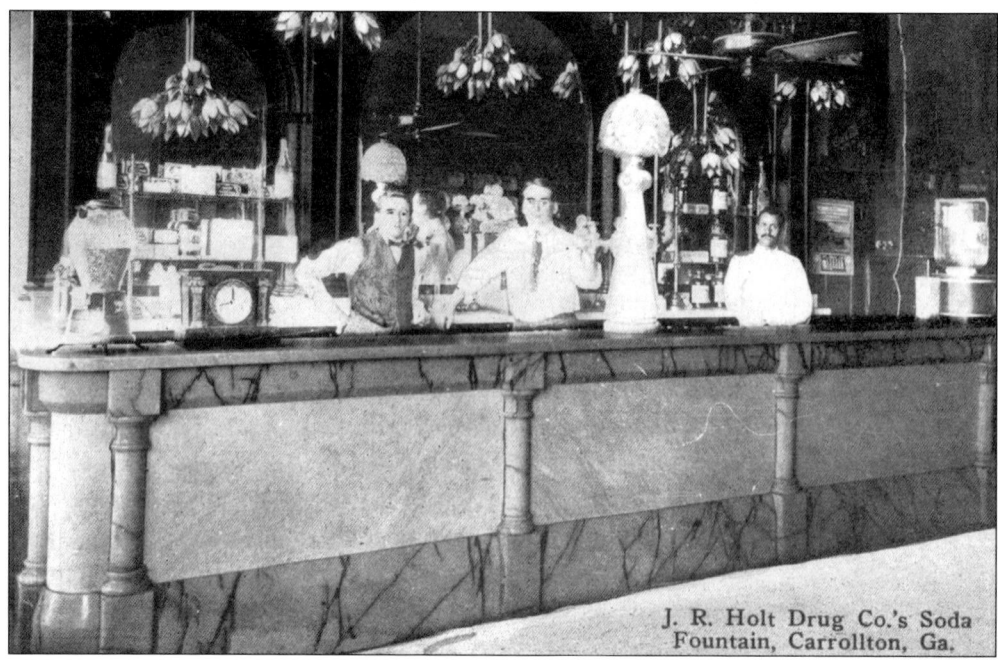

J. R. Holt Drug Co.'s Soda Fountain, Carrollton, Ga.

Located on the corner in the northeast quadrant of the square and next to Newnan Street was the J.R. Holt Drug Co. Featured in this postcard is a fancy soda fountain with ornate fixtures and what appears to be a marble counter. (Courtesy of Gary Doster.)

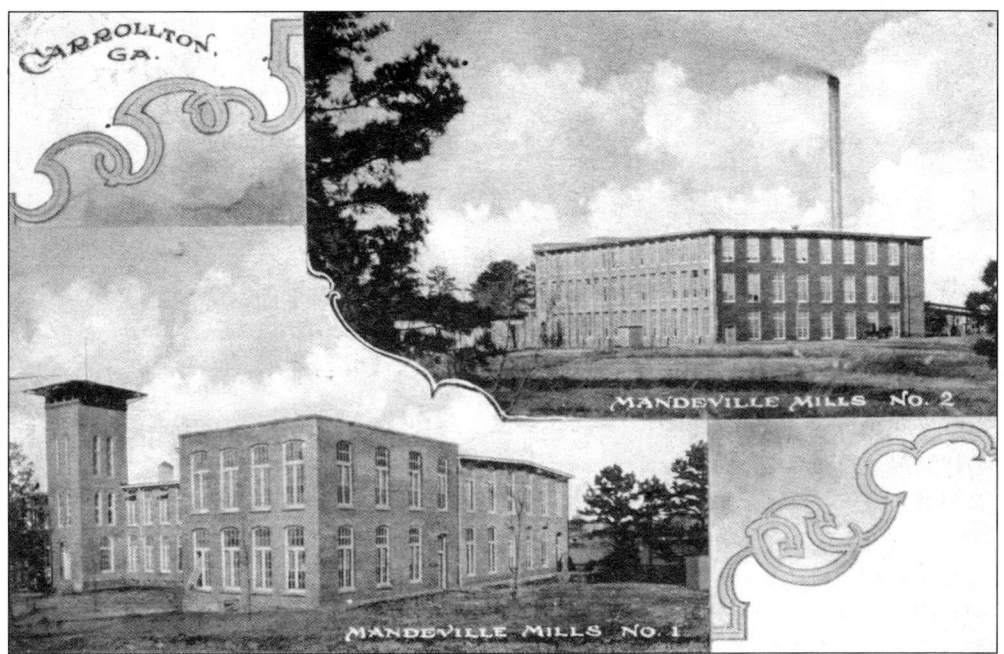

Postmarked June 1910, this photo card features two early views of the Mandeville Mills complex with buildings #1 and #2. In 1898, L.C. Mandeville (president and treasurer), H.O Lovvorn (secretary), and J.A. Aycock (general manager) chartered Carrollton Oil Mills. This was the beginning of Carroll County's biggest employer in the early 1900s. In the 1920s, mill #1 had 15,000 spindles and mill #2 had 20,000.

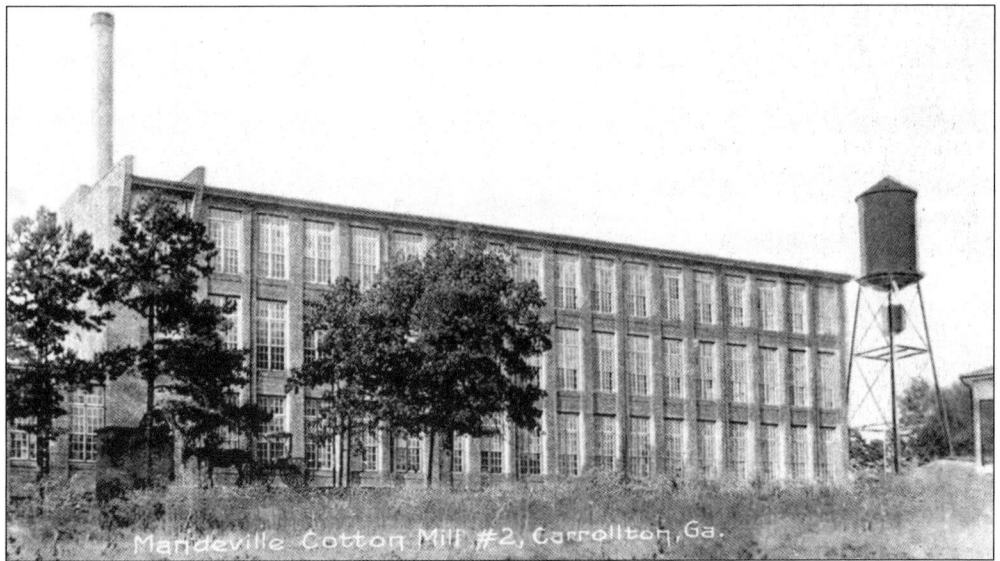

This view of the Mandeville Cotton Mill #2 was published by N.A. Horton of Carrollton and printed in Germany. L.C. Mandeville, for whom the mills were named, was born in Carrollton in 1851 and was one of the town's leading citizens. He organized the first bank, the oil mill, the cotton mills, the fertilizer works, a canning factory, and other businesses. His money and influence were largely responsible for securing the A&M School for Carrollton.

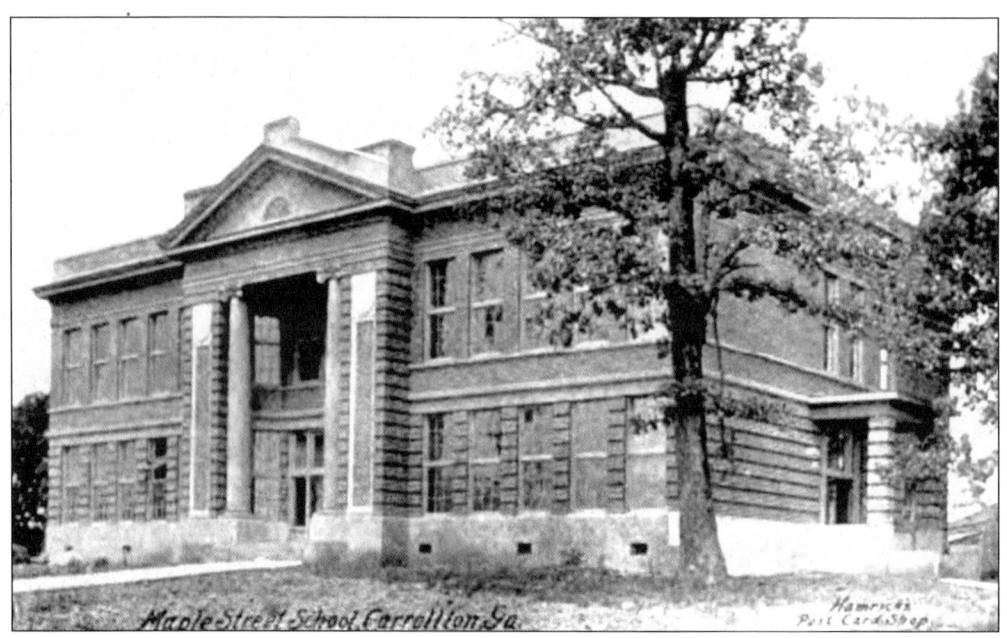

Maple Street School was built in 1913 and destroyed by fire in 1947. This view is postmarked 1916 and was published by Hamricks Post Card Shop. The children who attended the Westview School, which was built for the children of Mandeville Mills, were allowed to attend Maple Street starting in 1922–1923.

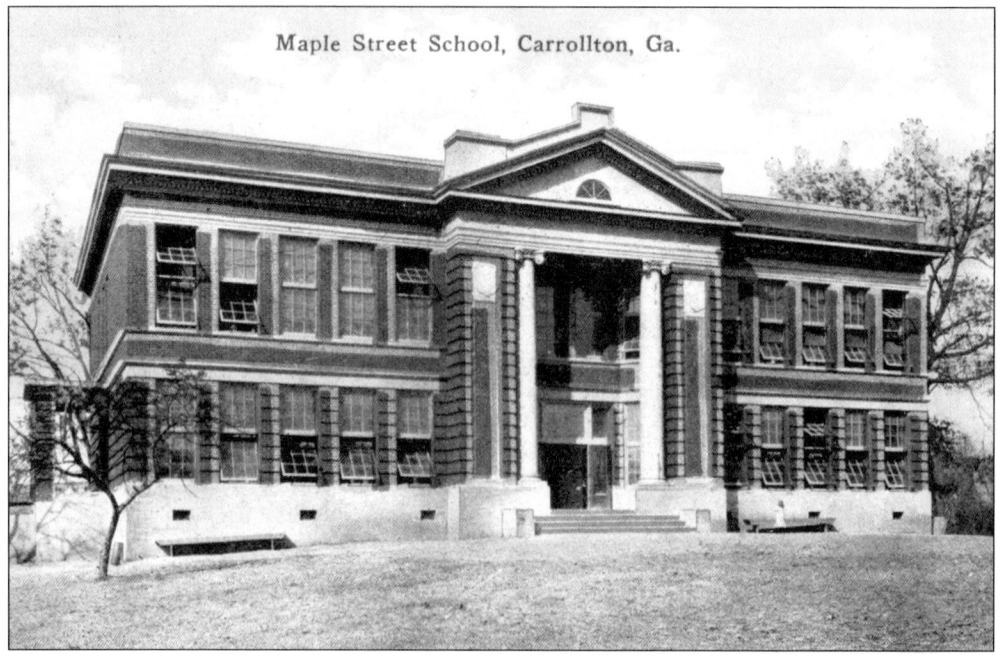

Another view of the two-story Maple Street School is postmarked July 6, 1914. The Carrollton community has a long-standing desire to have fine schools and is known for their commitment to excellence. While most schools of the time were one- or two-room wooden structures, Carrollton moved to brick buildings early on.

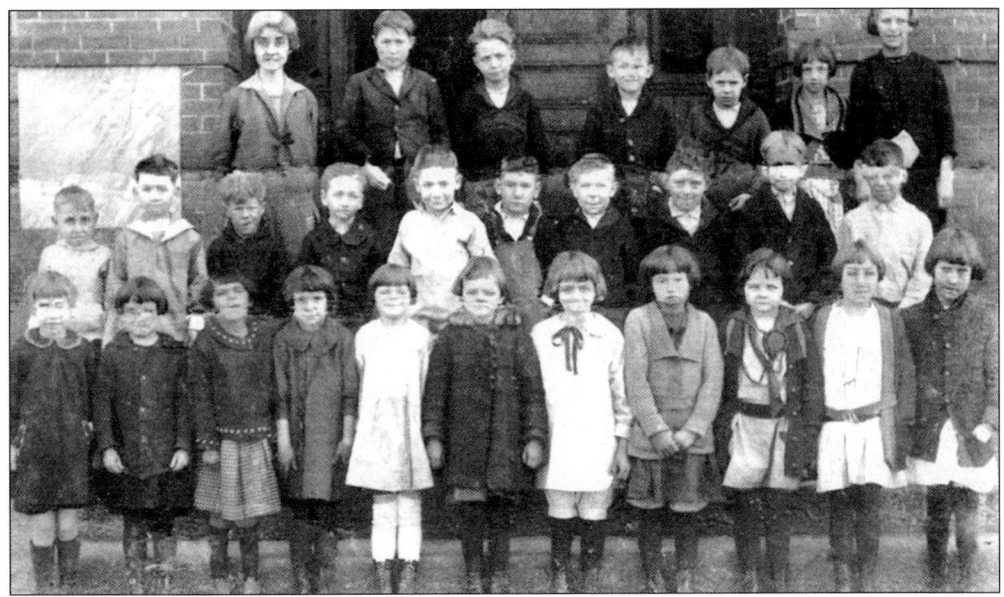

Miss Kate Slade's first grade class at College Street Grammar School is featured here. In the front row at far left is Kennon Henderson (Patton), granddaughter of Charles K. Henderson Sr., a leading citizen. At age four she started at Maple Street School. Due to overcrowding, she was sent to College Street, but she returned to Maple Street the following year. To Kennon's right is Etta Williamson (Massey) and Selma Steinbach. Edna Earl Brown (Eason), third from the right in the first row, is wearing a hearing aid. (Courtesy of Susan Patton Hamersky.)

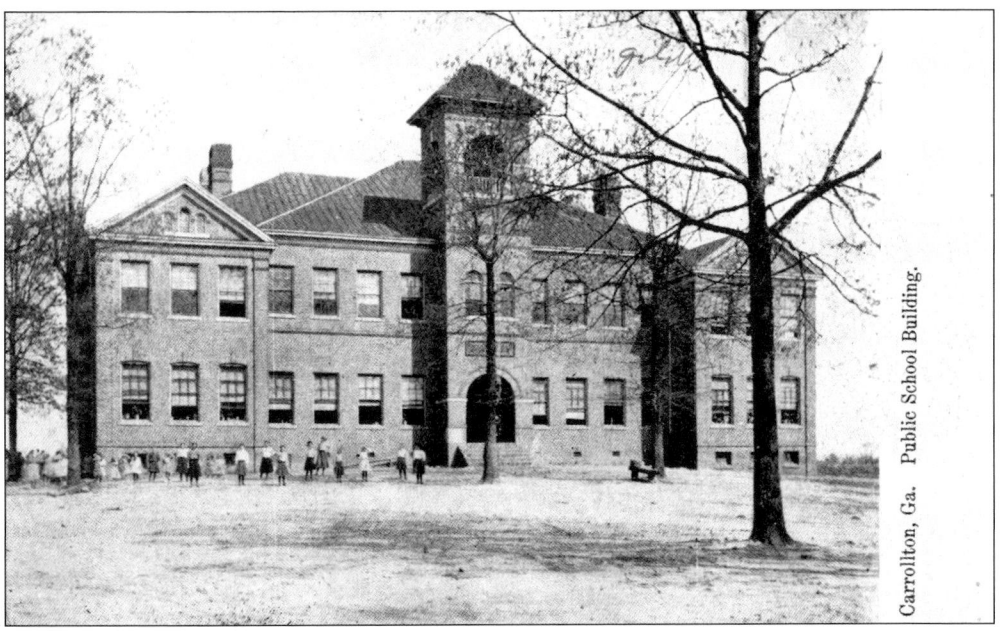

Carrollton Public School was built in 1897 on the previous site of private schools Carrollton Seminary and the Carrollton Masonic Institute. This view, published by MacGown-Cooke Printing of Chattanooga, was postmarked June 1911. The 11th grade was added to the school in 1911.

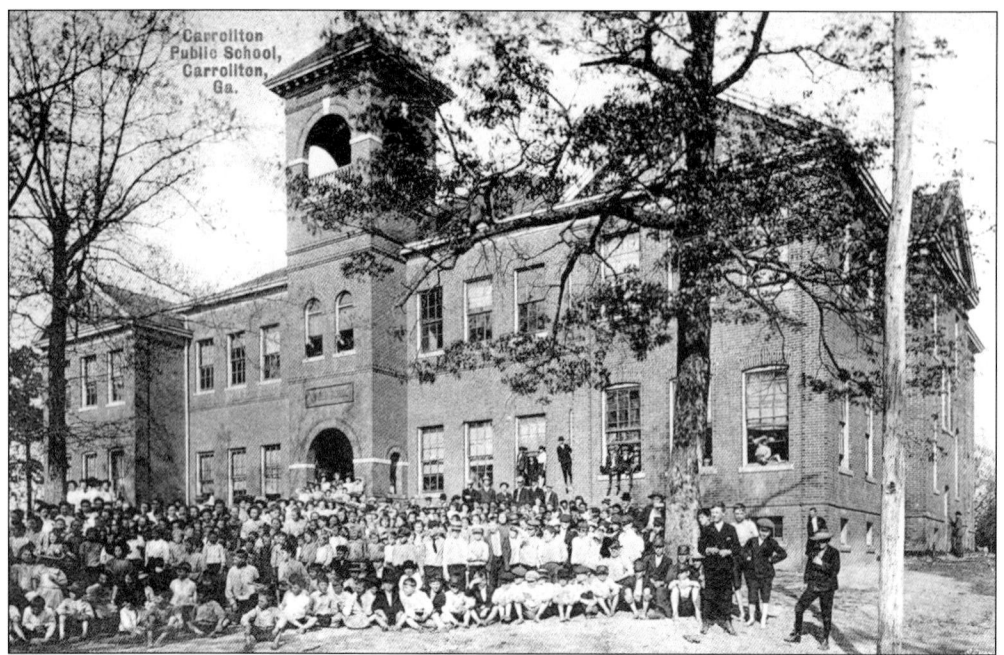

Postmarked July 17, 1911, this view of the Carrollton Public School on College Street features a large number of students on the grounds. The Williams Cash Store of Carrollton published the card.

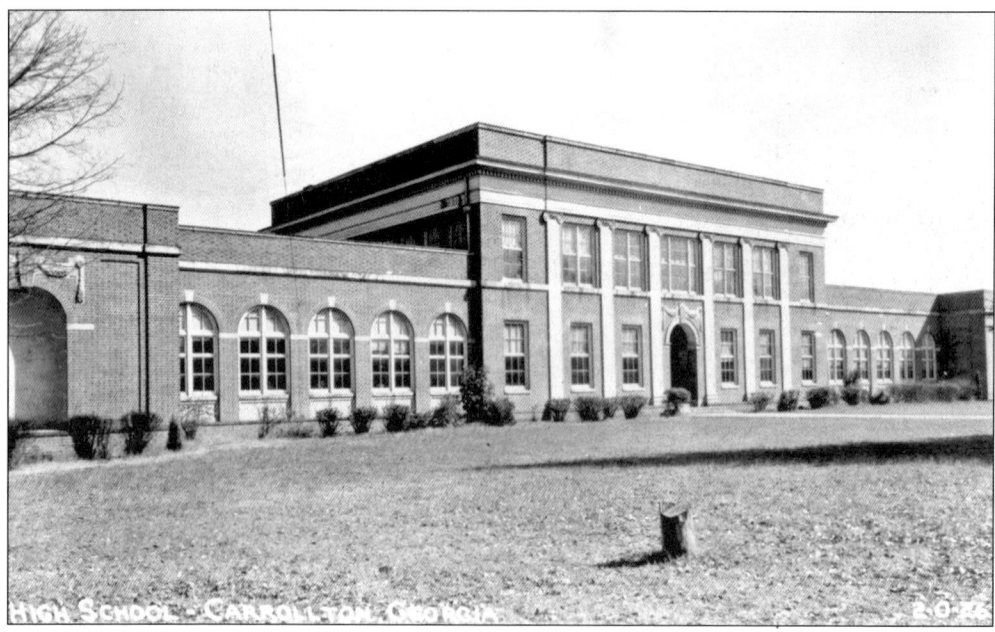

Carrollton High School was built in the 1921–1922 school year at a cost of $100,000. This view of the school is from the 1940s. The opening of a new high school in 1962–1963 forced the school to become a junior high. In 1986, with the addition of a new junior high school, the building became the Carrollton Community Activities Center.

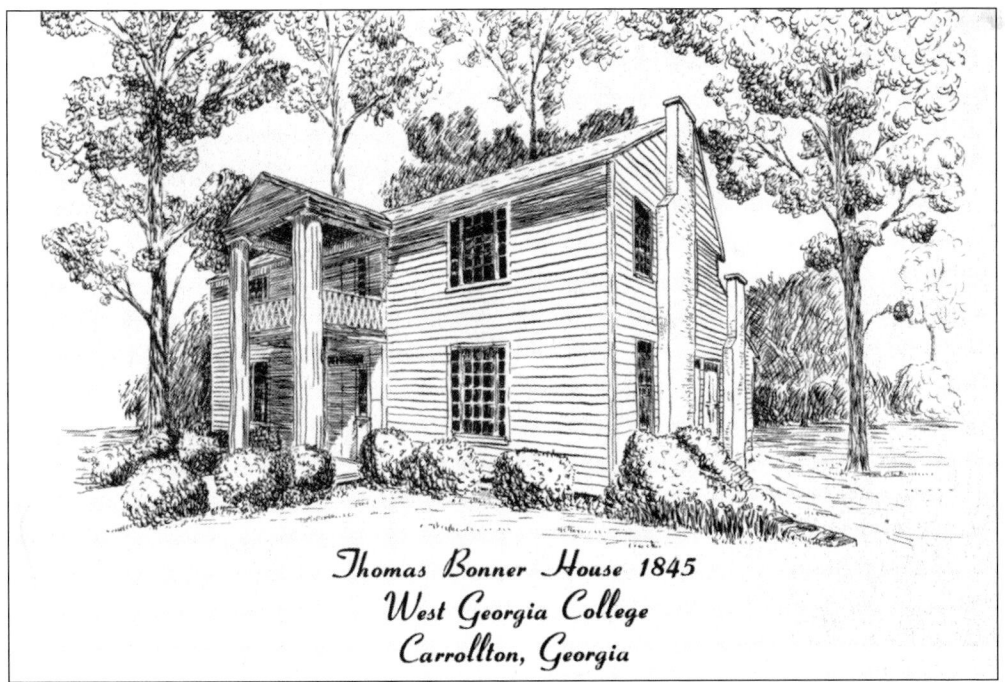

This pen-and-ink card done by John Beckvermitt illustrates the Thomas Bonner House built in 1845. The Bonner plantation is part of the land on which the State University of West Georgia now sits. The land was purchased in 1906 at a cost of $9,000 from B.A. Sharp. The house was moved from its original site several hundred yards east in 1913. It is still in existence today.

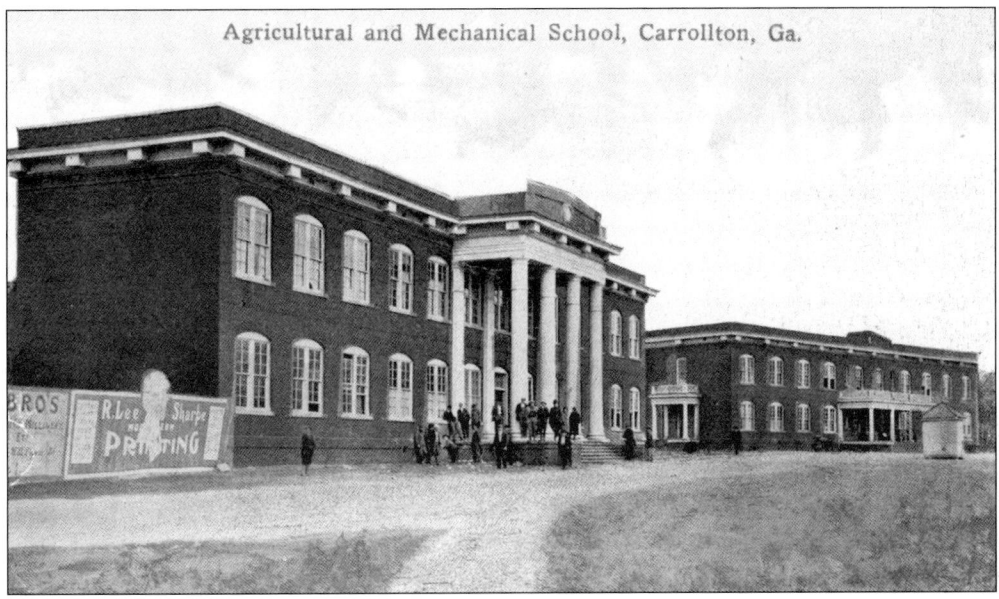

Mailed September 1916, this card shows a very early view of the A&M School. The school served students from 1908 to 1933. The two original buildings—the academic building and the boys' dormitory—and what appears to be a well house can all be seen in the card. Note the sign to the left that advertises R.Lee Sharpe Printing.

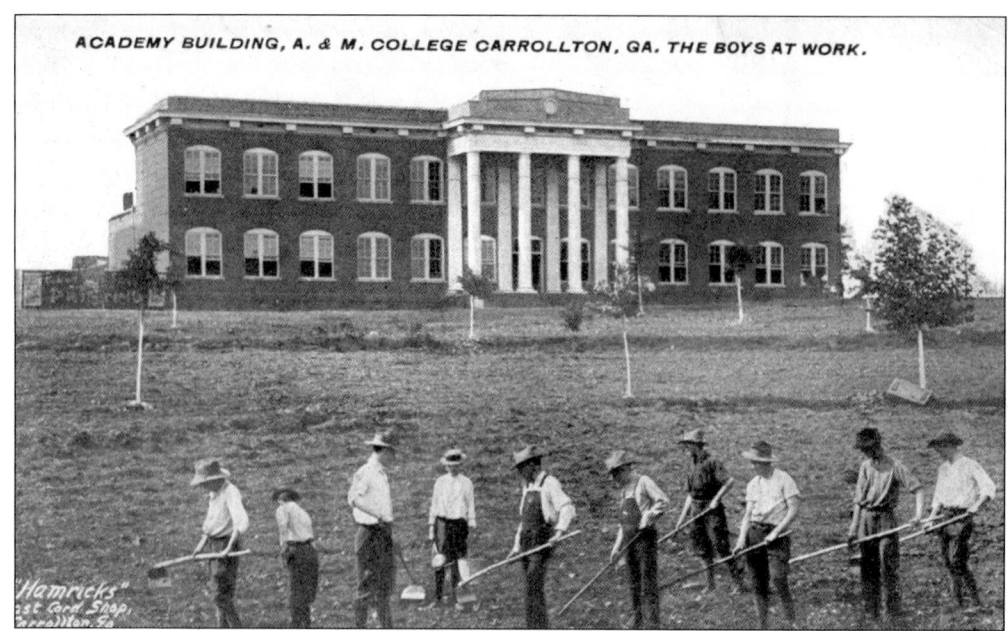

The message on the back of this card reads, "If our plans materialize, we expect to have free courses in Agriculture and Domestic Science for adults at the A&M for the month of August. 50 men and 50 women can be accommodated. Good strong teachers can be employed. We should like to have you for one of the hundred. If you are interested, let me hear from you. J.H. Melson, Principal." In pencil is noted the name C. Chestnut.

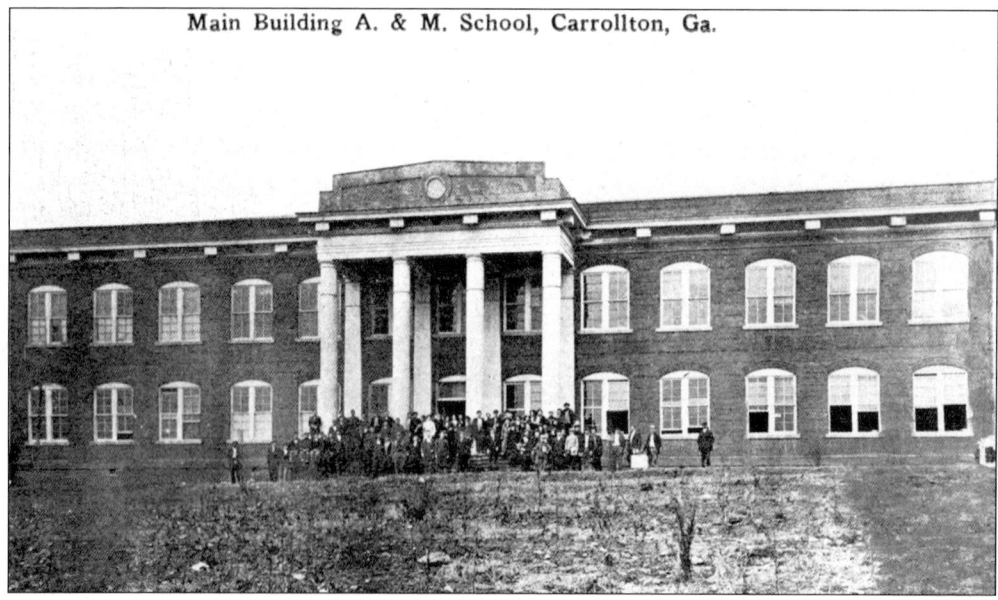

Another early view of the academic building is shown here. By 1910, the A&M school had a farm of 275 acres, three brick buildings erected at a cost of $30,000, and a two-story framed house used as a girls' dormitory and barn. About 100 of the acres were in cultivation. Two names associated with the building of the school were L.C. Mandeville and J.A. Aycock. Buildings on campus were later named in their honor.

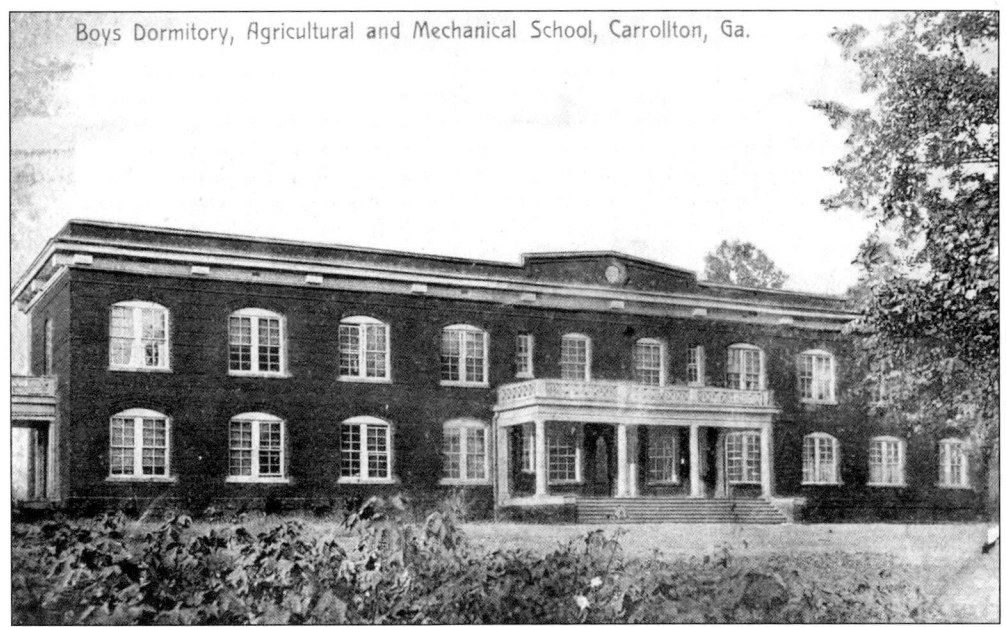

Mailed February 14, 1909, from Carrollton and published by N.A. Horton of Carrollton, this card shows the boys' dormitory building. The building featured 42 living rooms that could each house two male students, bath rooms, and closets. The academic building had six large recitation rooms, an auditorium that could seat 500, a sewing room, and a library.

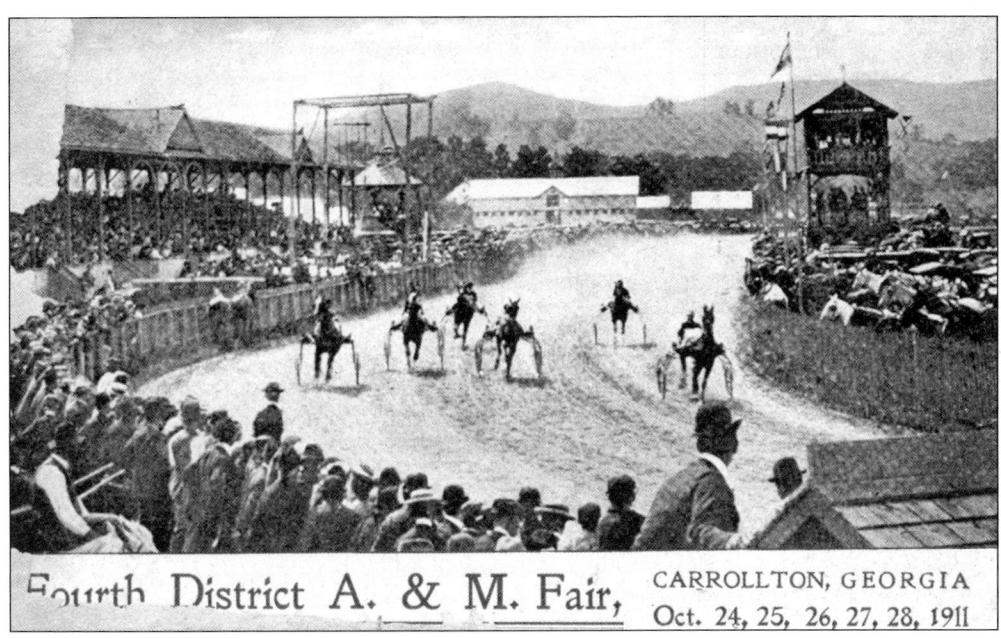

A rare advertisement card for the Fourth District A&M Fair, held in October 1911, features a view of a racetrack. The A&M School Fair Association was organized in 1909, and its object was "to encourage and promote agriculture, stock raising, horticulture, arborculture, and conservation of natural resources." Over 16,000 people attended the first fair. The fair was reorganized in 1921 as the Carroll County Fair. (Courtesy of Gary Doster.)

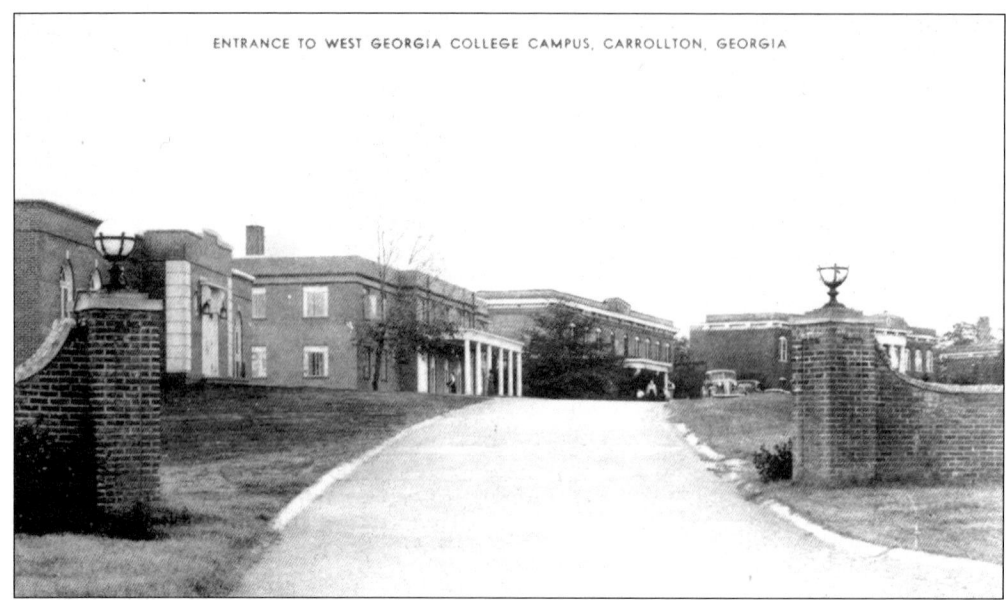

In 1933, West Georgia College was created after funding for the statewide A&M schools stopped. Dr. Irvine S. Ingram served as the last principal of the A&M School and became the first president of West Georgia College, a junior college. In 1957, West Georgia College became a senior college with President Ingram serving the school from 1920 to 1960. The current library at the state university is named in honor of Dr. Ingram.

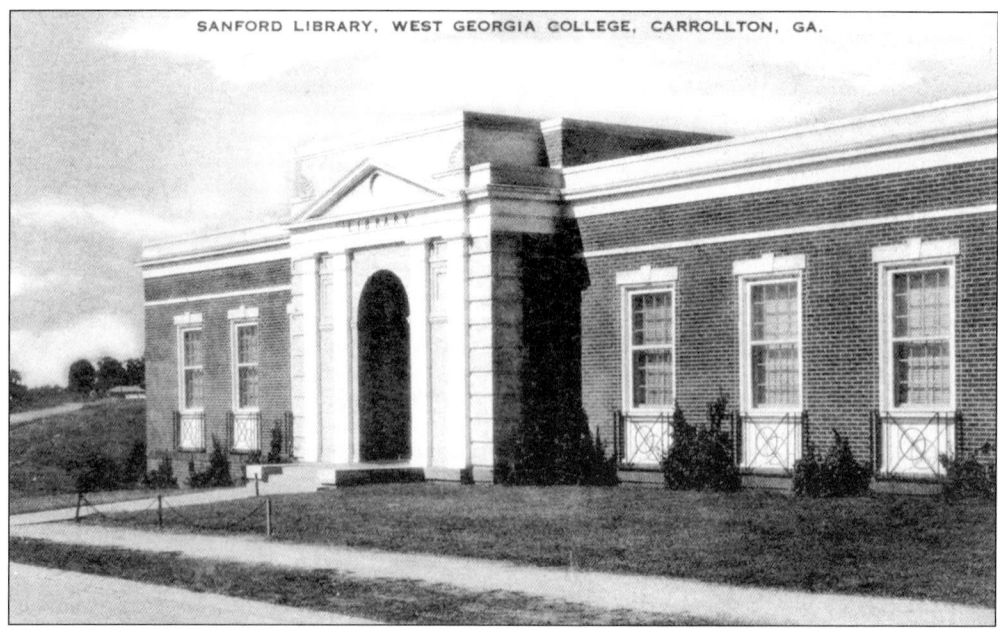

Postmarked June 17, 1944, this postcard shows the front of the Sanford Library at West Georgia College. Built in 1938, the library was named for Steadman V. Sanford, a chancellor of the University System. The college library was located on the first floor from 1944 until the 1960s, and the West Georgia Regional Library was located in the basement. Today, it is known as Sanford Hall and houses administrative offices.

The First Baptist Church is located on the corner of Dixie and Newnan Streets across from the Carroll County Courthouse. Records indicate that church services were held at this site since 1875–1876, but this brick church building was built in 1908. Published by N.A. Horton of Carrollton, the card was addressed and mailed *c.* 1912 to Miss Delphia Wester and encouraged her to purchase striped pink and crepe material for a dress.

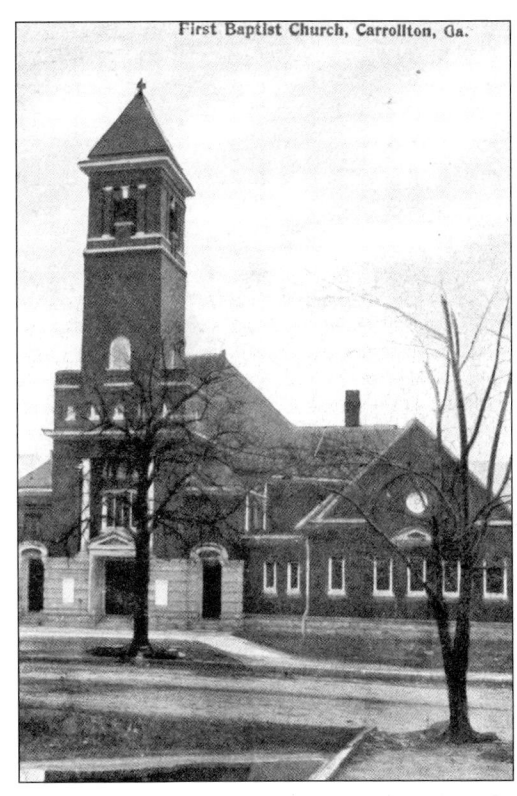

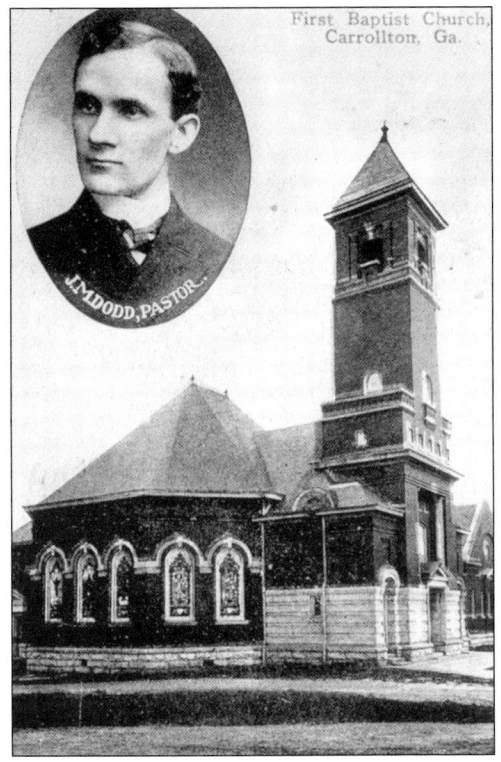

This is a side view of the First Baptist Church from Newnan Street. This early view of a church is unusual in that it features a picture of the pastor, J.M. Dodd. This view shows the ornate Tiffany stained-glass windows and the impressive bell tower.

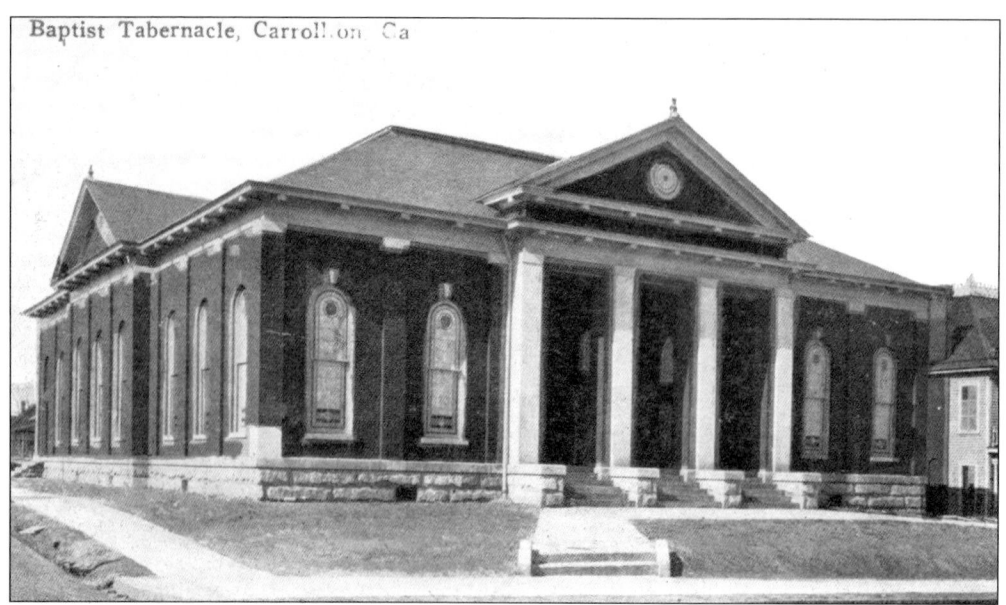

The Baptist Tabernacle Church was created when a split took place within the Baptist community. The Central Baptist Church, later known as the Tabernacle Church, was thus established. The church pictured was built in 1913 on Depot Street. It was claimed that the church auditorium was the largest in the state when it was built. The Tabernacle congregation moved to their new building in 1989. Today, this is the site of Carrollton City Hall.

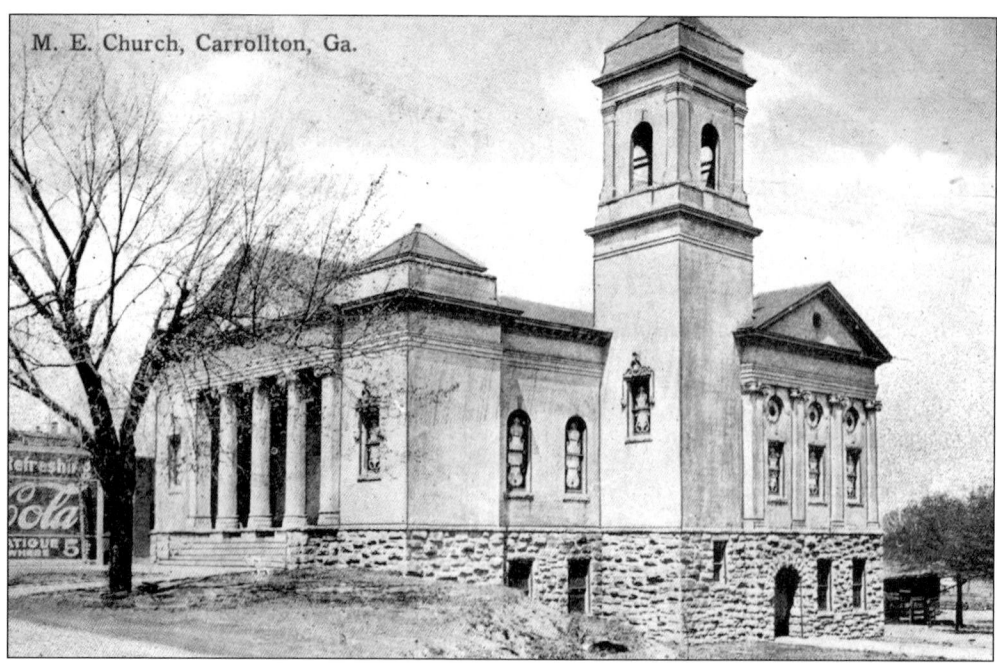

Today known as the First United Methodist Church, the M.E. Church located on Newnan Street was dedicated by Bishop Warren Candler, formerly of Villa Rica, in a sermon in 1906. This building replaced a wooden church on the same site that had served the congregation. The Williams Cash Store of Carrollton published this card.

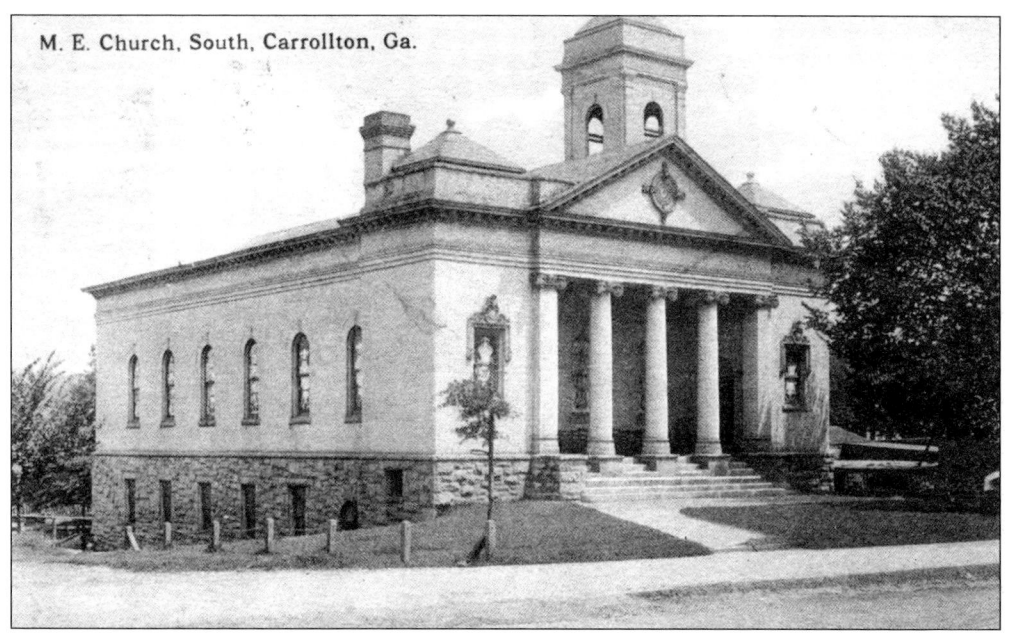

Published by Horton's Book Store and postmarked January 27, 1918, this card is another view of the M.E. Church. Addressed to Rev. A.E. Sansborn from a sender named Laura, the message concerns a missionary conference.

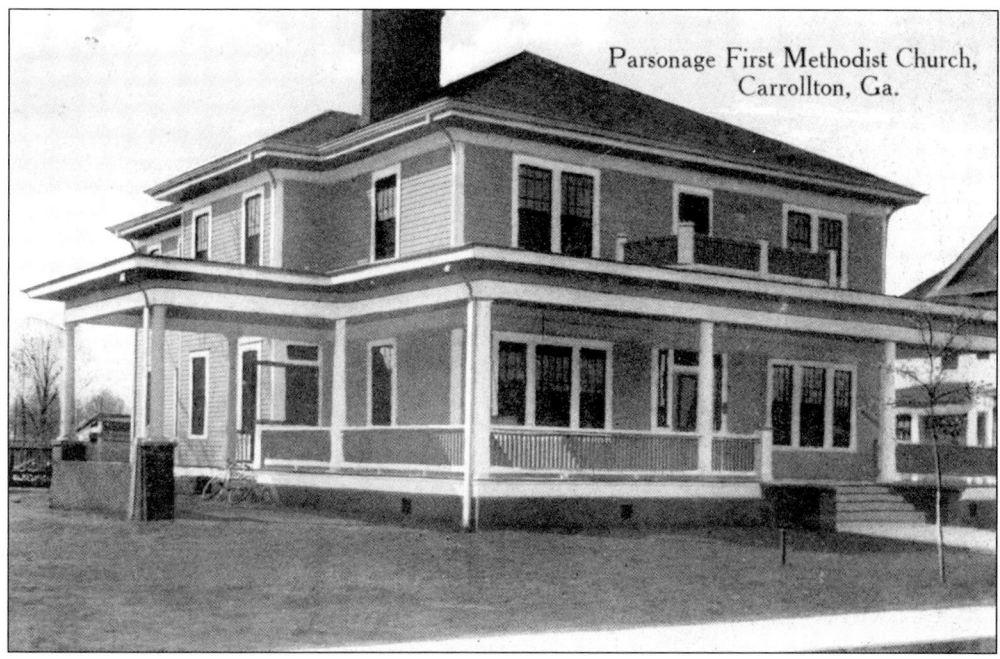

This card is a view of the parsonage of the First Methodist Church in Carrollton. Postmarked January 26, 1918, and addressed to Rev. A.E. Sansborn from a woman named Laura, she warns the reverend not to eat the food in the "ice box."

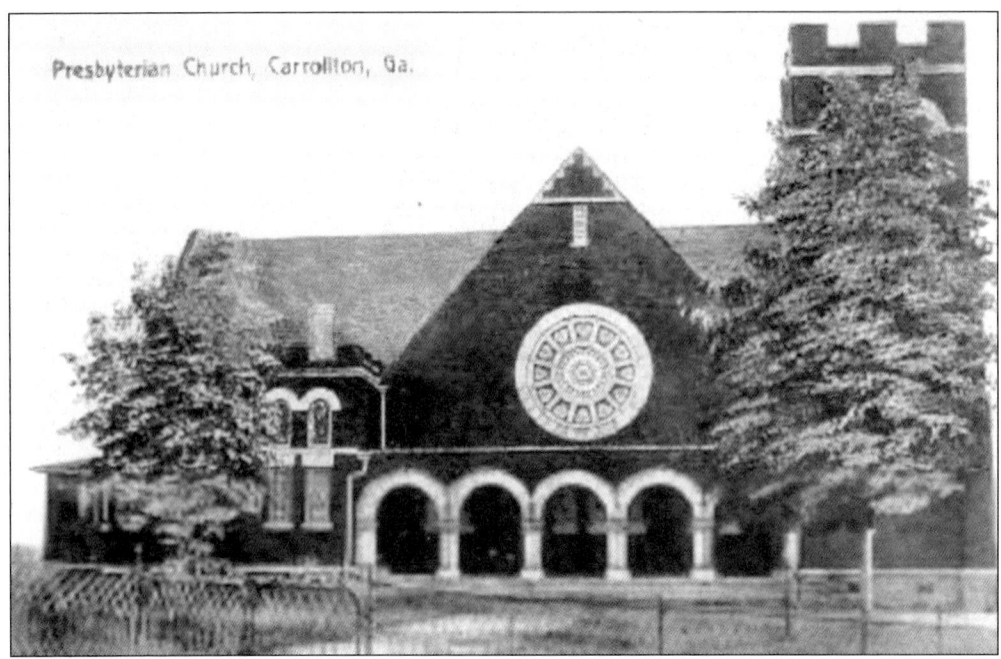

The Presbyterian Church of Carrollton was organized in 1841, and the present structure was built in 1902. The building committee consisted of L.C. Mandeville, J.A. Aycock, and A.A. Simonton, with the Reverend Cozier serving as an ex-officio member. This card was postmarked 1909 and was published by N.A. Horton of Carrollton.

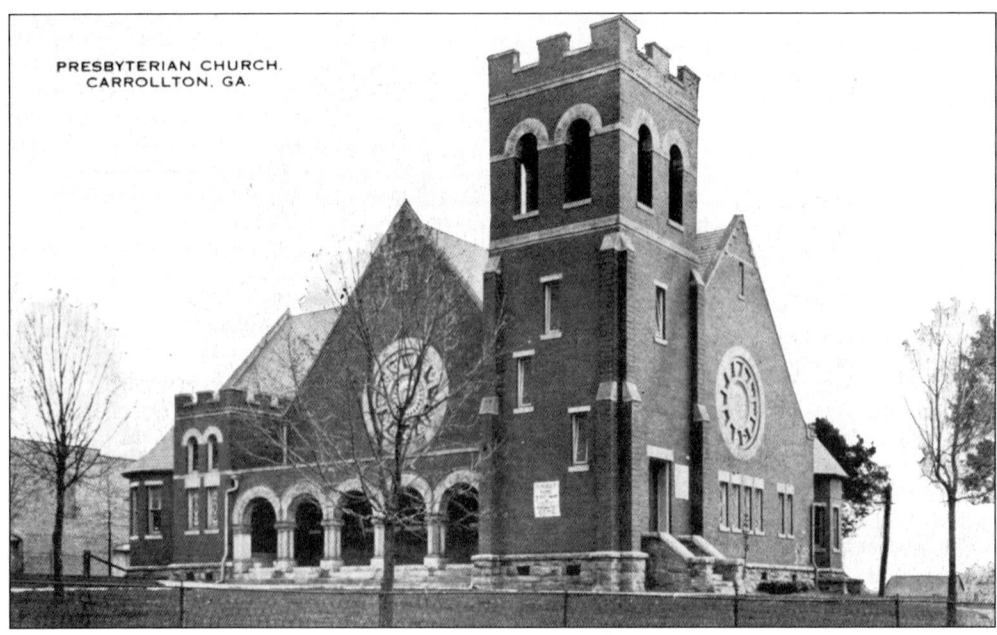

A different view of the Presbyterian Church of Carrollton is shown above. Reverend Cozier served the church as pastor from 1894 to 1915 and was the first pastor in the 1902 building. The church building is known for its beautiful, large and round stained-glass windows.

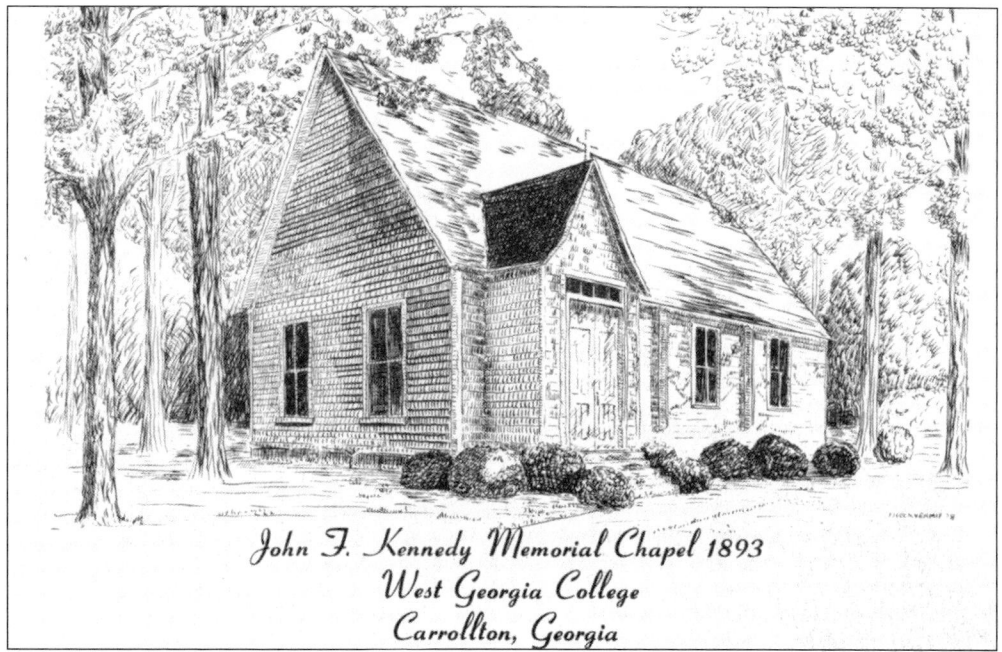

This pen-and-ink notecard by local artist John Beckvermitt shows the John F. Kennedy Memorial Chapel, which was built in 1893 as an Episcopal church. The white-framed building was used as a Catholic church from 1954 to 1962 and was donated and moved to West Georgia College in 1964 as an interfaith chapel. Named in memory of President Kennedy, his brother Robert gave the dedication address.

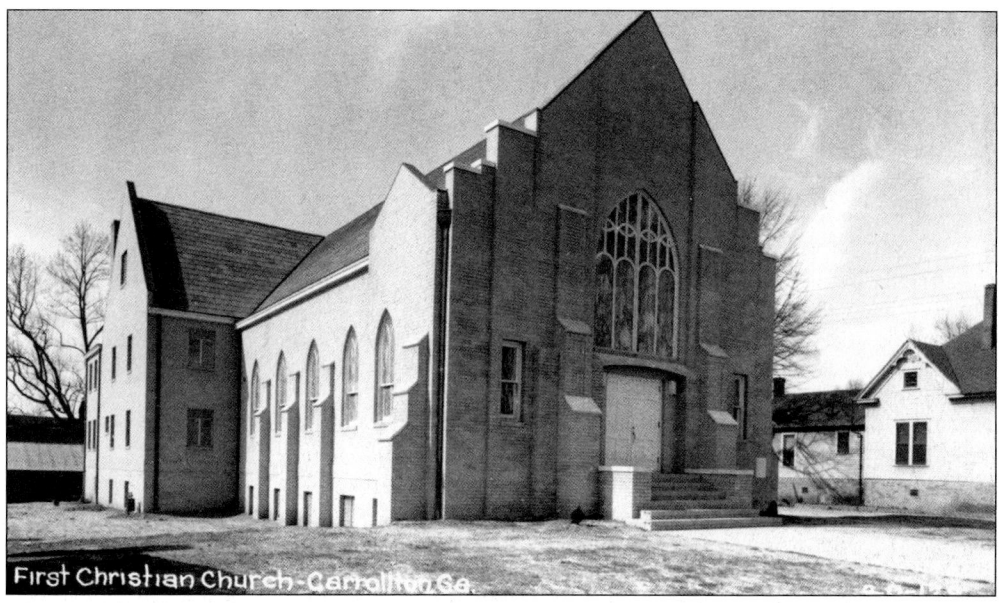

The First Christian Church of Carrollton was built on the corner of Ward and College Streets on March 19, 1946. George Carter constructed the Gothic, buff brick building. The building committee consisted of W.J. Aldridge, Grady Cole, Lester Reeves, Elbert Traylor, and Mayor William Traylor. A Mr. Morgan served as chairman.

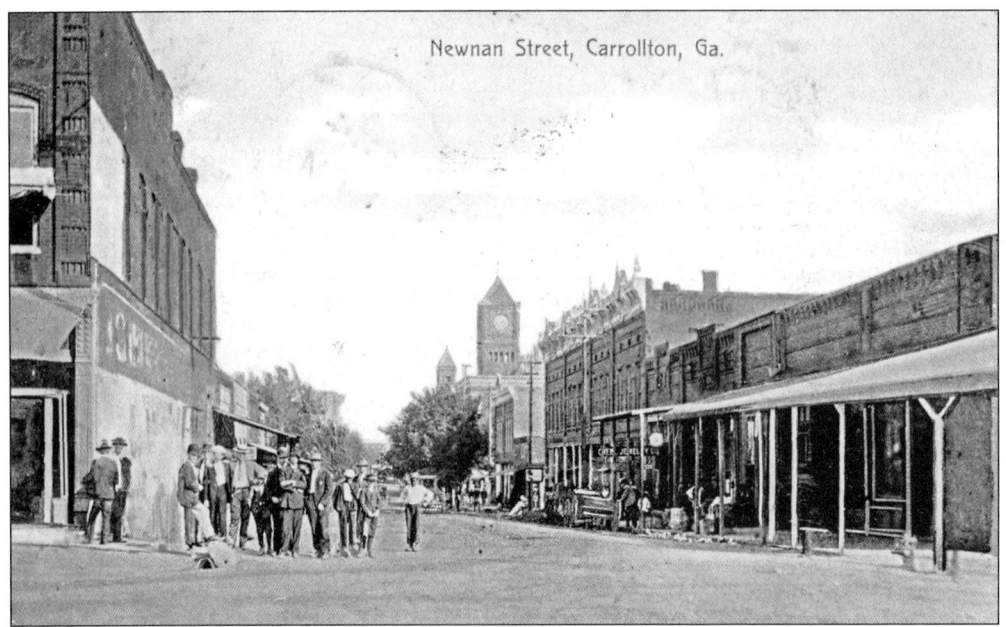

This is a street scene, looking down Newnan Street from the center of the square in Carrollton, c. 1910. Located on the right side of the card is a Creel Jewelry sign. The Roop Building, the Holderness Building, and the Masonic Building can be seen in front of the courthouse and First Baptist Church towers.

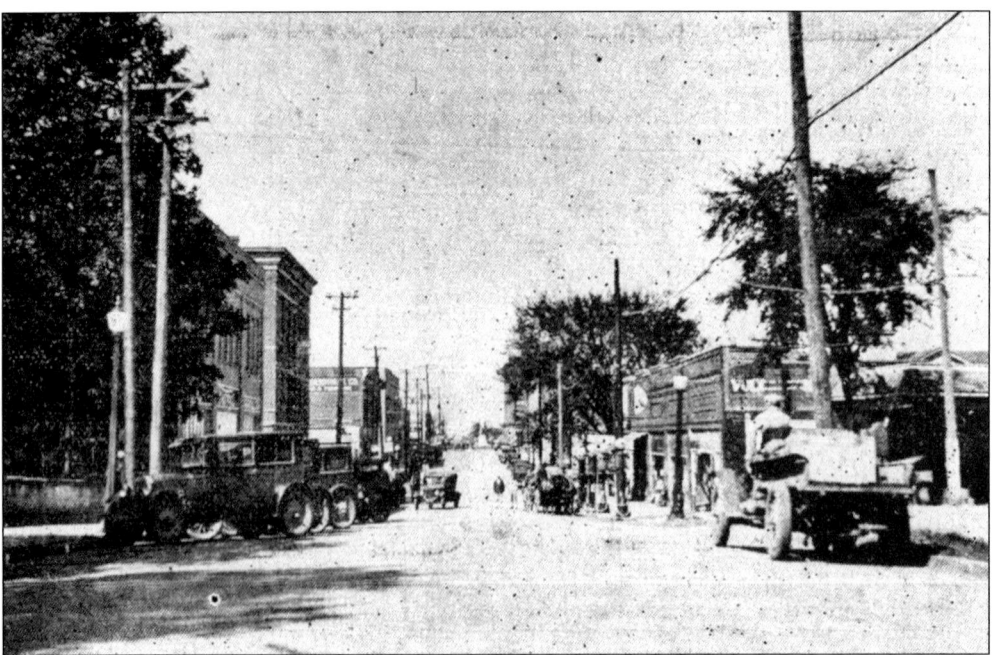

This 1928 view of Newnan Street looks toward the square. Located in the center of the square is the Confederate monument. To the left can be seen the Folds Motor Company Building and then the Masonic Building. Across the street is an early gas station with gas pumps located on the curb.

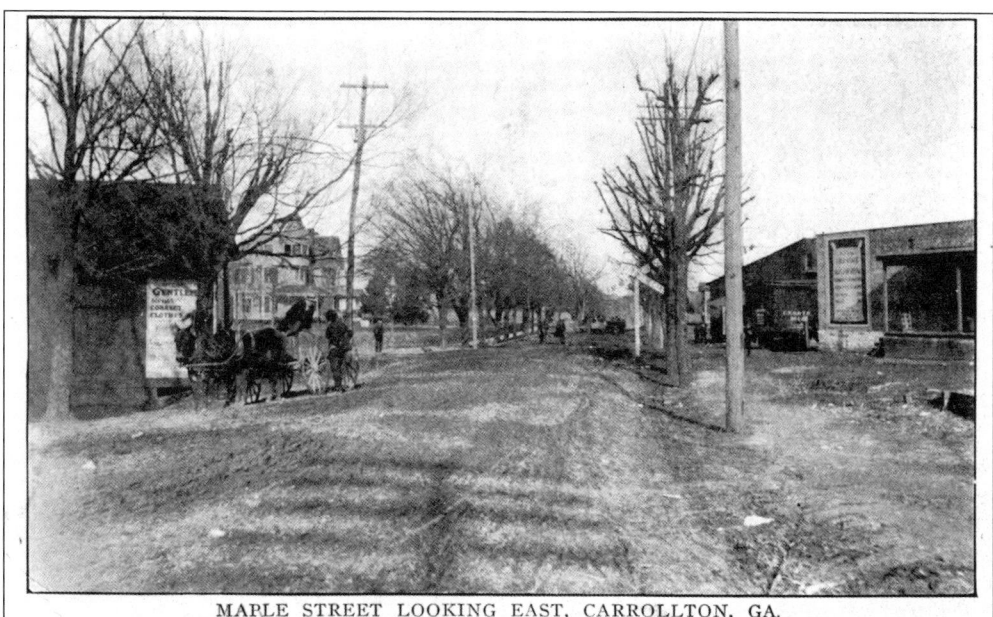

MAPLE STREET LOOKING EAST, CARROLLTON, GA.

Maple Street looking east towards downtown is the focus of this postcard, *c.* 1915. The crossed wooden sign reads, "Look Out The Cars and Railroad Cross." Note the large Victorian home to the left, which was the home of L.C. Mandeville, completed in 1890. Today, this home is known as the Maple Street Mansion. Originally known as Bowdon Street, Maple Street got its name from the maple trees planted by Appleton Mandeville.

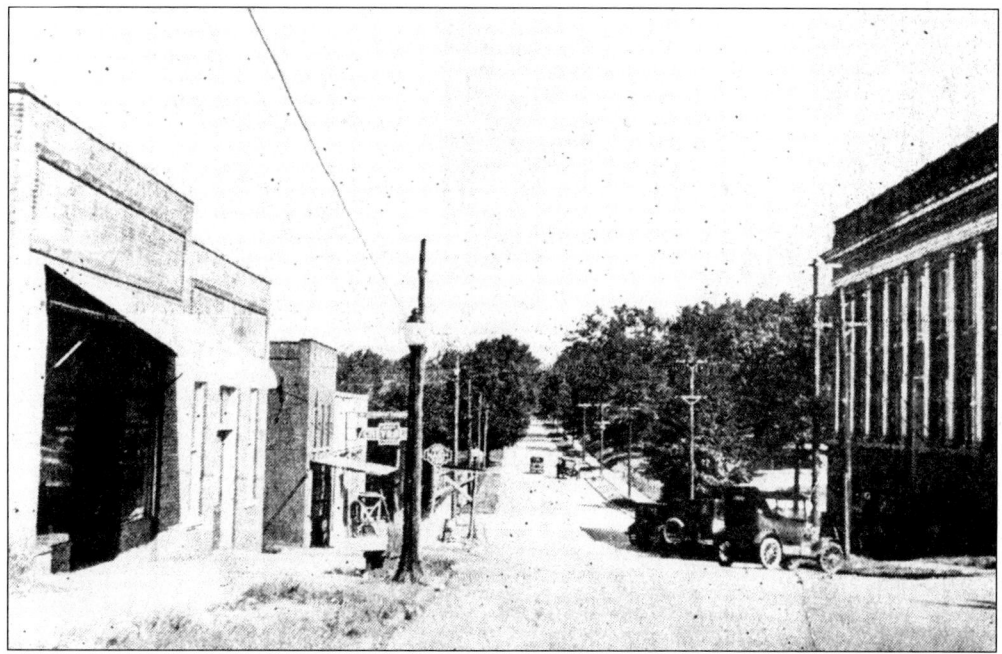

Here, a view of Rome Street looks north from the square. On the right, the rear of city hall is visible. On the left is the Carroll Chevrolet Company, which opened in the building in 1927, and the Bonner & Tuggle Nash Dealership. This view is from 1928.

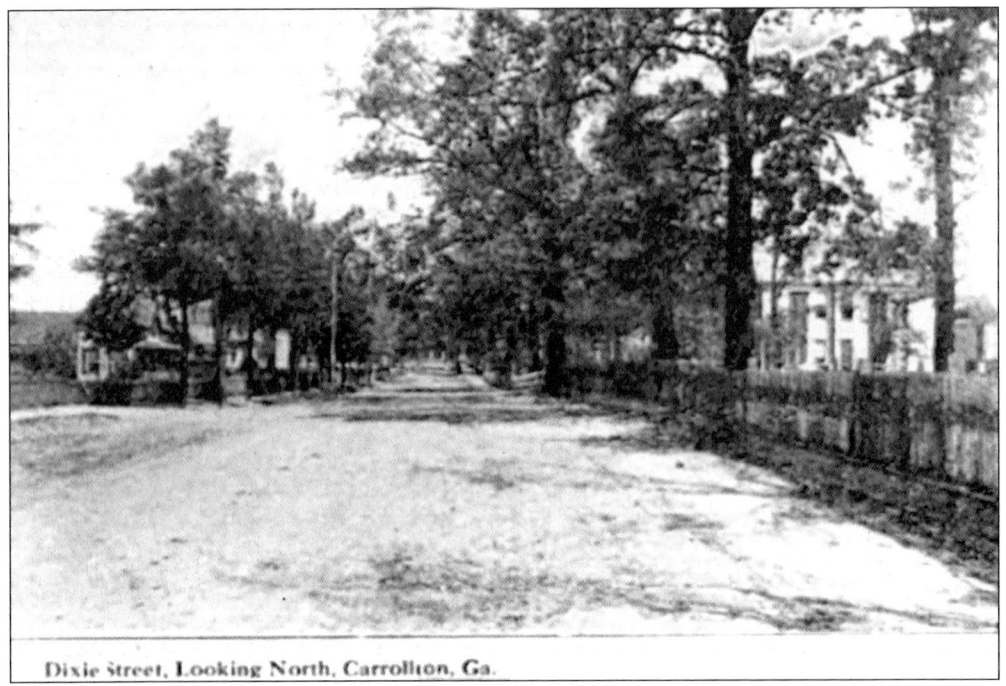

Dixie Street, Looking North, Carrollton, Ga.

Dixie Street has always had some of Carrollton's oldest and finest homes. Today, known for its beautiful, sidewalk-lining azaleas, the street owes its names to Civil War times when Yankee raiders attacked the town. Southern troops approaching from the south were said to have been singing "Dixie." The sounds drove off the raiders and saved much of the town, and the street was given the name Dixie in honor of the troops' gallant efforts to save the town.

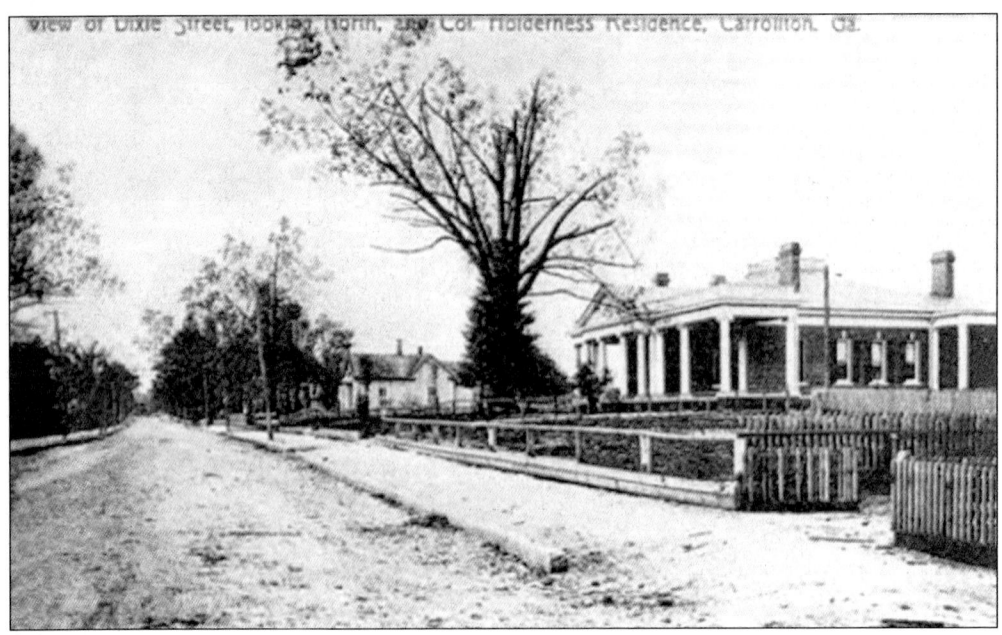

View of Dixie Street, looking North, and Col. Holderness Residence, Carrollton, Ga.

This is a view of Dixie Street looking north, with the Col. Sidney Holderness residence on the right.

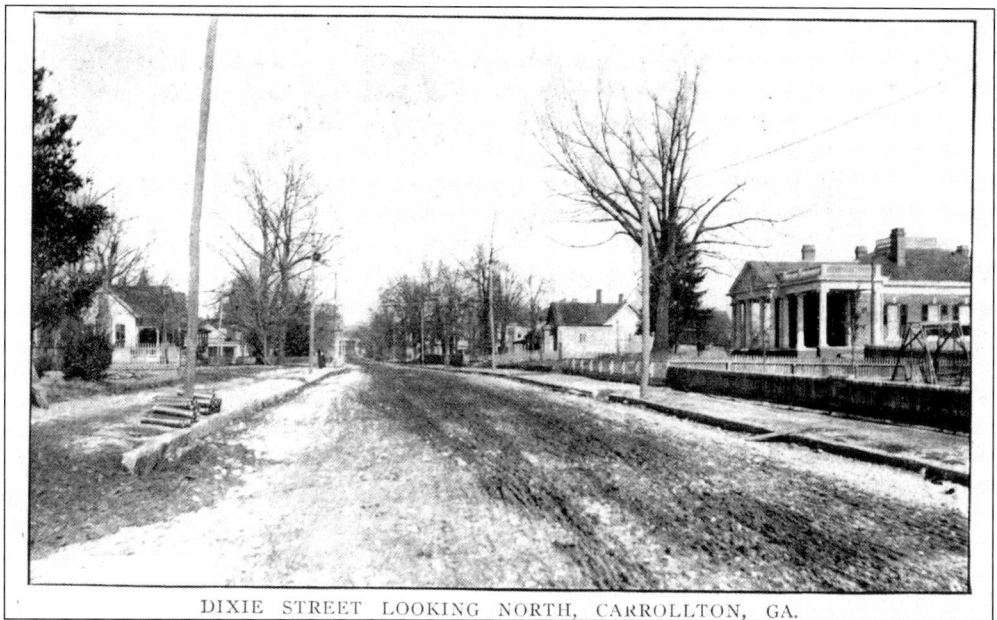

DIXIE STREET LOOKING NORTH, CARROLLTON, GA.

This is another view of Dixie Street looking north with the Col. Sidney Holderness residence on the right.

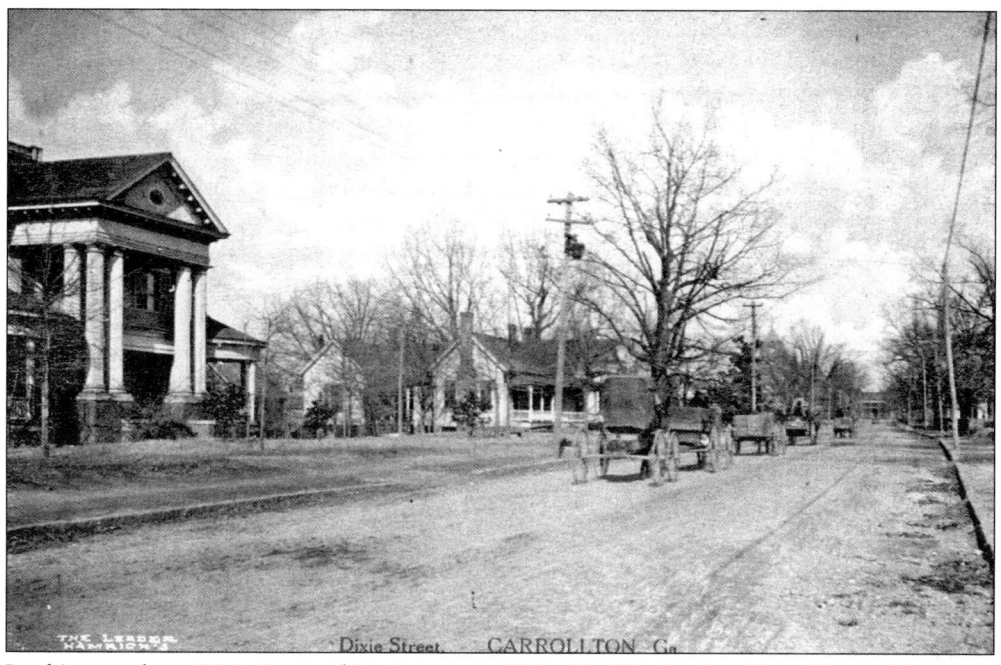

Looking north on Dixie Street, this view was published by The Leader, Hamricks, and features a group of wagons and horse-and-buggies going towards town. The large house to the left once belonged to Dr. Henry J. Goodwyn. The Southland Hotel is believed to be seen at the end of the street.

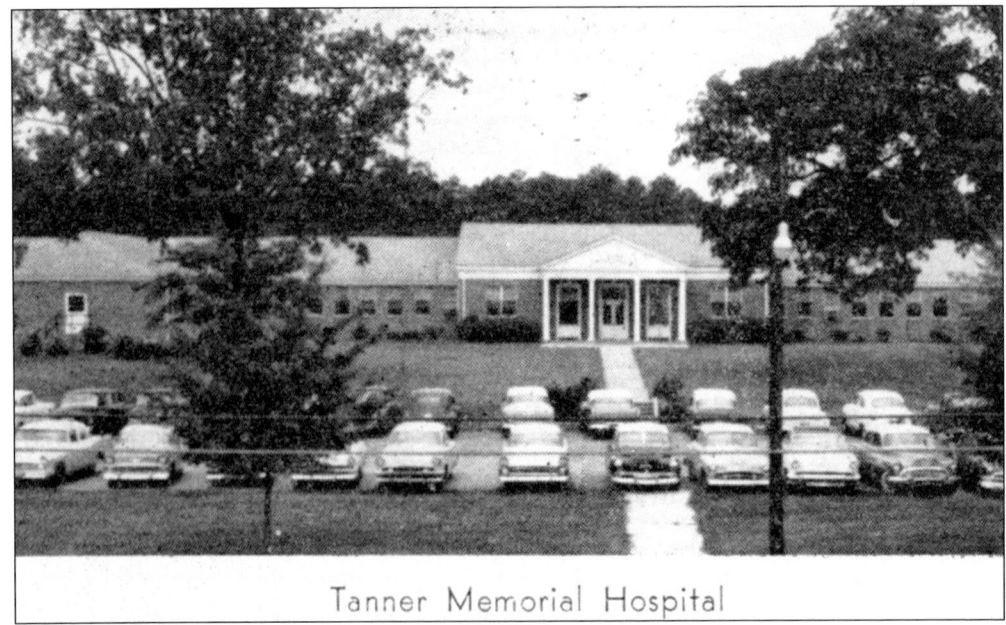

Tanner Memorial Hospital

Tanner Memorial Hospital is featured in this Carrollton Chamber of Commerce view from 1956. The card reads, "Tanner Memorial Hospital, completely new and modern, is equipped with modern operating room, obstetrical facilities and complete clinical equipment. Staffed by fifteen physicians, including many specialists. County Health Center located adjacent to the hospital." The hospital was named for its largest benefactor and leading citizen, C.M. Tanner.

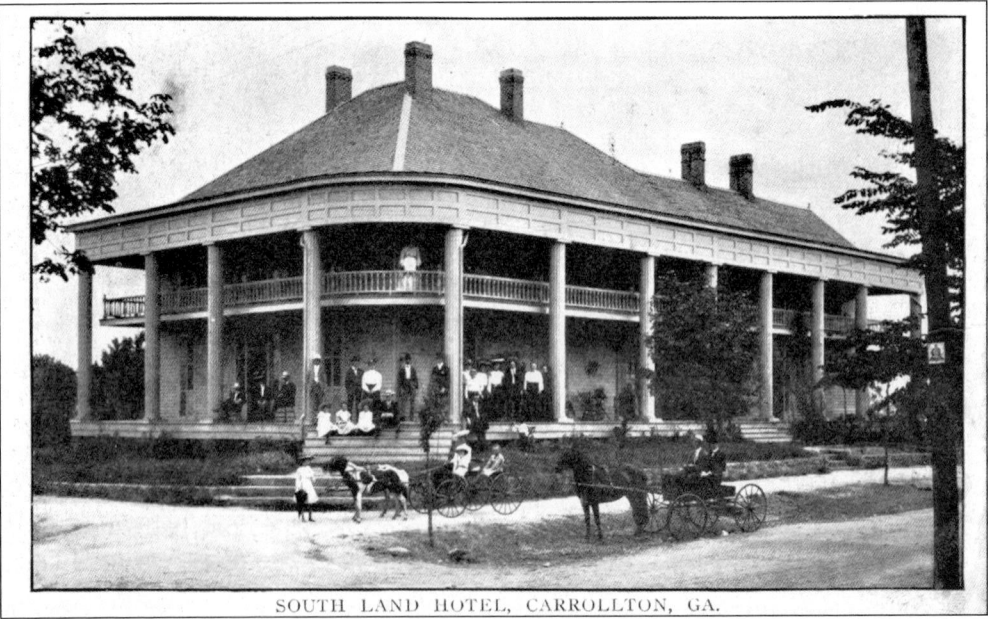

SOUTH LAND HOTEL, CARROLLTON, GA.

The Southland Hotel was originally built across the street from the Carrollton Presbyterian Church but burned and was rebuilt on Newnan Street across from the First Baptist Church. Postmarked May 1908, the card shows the hotel with the large, beautiful porch that encircled the second floor. Early photographs show that the hotel was located next to the post office.

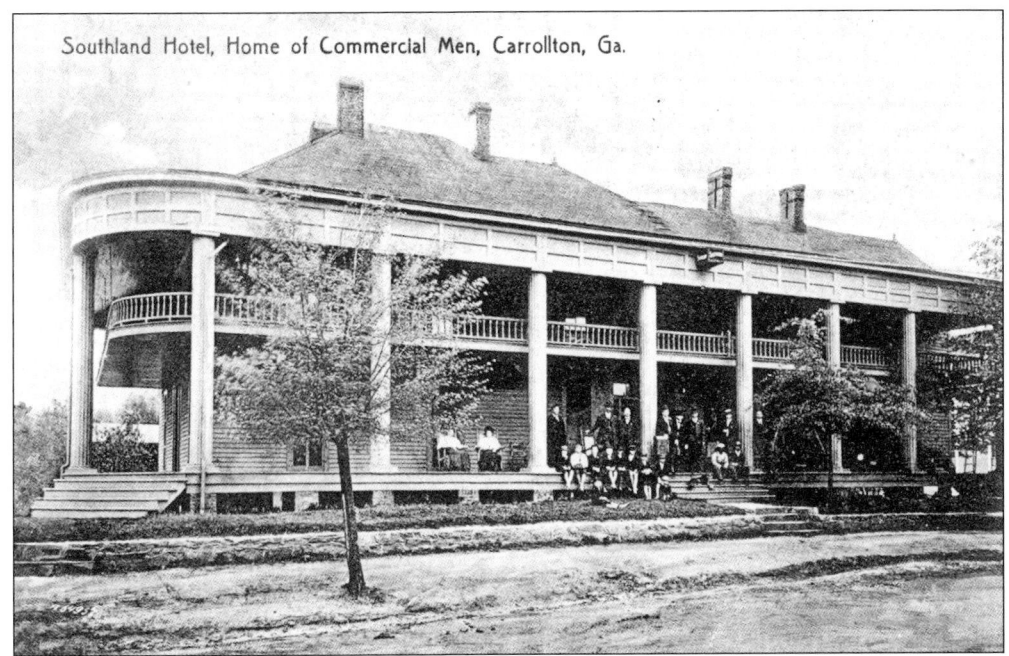

This advertisement card claims the Southland Hotel is the home of commercial men. This card was signed by Jas Roy Beall, and he wrote, "Beall and Brown in town. Don't you know we are painting this North Ga. town red?" The card was published by Holt & Cates Co. of Newnan and was made in Germany.

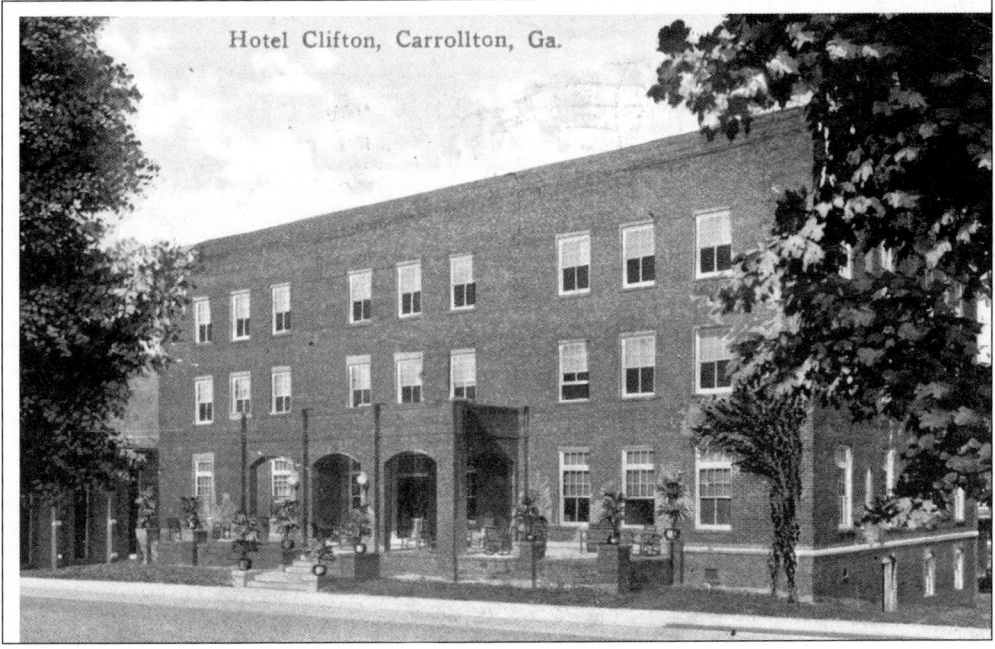

Hotel Clifton was built on the site of the burned Southland Hotel. The hotel served the Carrollton community from 1911 to the 1940s. A simple message on the back reads, "A very nice day, 11–22–21." (Courtesy of Gary Doster.)

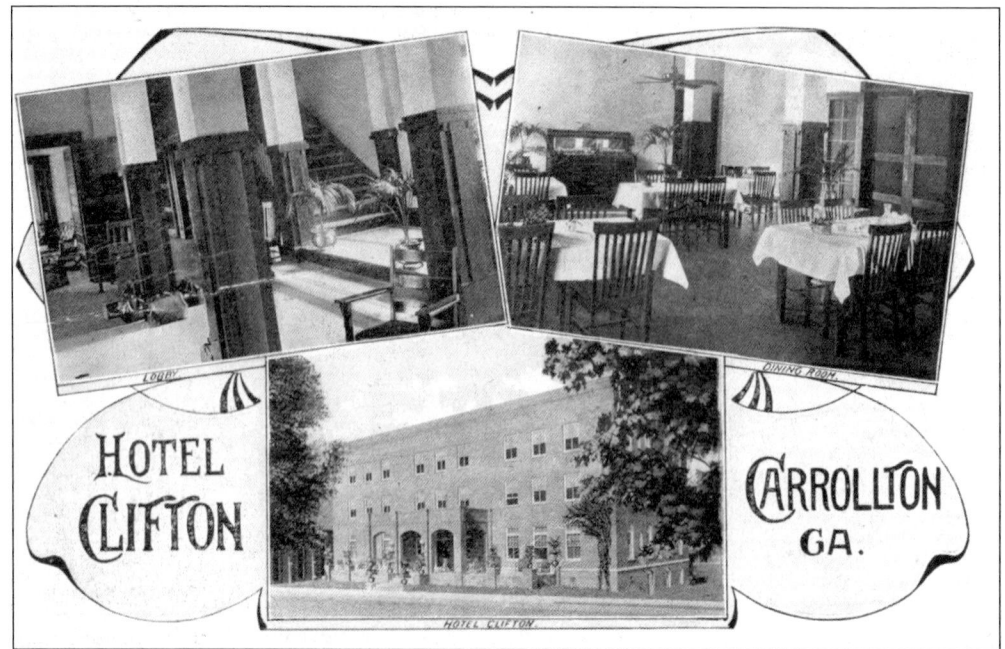

This card depicts scenes of the interior of the Hotel Clifton. It is postmarked 1917 and features the lobby and dining room. (Courtesy of Gary Doster.)

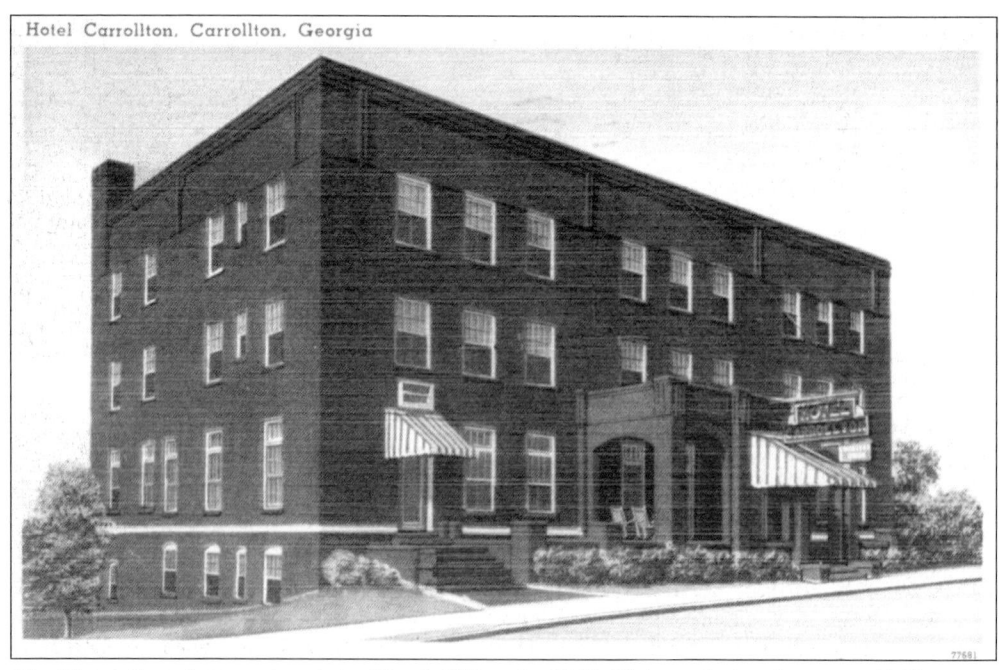

The Hotel Carrollton replaced the Hotel Clifton in 1947. This card, dated January 1948, states, "West Georgia's finest Hotel, Home of Carrollton's Civic Clubs, Coffee Shop and Dining Room. Every room with bath. On U.S. 27." Today, the building is the United Community Bank.

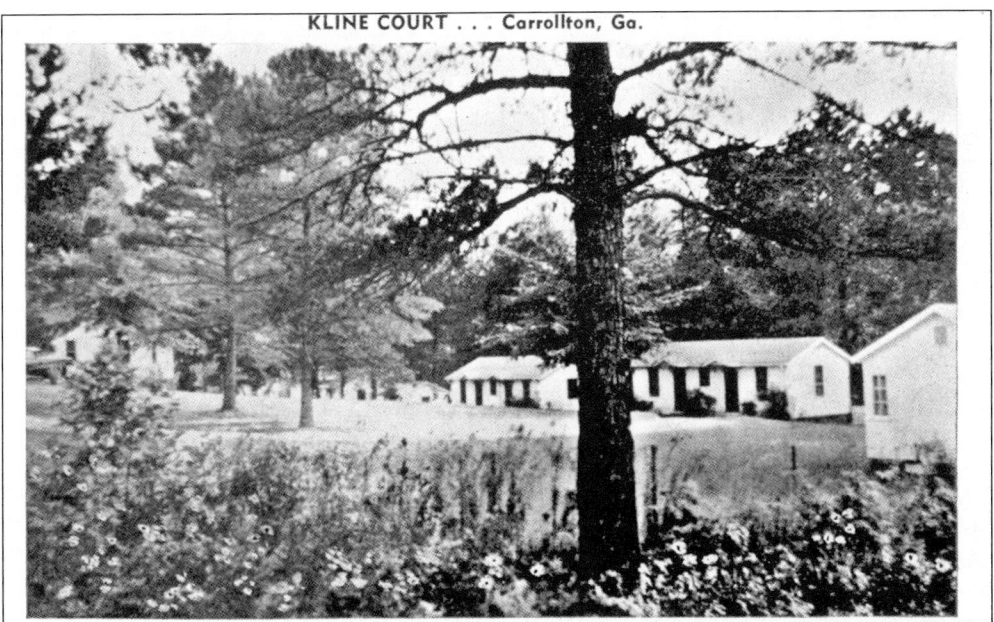

The back of the Kline Court card, published by Kroop Co. of Milwaukee, reads, "Located U.S. Highway 27, ? mile north of Carrollton, Ga. City water, all modern rooms, stop and look, approved only by you. Owner operated by Mr. and Mrs. L.M. Kline, phone 1422W."

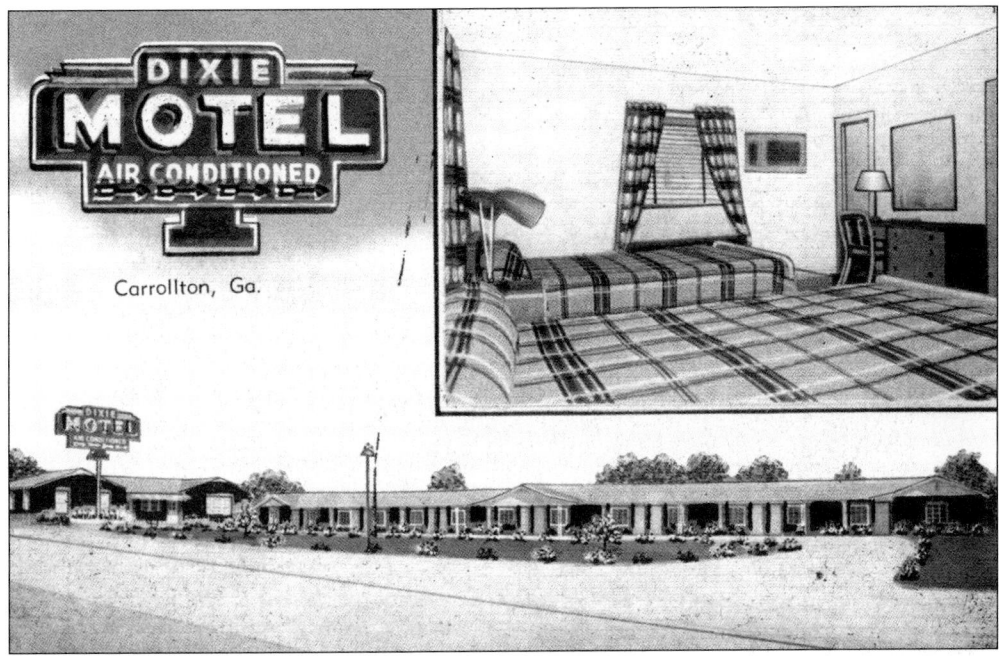

The back of this card, published by the Kroop Co., reads as follows: "Dixie Motel. 100% Air Conditioned. In city limits, Dixie St. Fed. Hwy 27 South—All city conveniences—nearby to churches—theatres and business district. New—Modern. Brick construction—circulating water heat—Simmons Beauty Rest Mattresses—wall to wall carpet floor—all tile baths. Phone 1797. Proprietor Seaman Baskin. Resident Manager Mrs. Leola Sampler."

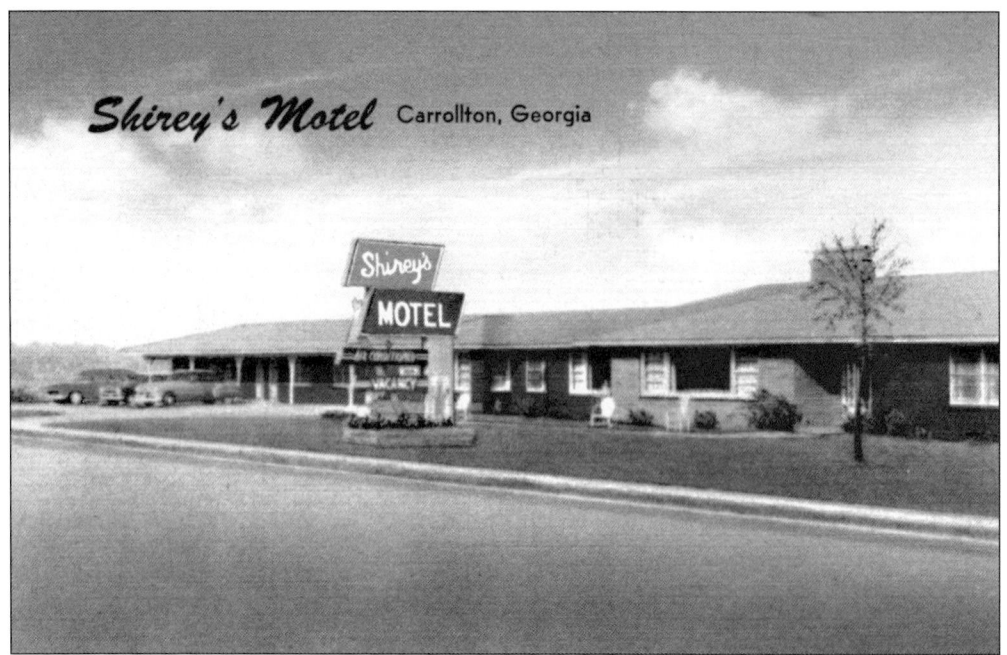

This card reads, "Shirey's Motel Up-Town. Tourist Lounge with Television. Latest Thing in Motels. Hi-Way 27. Carrollton, Ga. Tel. 2–3102. Mr. and Mrs. Opal Shirey, Owners and Operators."

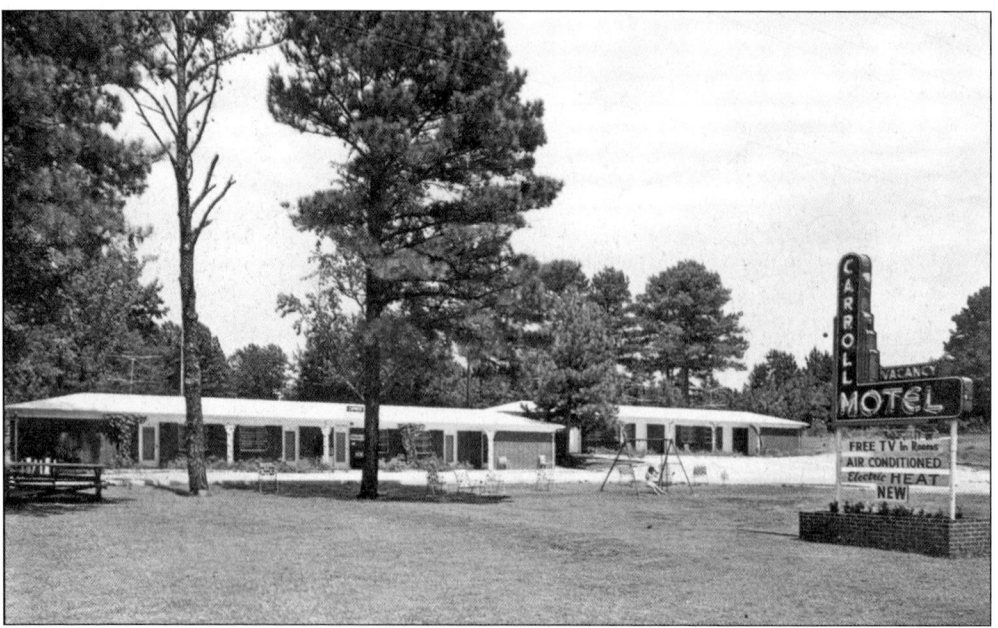

This card reads as follows: "Carroll Motel. North on U.S. 27. Carrollton Ga. Carrollton's newest motel, all rooms free TV, 100% air-conditioned, 16 brick units, electric heat, tile tub and shower combination, family units, restaurant near. Phone Terrace 2–6062. Mr. and Mrs. Gerald R. Batchler, Owner-Managers."

This 1908 card features a view of Carrollton's pumping station on the bank of the Tallapoosa River.

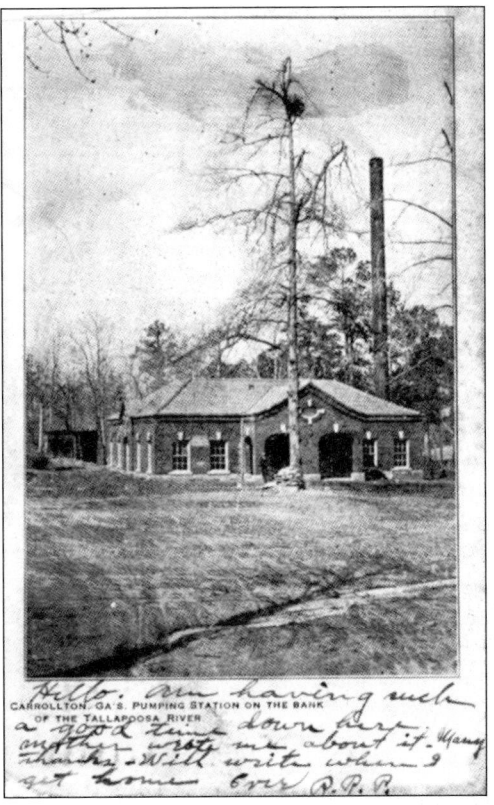

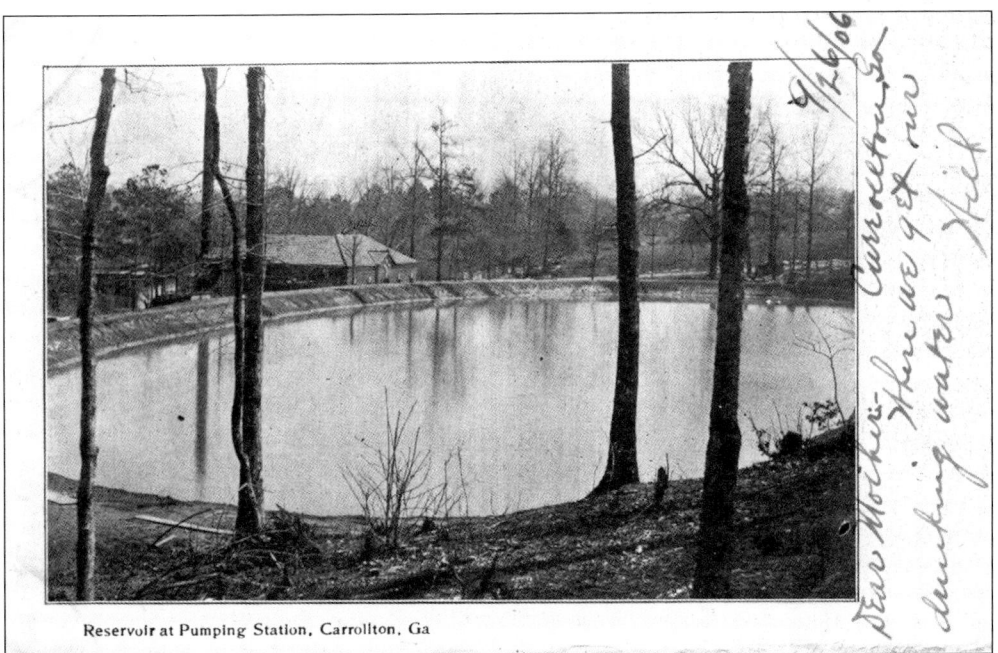

This card from 1906 shows the reservoir at the pumping station in Carrollton. The message reads, "Dear Mother, Where we get our drinking water. Niel."

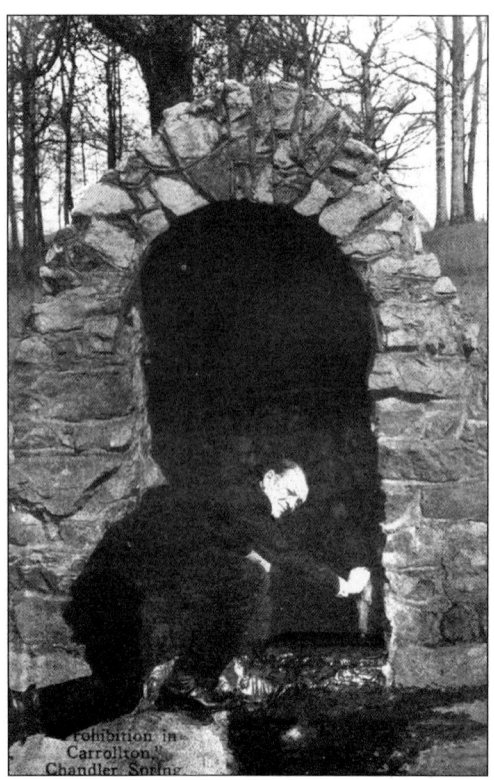

The caption on this card is, "Prohibition in Carrollton, Chandler Spring." This 1920s card shows a gentleman lifting what appears to be a bottle out of Chandler Spring. It is unknown if the card represents a revenuer who made a bust or if it was meant as a comic card showing where the contraband was hidden. Some locals swore to the medicinal value of the water of the springs.

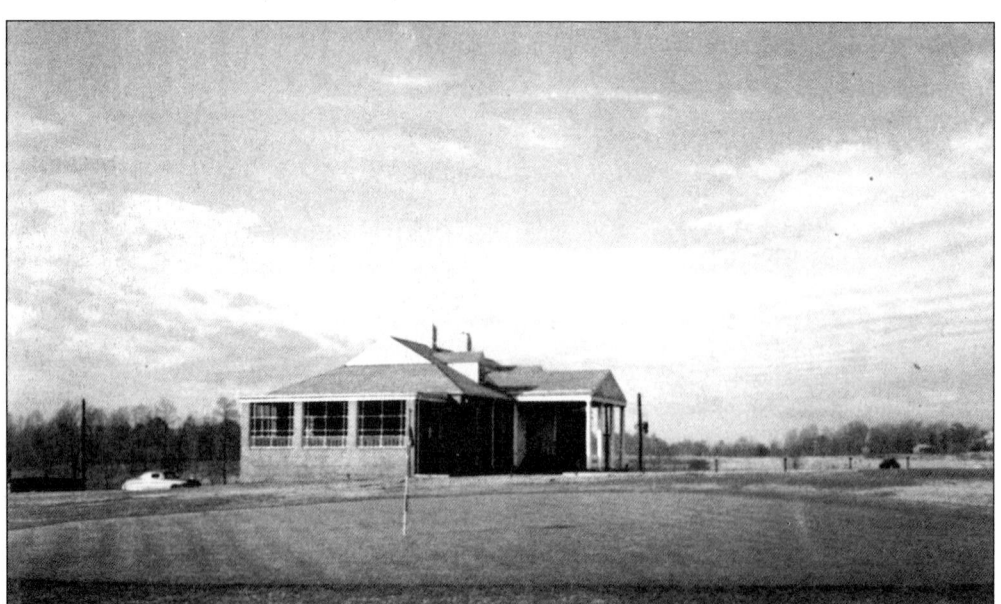

Published by the Carroll Service Council, this card features the newly constructed Sunset Hills Country Club. The back of the card reads, "Sunset Hills Country Club, Carrollton, Ga., Climate where you never have a sleepless night." The original course was a nine-hole golf course designed by Robert Trent Jones in the late 1940s. J. Taylor took the photo that appears on the card.

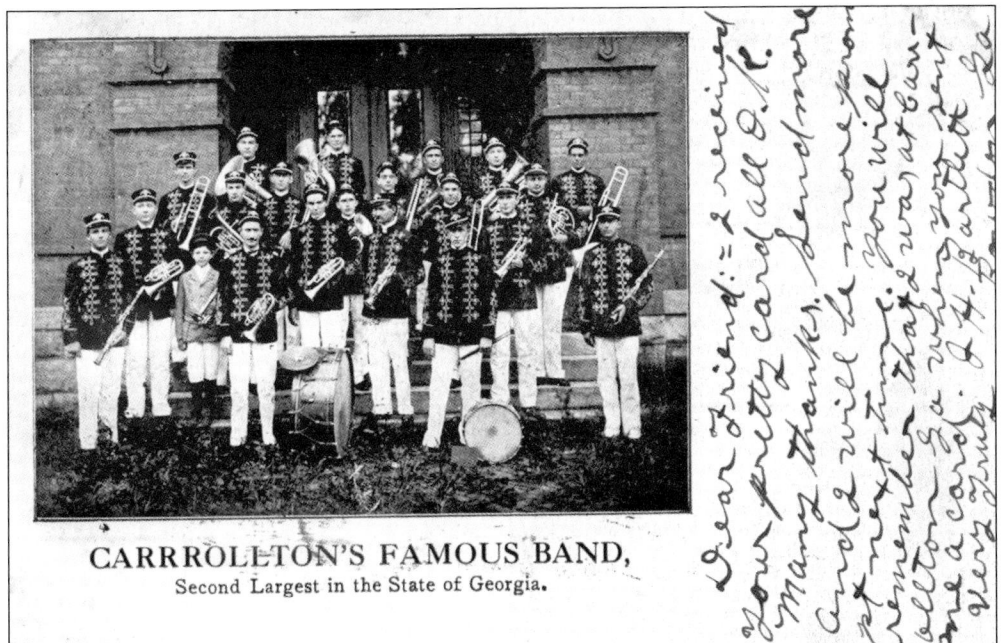

CARRROLLTON'S FAMOUS BAND,
Second Largest in the State of Georgia.

This card features a real photo of Carrollton's Famous Band, the second largest in the state. Addressed to Miss Marion Whipple in Massachusetts from J.H. Bartlett of Bowdon and dated January 1907, the card was published by Modern Postals, R. Lee Sharpe of Carrollton. On another card with the same image, G.J. Gray is listed as the band director.

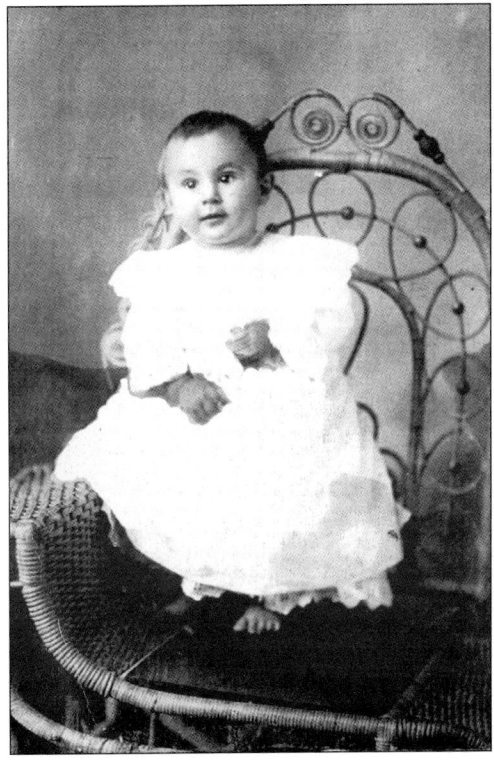

Jesse Terrell Harris, born January 29, 1905, lived his whole life in Carroll County (1905–1985). He married Elma Patterson on December 23, 1925, and they had 10 children—7 girls and 3 boys—between 1926 and 1949. He was a hard-working man and always had a big garden that provided plenty of good food for his family. It was his goal each year to have fresh, sweet corn before July 4th. (Courtesy of Violette Denney.)

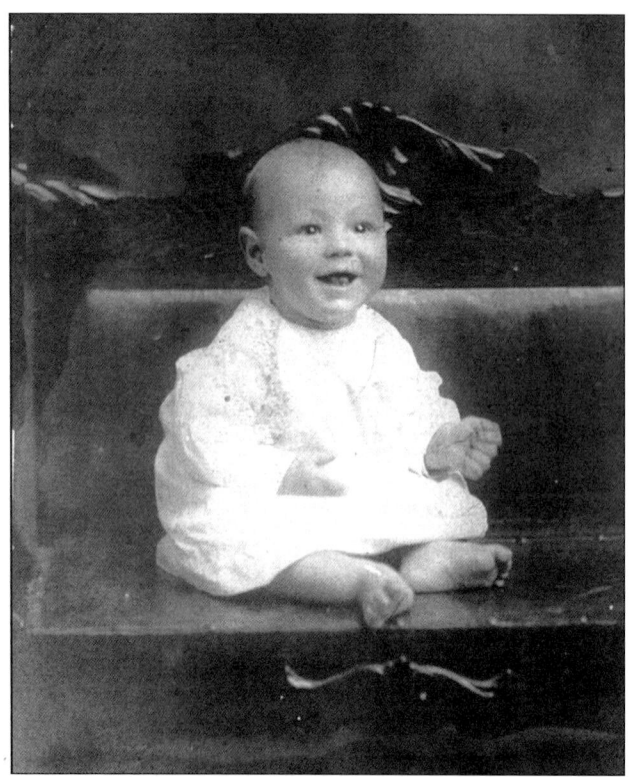

As the son of L.G. and Susie Mae Shadinger Denney, Donald was the youngest child and because of this was always introduced as "the baby." He had three brothers and two sisters. At age 17, he joined his three brothers in the United States Navy to serve his country until World War II was over. From 1949 to 1980, he worked at General Motors in Doraville. In 1951, he married Violette Harris, and they have two sons. (Courtesy of Violette Denney.)

These four Harris boys—identified from left to right as Melvin (b. 1898), Terrell (b. 1905), Harvey (b. 1900), and Marvin (b. 1896)—were children of William Samuel and Martha Lee "Mattie" Mobley Harris. The family lived on a farm east of Carrollton and owned several hundred acres. William purchased a portion of his farm from his father, William Washington Harris, in January 1894. Some of that land remains in his family in 2004. The couple also had four girls—Myrtie (b. 1887), Lula (b. 1889), Ethel (b. 1891), and Lilly (b. 1893). (Courtesy of Violette Denney.)

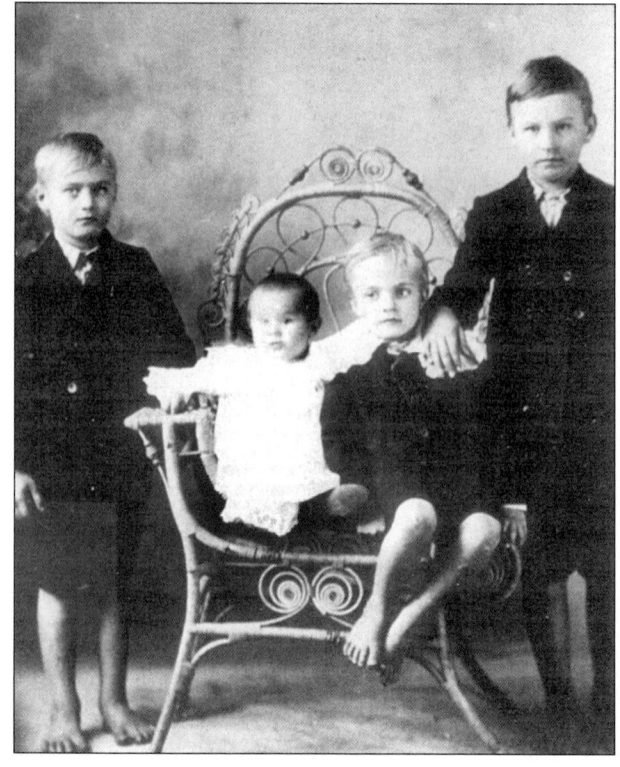

C.W. Chatham (1886–1966) always aspired to be a train engineer, and he carried a railroad watch to remind him of his dream. At his mother's request not to work for the railroad, he never fulfilled his dream. C.W. peddled farm products as far as Atlanta and then went to work for the National Biscuit Company in Atlanta. (Courtesy of the Spivey Collection.)

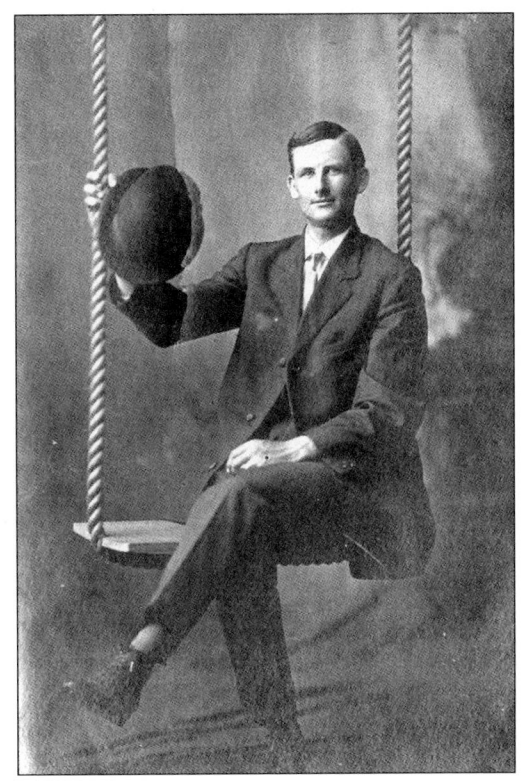

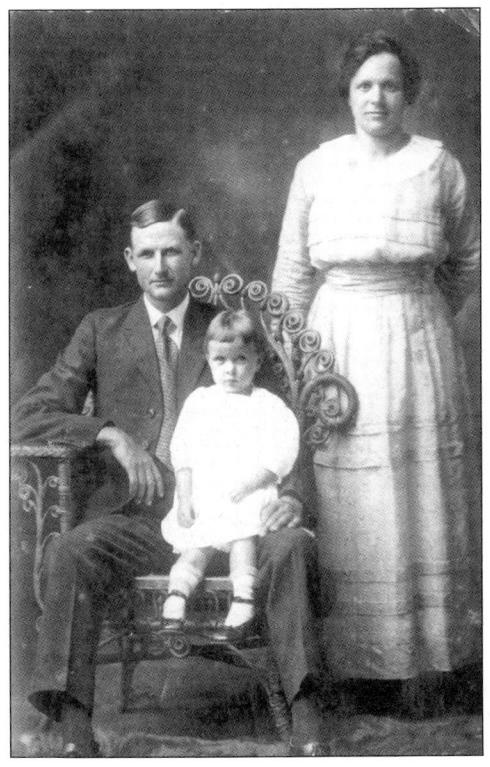

C.W. Chatham (1886–1996), Alma S. Chatham (1893–1992), and Florrye Chatham (b. 1916), who is the oldest of their two children, are seen in this card. They lived on a farm bought from C.W. Chatham's brother, George Washington Chatham, for $600. The farm was located at the edge of Carroll County, now bound by the St. Andrew's Golf Course. In 1946, he sold the family farm and purchased land on Highway 27, two miles south of the Carrollton Courthouse. (Courtesy of the Spivey Collection.)

Cornwalis W. Chatham, born in 1886, received this draft notice of classification of 4A from the local Carroll draft board in November 1918. It was erroneously addressed to Cornelius Chatham. According to family members, he was not drafted and he missed World War I due to his age. Today, the classification of 4A means a registrant who has completed service or is a sole surviving son. (Courtesy of the Spivey Collection.)

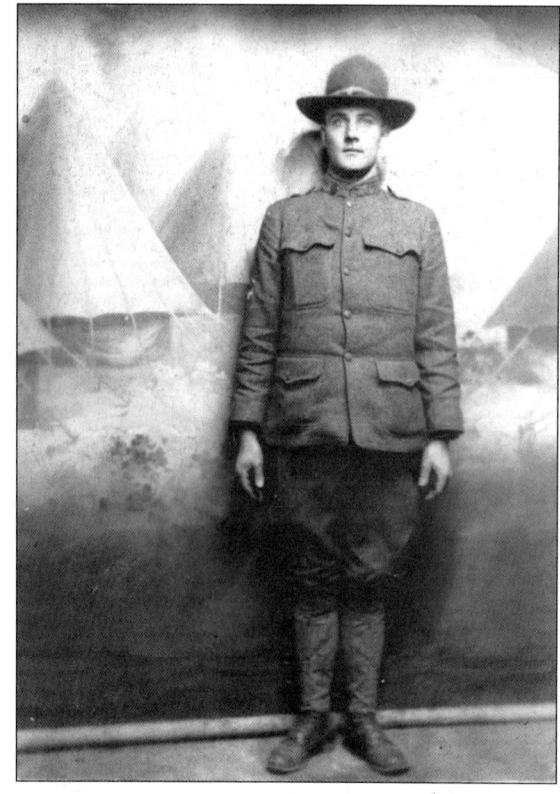

Sgt. Walter Lloyd Barnes (1895–1961) served during World War I at Camp Gordon, Georgia, at the Remount Station Quartermasters Department. On the day he was discharged, he bought three mules and walked them from Fort McPherson to Carrollton. He married Willie Lessie Winder, and they had three children: Walter Howard, James Hansel, and Lessie Doris (Poteat). His second wife was Ester Mae Ledford. Dated 1918, this card was sent to Walt's uncle Frank Barnes and was passed down to his great granddaughter. (Courtesy of Carol Barnes McWhorter.)

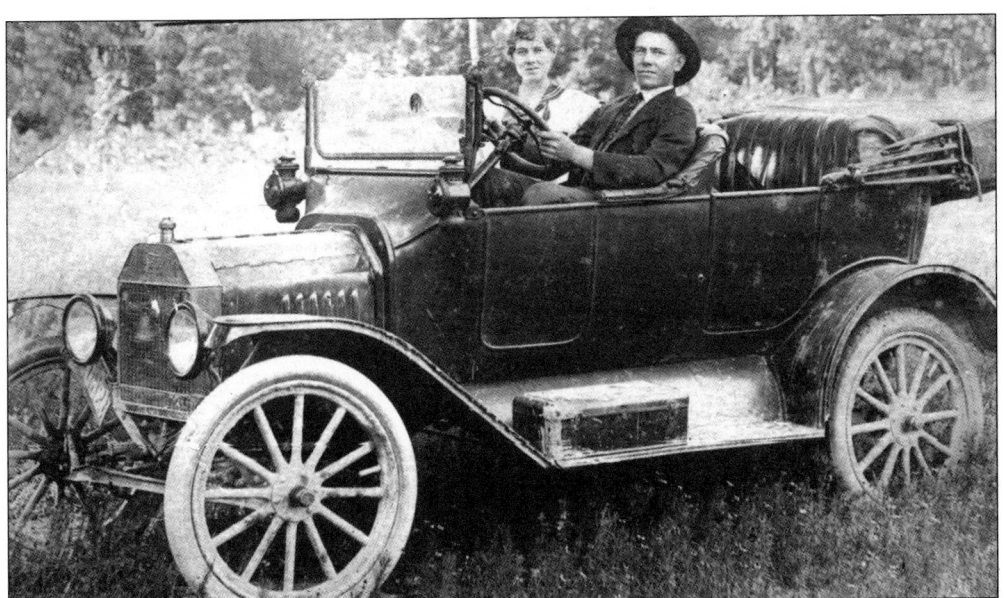

Retha and Wylie Russell, brother and sister, are seen in this real photo card, c. 1910. They were two of the children of Mollie Handley and Marvin E. Russell of Carrollton. Wylie and his wife moved to Little Rock, Arkansas, where he sold used cars. Retha married Glen Armstrong and moved to Cape Gerard, Missouri, and had two daughters, Aline and Mildred (Limbaugh). Mildred's son is the noted Rush Limbaugh. (Courtesy of Carol Barnes McWhorter.)

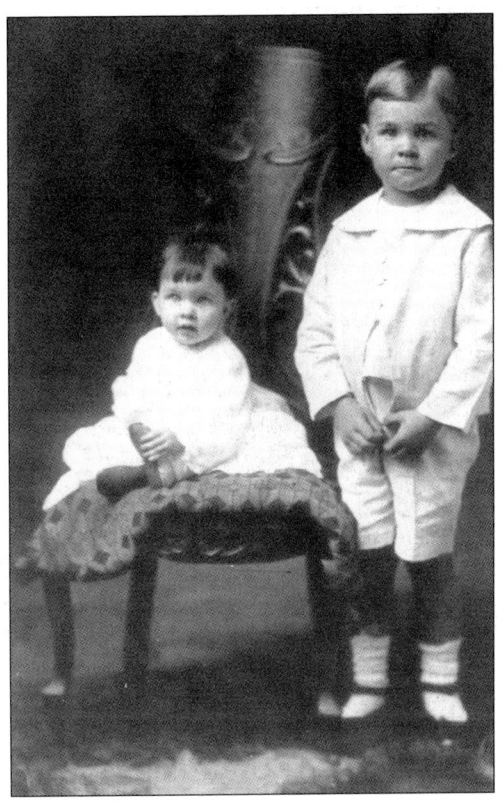

Shown here are siblings Mary Ruby Walker (Pyle) on the left, born January 6, 1915, and William Ralph Walker on the right, born November 6, 1912. A younger sister, Vera Winnie Walker, was born on September 6, 1918. They were the children of Larkin LaFayette (Fate) and Avva Orilla Johnson Walker. They were born on the family farm in the Striplin Chapel community. This photo card was taken in Carrollton in 1916. (Courtesy of Sam Pyle.)

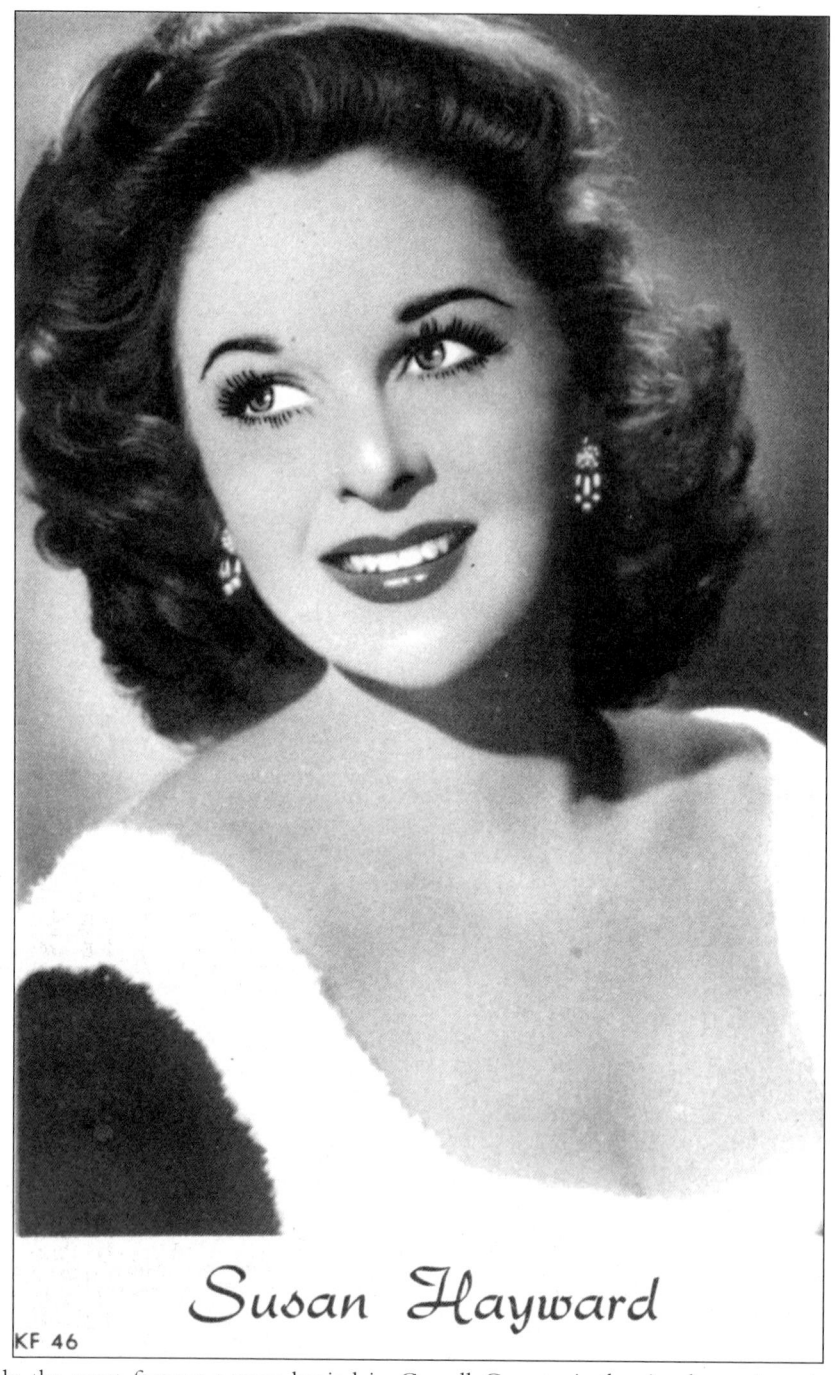

Susan Hayward

Arguably the most famous person buried in Carroll County is the Academy Award–winning actress Susan Hayward (1917–1975). Born Edythe Marrenner on June 30, 1919, in New York, she was to become known around the world as the movie star Susan Hayward. In 1957, she married Eaton Chalkley, the owner of the Chevrolet-Oldsmobile-Cadillac dealership in Carrollton. They built a beautiful home between Carrollton and Temple. Mrs. Chalkley's marker is located next to her husband in Our Lady of Perpetual Help Catholic Church Cemetery.

Three
ROOPVILLE

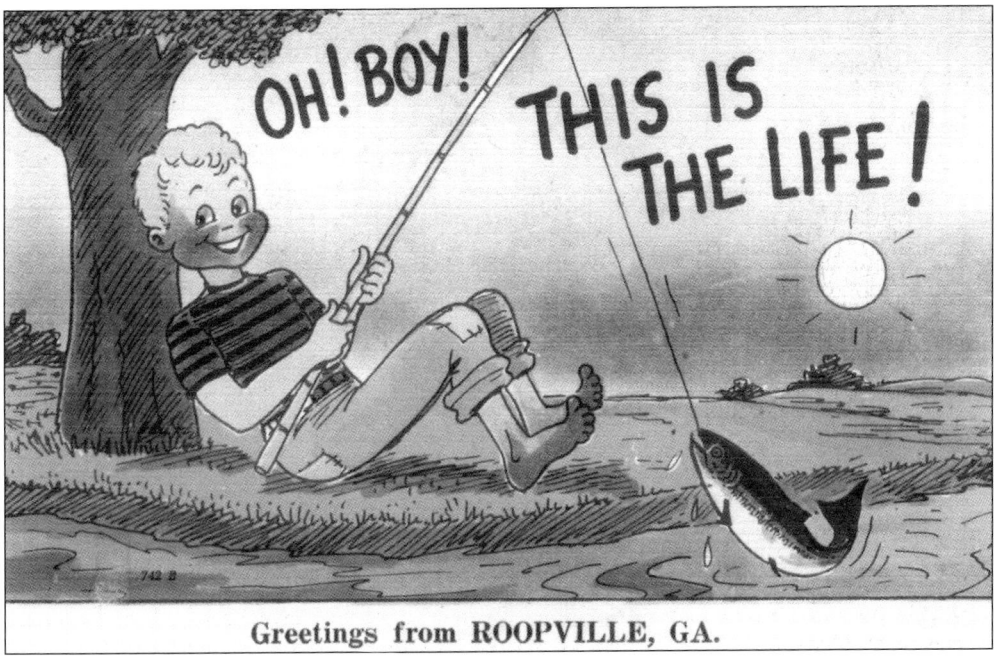

This is one of a series of comic cards that was used to greet people from a community. "Oh Boy! This is the Life!" epitomizes the life of the small community of Roopville. The name Roopville was chosen in honor of Martin Roop by his sons, who were early settlers of the community. (Courtesy of the Spivey Collection.)

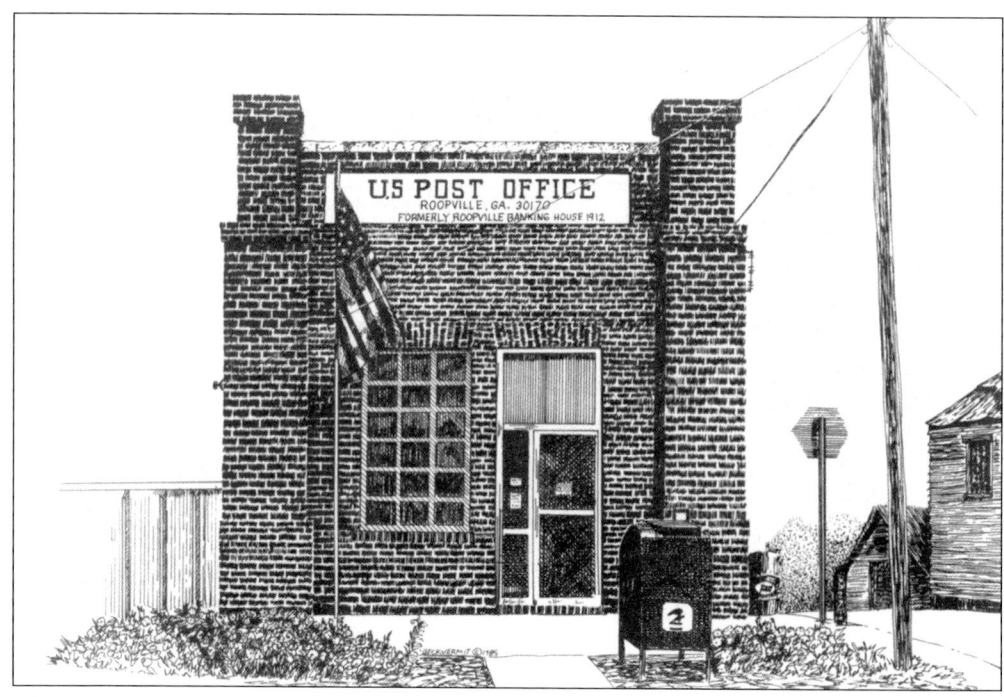

This pen-and-ink postcard features the U.S. Post Office in Roopville. The post office was originally located in a shoe shop and general store, but when the Roopville Bank closed in 1927, the post office moved there. Local artist John Beckvermitt produced a series of Roopville cards in 1985 that are presented here with his permission.

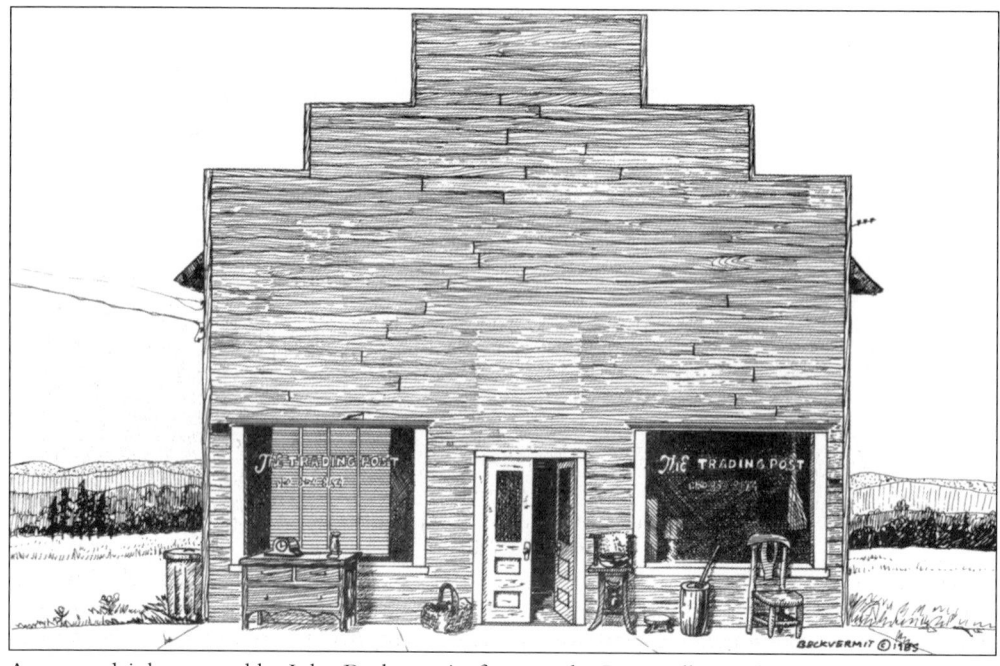

A pen-and-ink postcard by John Beckvermitt features the Roopville Trading Post.

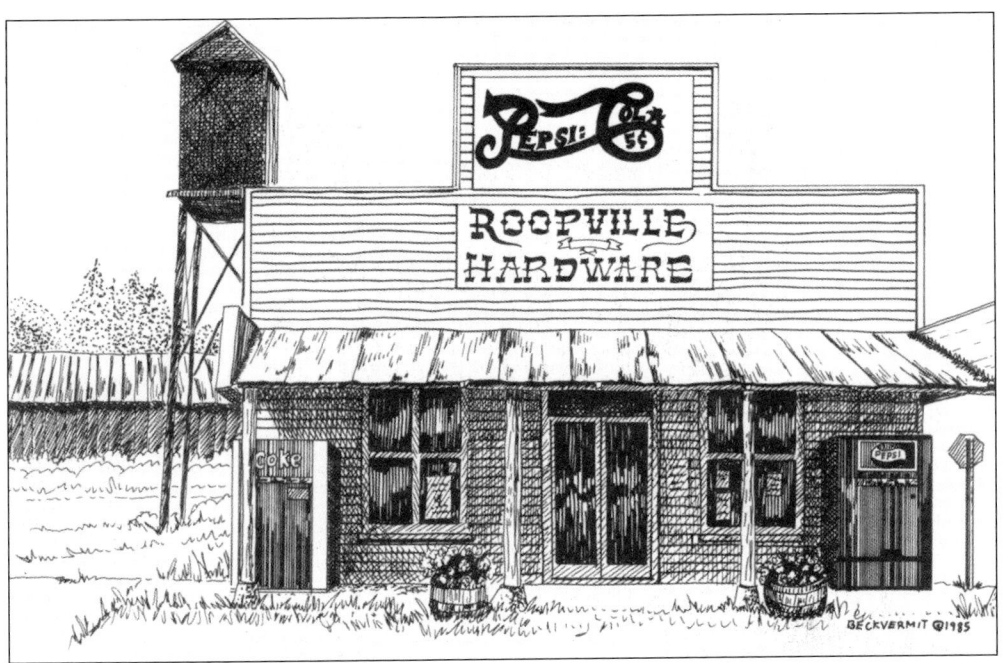

Here is another pen-and-ink postcard by John Beckvermitt. This one features the Roopville Hardware Store.

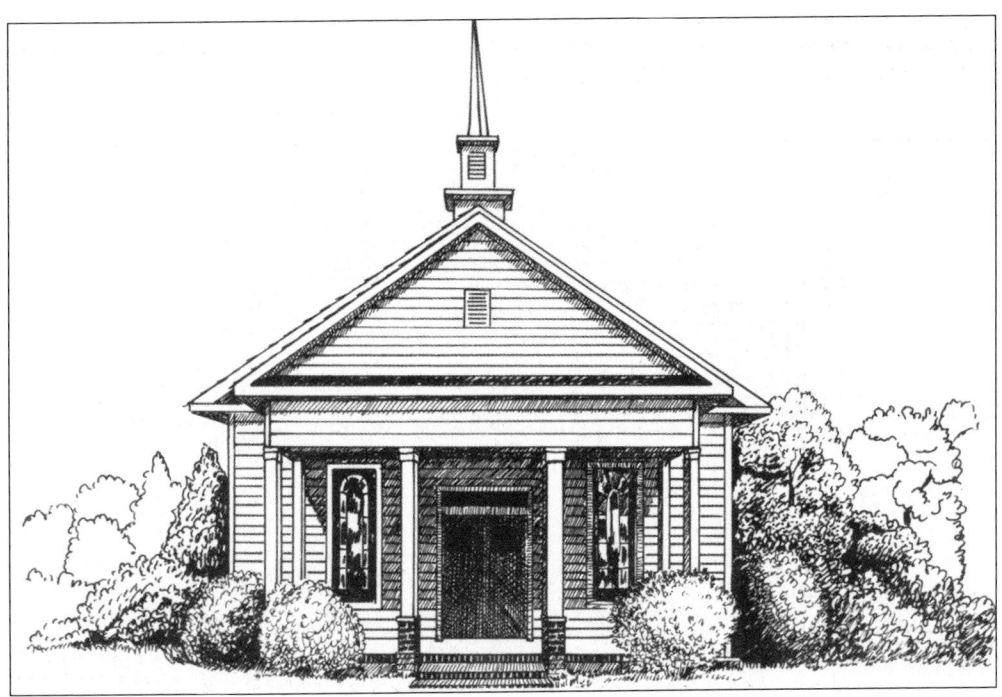

A pen-and-ink postcard by John Beckvermitt features the Roopville Baptist Church. The first service in the church was held on September 29, 1883. Built on the same site of the original church, the new church building (portrayed in the postcard) held its first services on November 3, 1940.

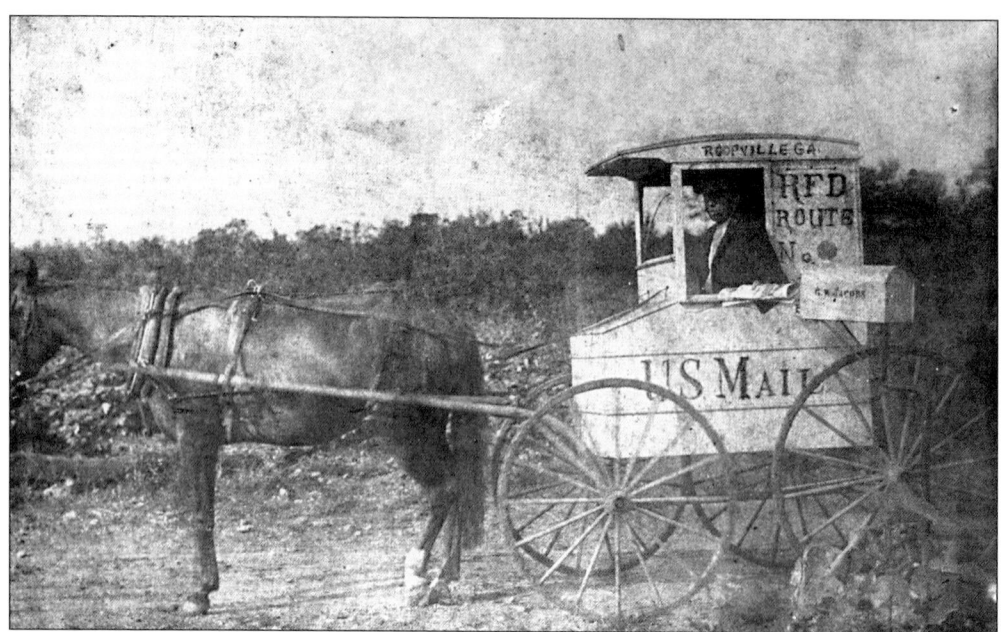

This commemorative postcard by the Roopville Historical Society features a United States mail wagon in 1904 that served the Roopville community. The message on the back reads, "Eight years after rural free delivery. Better than the Horseback days." The driver is believed to be Odus (Odie) Garrett.

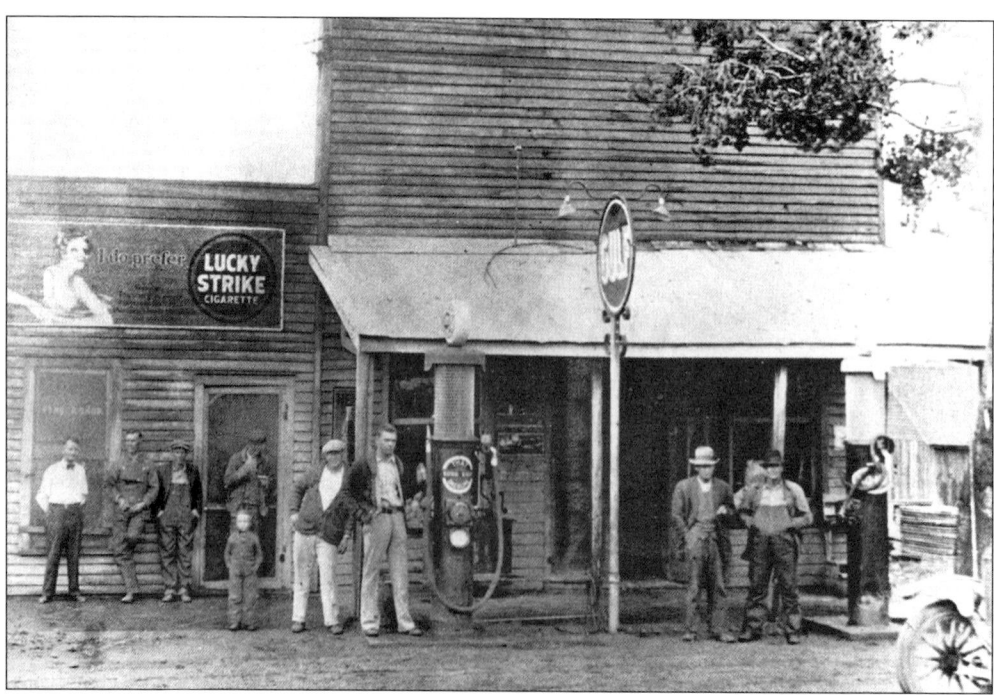

This commemorative postcard by the Roopville Historical Society features the Bell Store. "A typical scene in Roopville in the heyday of the Cotton Economy about 1927" is written on the reverse side of the card.

Four
TEMPLE

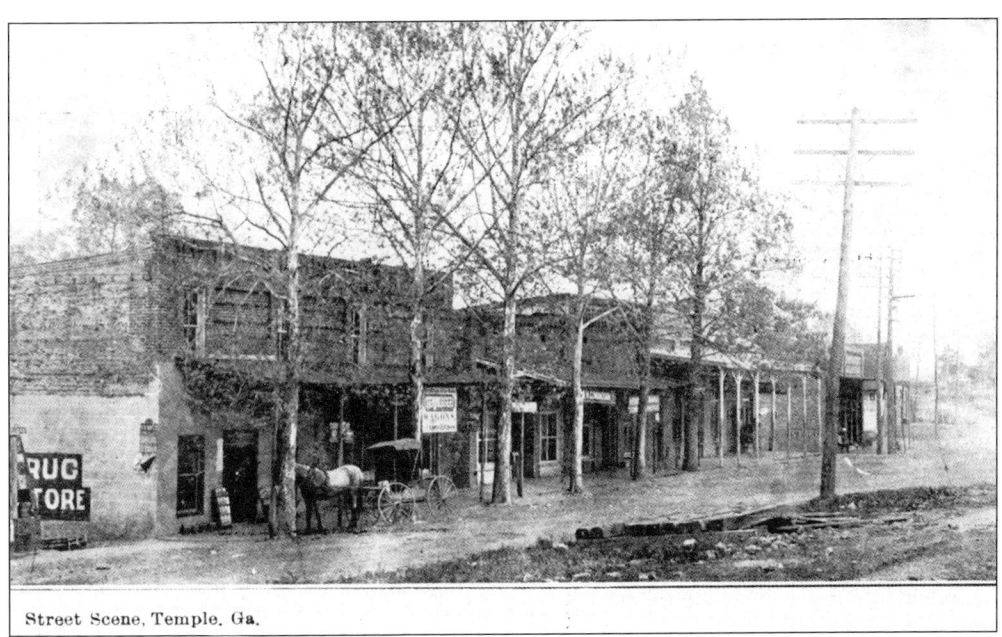

Street Scene, Temple, Ga.

The town of Temple was incorporated by an act of the state legislature on August 28, 1883, and Jesse Kinney was elected the first mayor. The town was named for Maj. Robert H. Temple (1831–1901), chief engineer of the Georgia Pacific Railroad. Postmarked January 1912 in Temple, this card shows the business district on W. Johnson Street.

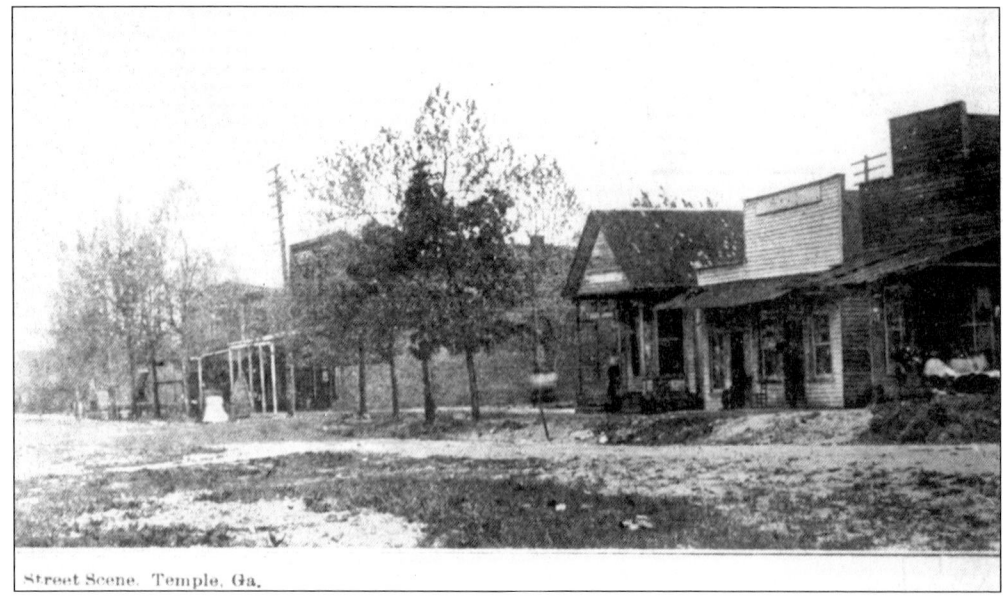

Another view of the Temple business district shows Sage Street, c. 1908. The first brick storehouse was built in the 1890s. In 1883, E. Lewis Connell, young schoolmaster at Temple Academy, wrote a poem entitled "Temple." The first verse reads, "Mid Carroll's rich and fertile lands / About one year ago / Where our little town stands / Was but a house or two." (Courtesy of Ruth Holder.)

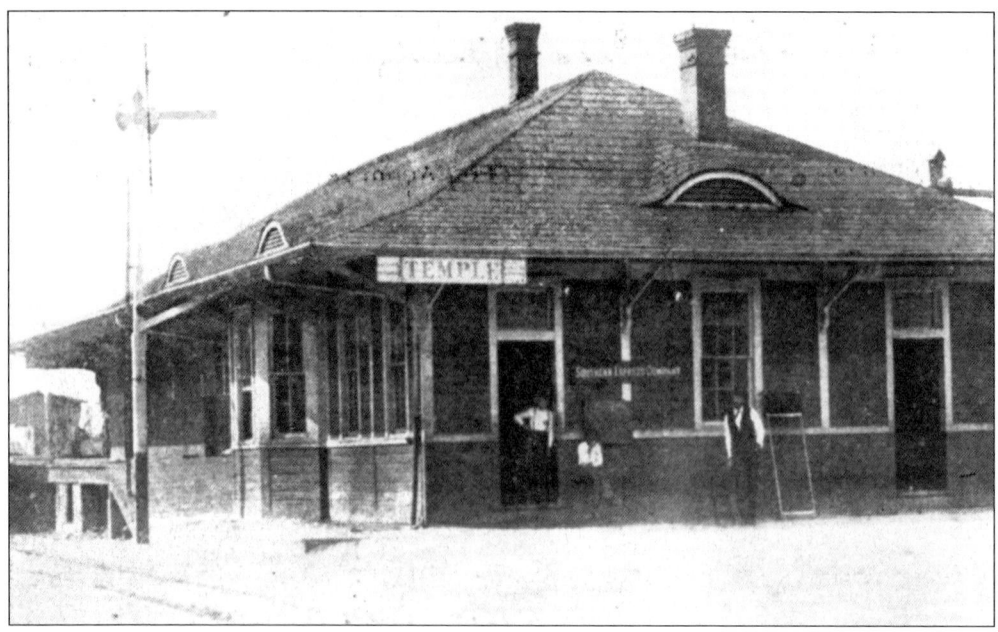

In 1983, Temple celebrated their centennial and several commemorative postcards were made. This commemorative card features Temple's Southern Railway depot. The back reads, "Built in 1906 after the original burned." The city grew up around the railroad when the Georgia Pacific Railway was built through the area in 1882. In 1894, the Georgia Pacific Railway was sold to Southern.

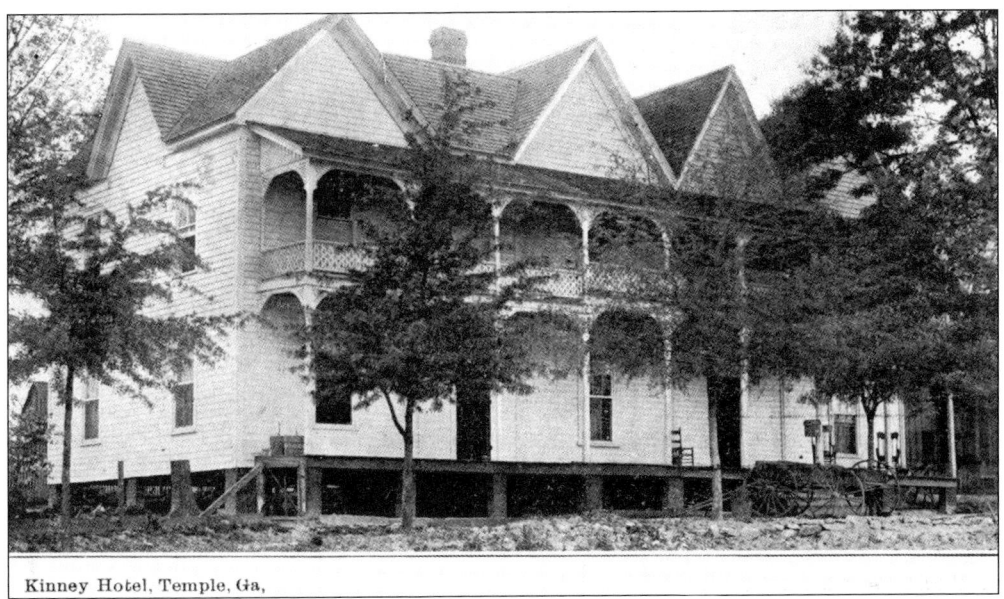

Kinney Hotel, Temple, Ga.

Originally known as the Walker Hotel, this hotel was built in 1895 by John and Lula Walker on W. Sage Street. There were 18 large rooms and a large lobby. Located across the street from the depot, it was also later known as both the Kinney Hotel and Lewis Hotel. Postmarked July, 1910, from Temple, this card has a simple message: "Hello Mr. Persons, You ought to be up here. Are having a h— of a time. Miss Pam."

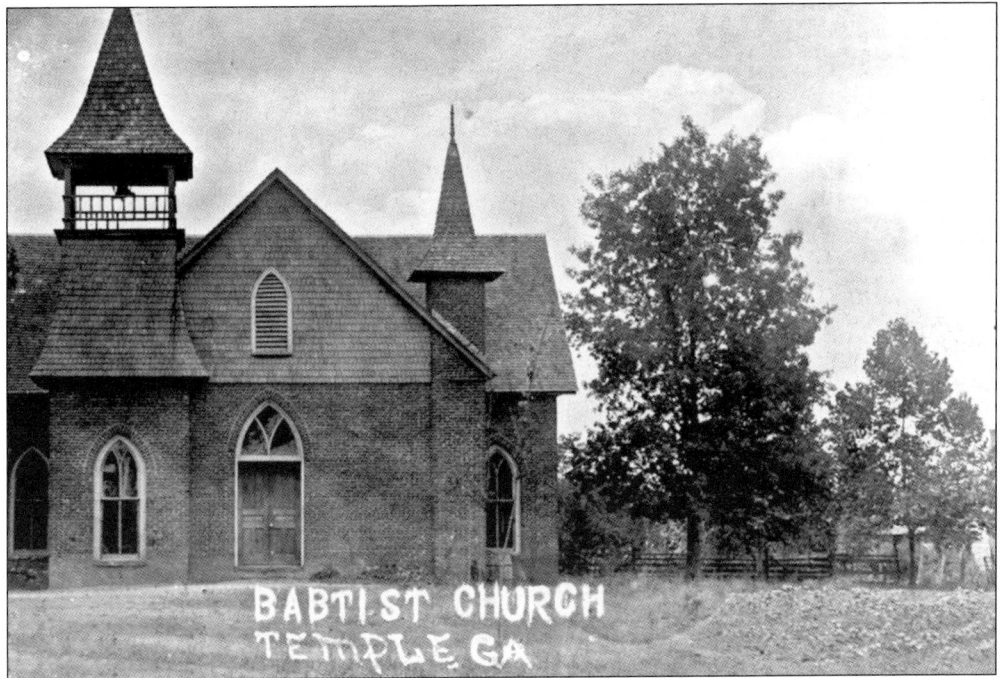

Baptists built a wood-frame sanctuary in 1884 that faced Buchanan Street. Along with a wood-frame Methodist church built that same year, they became Temple's first church buildings. This real photo card was postmarked June 1909 in Temple, Georgia.

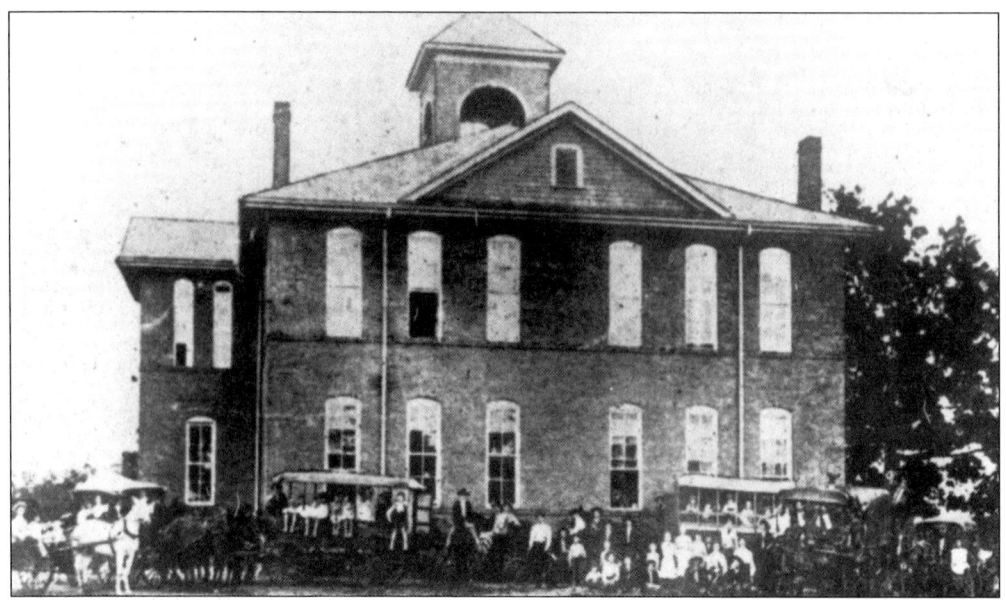

A centennial commemorative card features a view of the Temple Model School. The back reads, "Built in 1903–04 at the corner of James and Griffin Streets. The consolidated school operated a farm and horse-drawn school wagons." The two-story brick building featured four classrooms on the ground floor, an auditorium on the second floor, and shingles of slate.

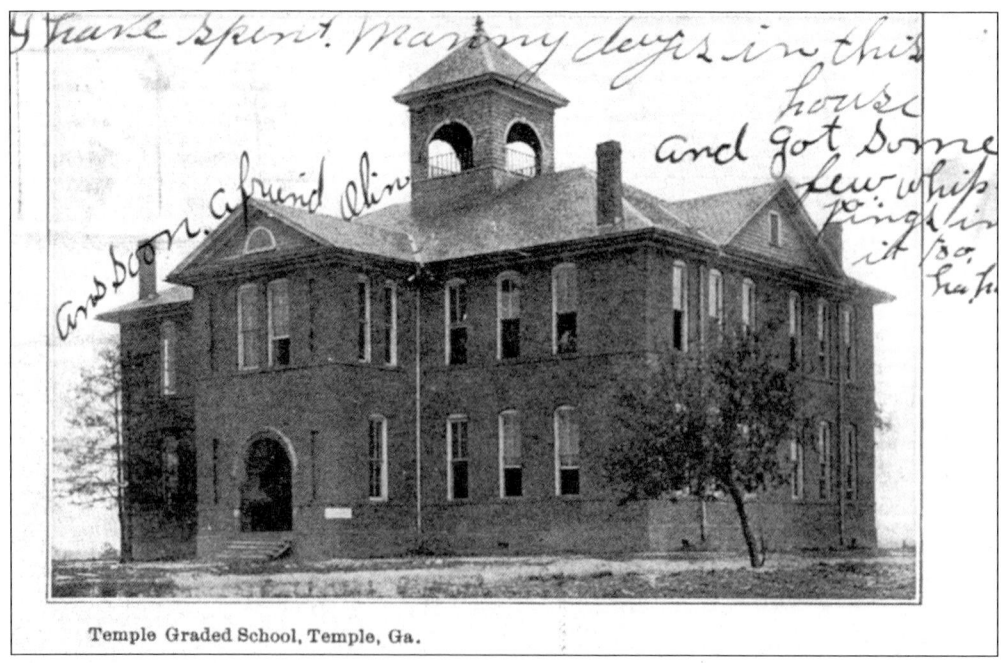

Postmarked from Temple in 1910, on the back of the card, the writer speaks of picking cotton and going to Carrollton for the fair the following week. Having run out of room on the back of the card, he writes the following on the front of the card about his tenure at the Temple Model School: "I have spent many days in this house and got some few whippings in it too. ha.ha. Ans. Soon. A friend. Olin." (Courtesy of Gary Doster.)

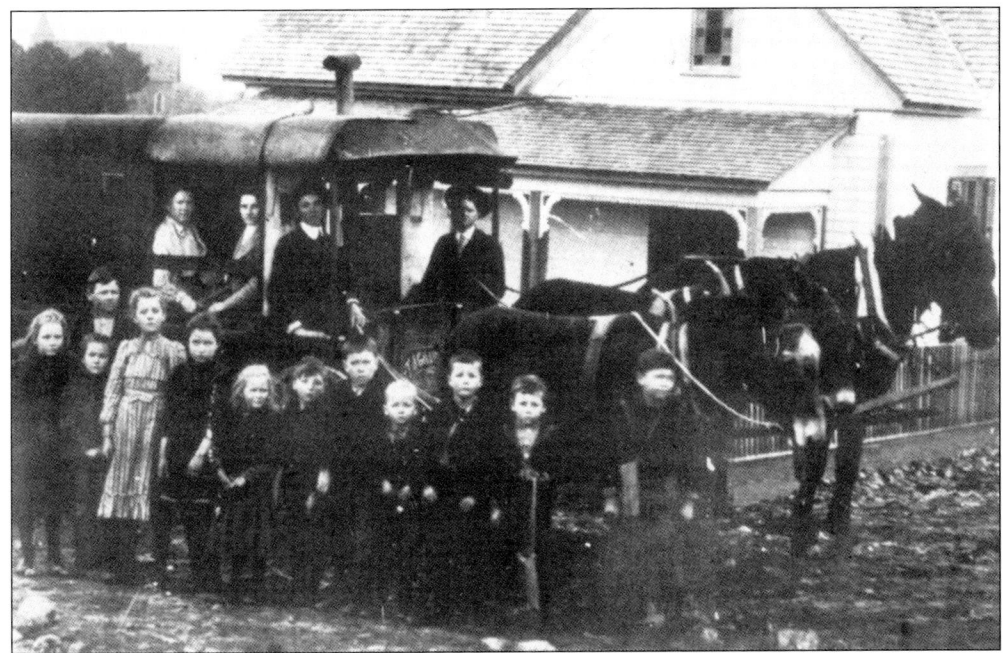

A centennial commemorative card reads, "Five horse-drawn wagons brought children from a 5-mile radius to the Temple Model School, 1904." The public school transportation system was the first in the state. The wagons were mule- and horse-drawn and featured a covered top and curtains on the sides for bad weather. It could seat about 20 children on long benches, and there were 2 drivers per wagon.

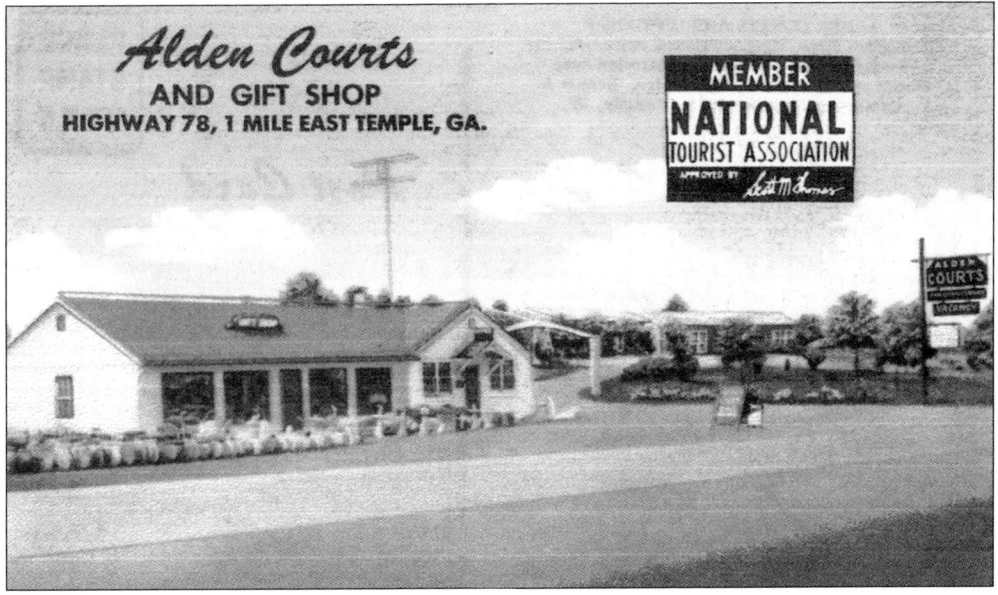

This *c.* 1950 card reads, "15 Modern Stone Air Conditioned Units. All individual. Automatic controlled heat. Owned and operated by Mr. & Mrs. Ernest A. Ortenburg. Phone 2071. Temple, Ga." The community around Alden's Motel became known as Aluminum Court, so named because the siding and roof of the motel were made of aluminum. (Courtesy of Ruth Holder.)

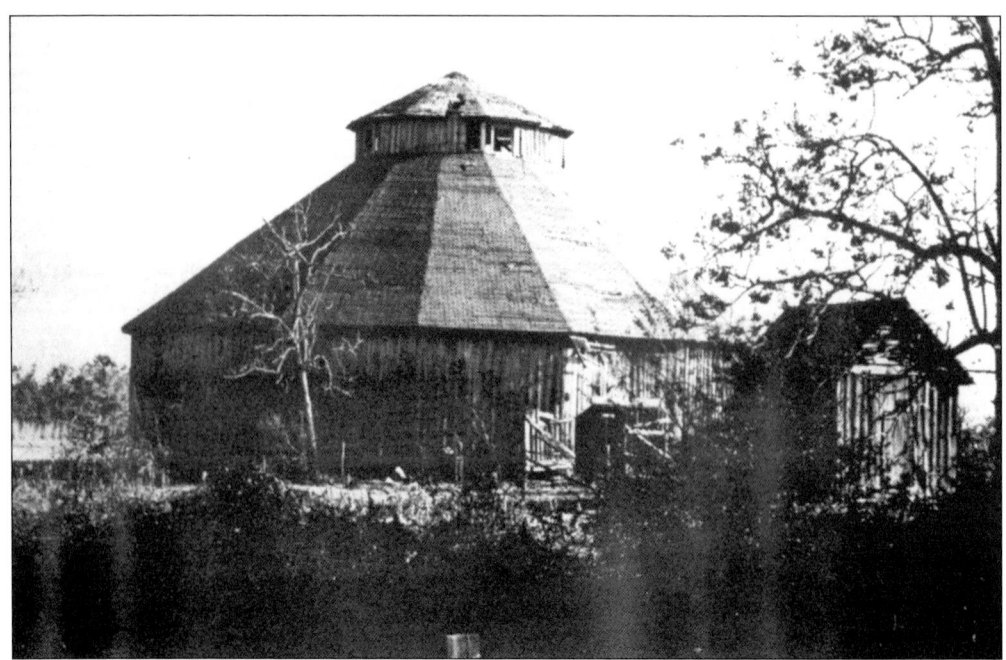

Another of the Temple commemorative cards depicting one of Carroll County's most recognizable landmarks, the round barn, reads, "Built in 1917 at Hickory Level by Floyd Lovell for E.W. Dorough. Placed on the National Register of Historic Places in 1980." A huge silo is located in the center of the barn, constructed of a concrete base and wood siding. Wood and metal doors the length of the silo allowed for movement of silage at different levels.

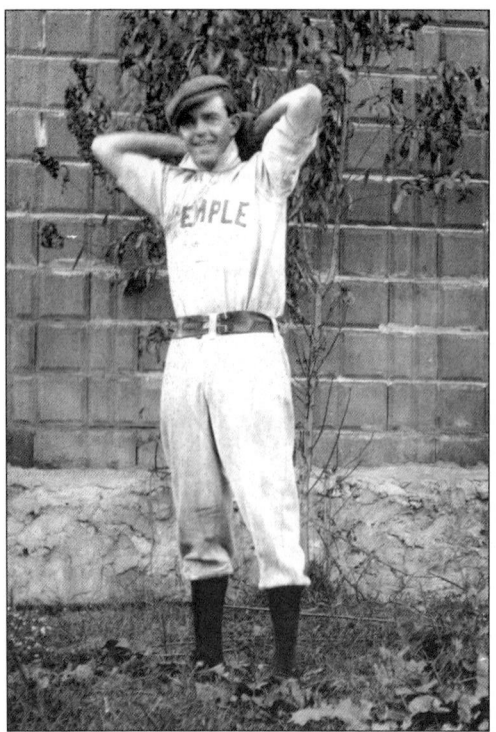

This postcard features a view of an unknown Temple baseball player from the early 1900s. The Georgia High School Association, which governs high-school athletics, had its beginnings in Temple in 1905.

Five
VILLA RICA

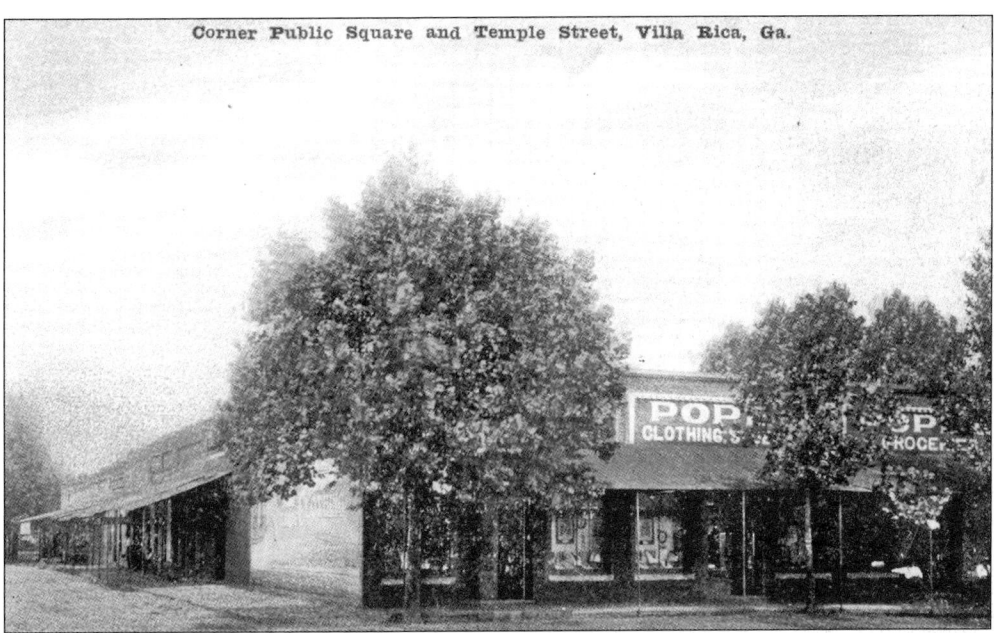

Pioneer gold miners were working in this area of the state by the mid-1820s. William Hix built a tavern and general store in the area, and it became known as Hixtown. In 1830, the town of Villa Rica, "Rich Village" or "City of Gold" was settled. This image, taken c. 1910, is published by the Marchman Pharmacy of Villa Rica and features the corner of the public square and Temple Street. (Courtesy of Gary Doster.)

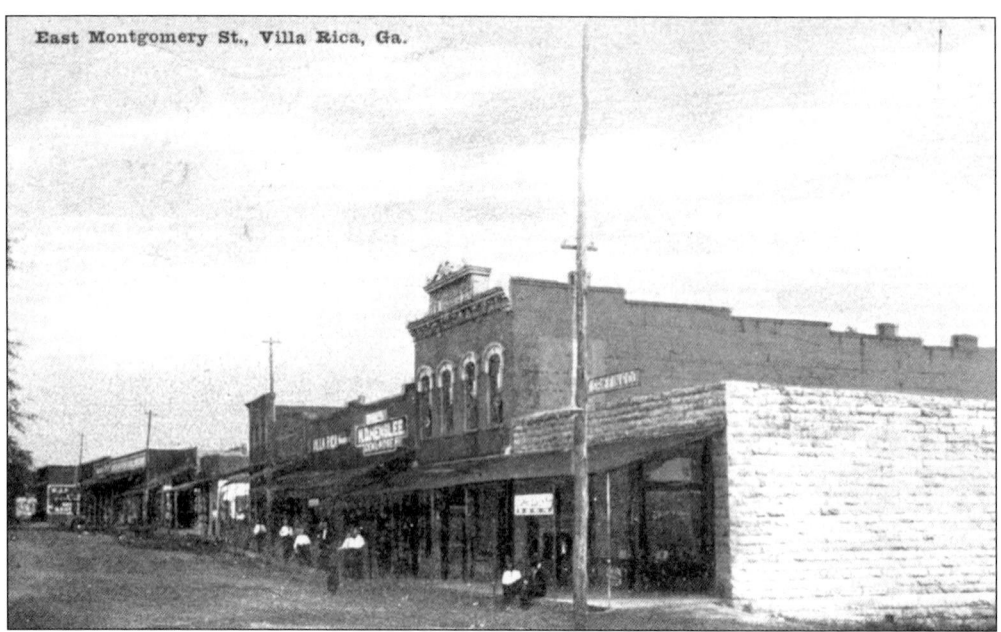

Mailed on April 25, 1912, this postcard of East Montgomery Street in Villa Rica shows the business district of the time. The building at the farthest right reads, "Griffin & Co." The large, two-story brick building is the Powell-Marchman Pharmacy and was built in 1895, with the second floor used as offices. The store sign next to it reads, "M.D. Henslee, Genl. Mdse." On December 5, 1957, a tragic gas explosion on this street leveled 4 stores, killing 12 and injuring 20.

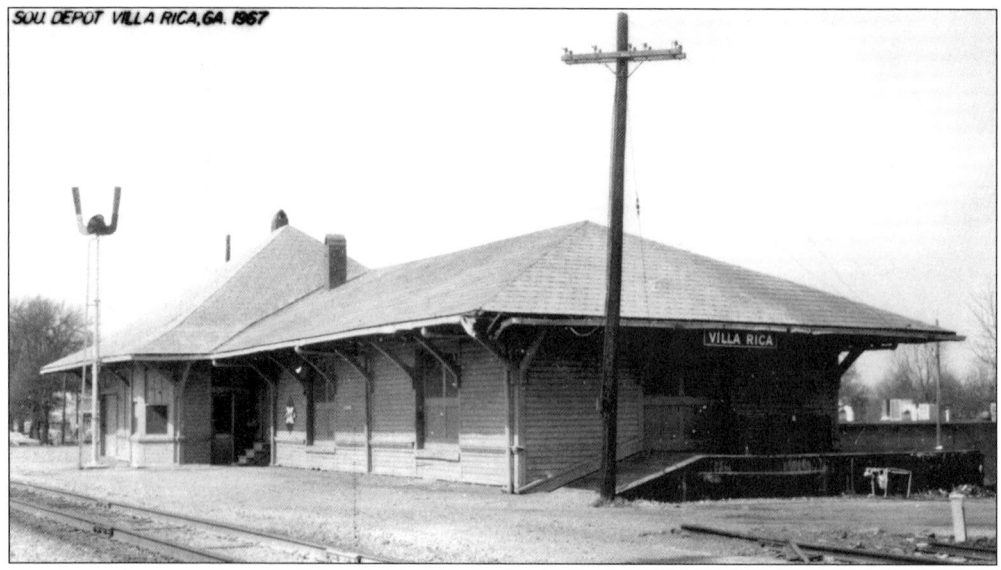

This view shows the Villa Rica Southern Depot in 1967. An event that took place in 1881 changed Villa Rica forever, when a large area of land known as Cheevestown, just to the south of "Old Villa Rica," struck another type of gold. Speculators sold land that the Central Railroad would cross, and a new Villa Rica was born, combining the two areas into one community, known as Villa Rica. The Georgia General Assembly incorporated Villa Rica on September 13, 1883.

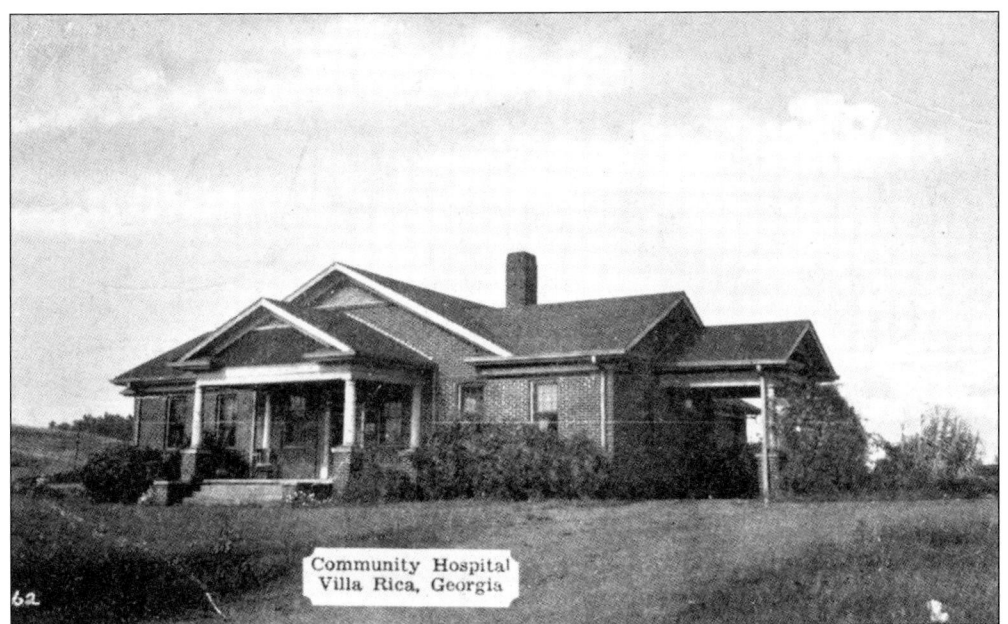

The Community Hospital was the predecessor to the Villa Rica Hospital. When this building was sold, the money went towards the Villa Rica Hospital that opened in July 1955. Postmarked November 28, 1942, this card reads, "I hope you can use this in your collection. Thanks for the cards you sent me. I rec'd about 40 new cards this week. In all I have save around 400. When you visit me I will show them to you."

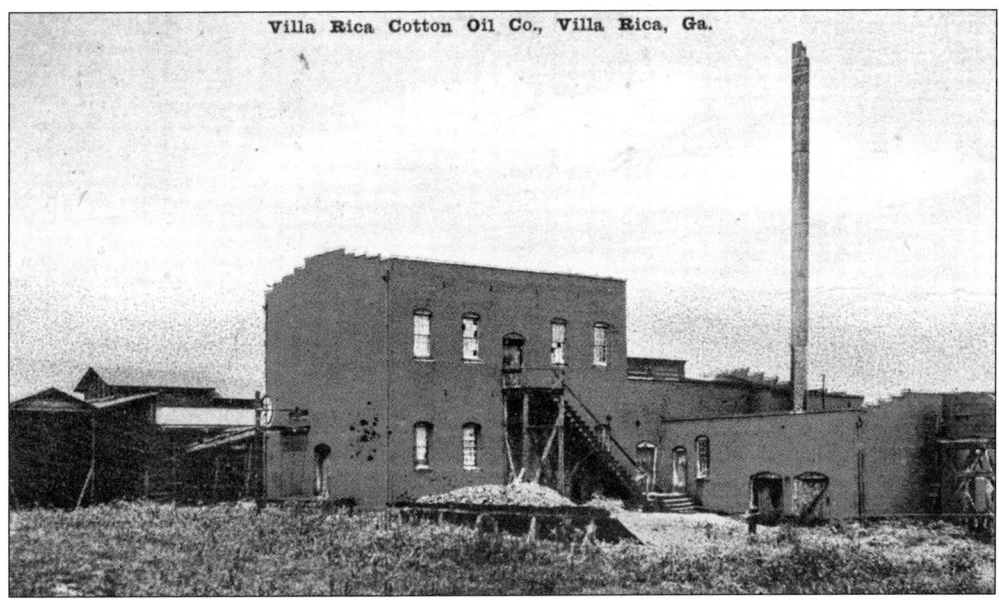

Published by the Powell-Marchman Pharmacy of Villa Rica and postmarked 1913, the message on this card reads, "Dear Bud, I saw lots of cotton here. Dad." The Villa Rica Cotton Oil Company came into being as early as 1902, and a fertilizer plant was added in 1908. From 1911 until 1928, W.B. Candler served as president, having taken over from Judson H. Fuller. The mill was the first in the state to install automatic hydraulic presses that double-cleaned cotton.

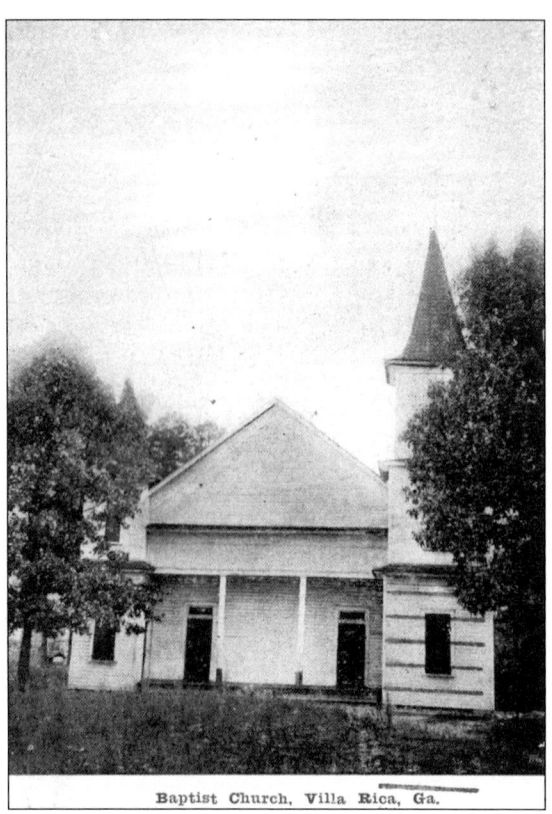

The Villa Rica Baptist Church was organized in a log schoolhouse around 1850 with the Rev. J.R.T. Brown as pastor. In 1885, Jack Jones donated land for the new building. Services were held once a month, and a Sunday school program was started at that time. The card was published by the Powell-Marchman Pharmacy. (Courtesy of Gary Doster.)

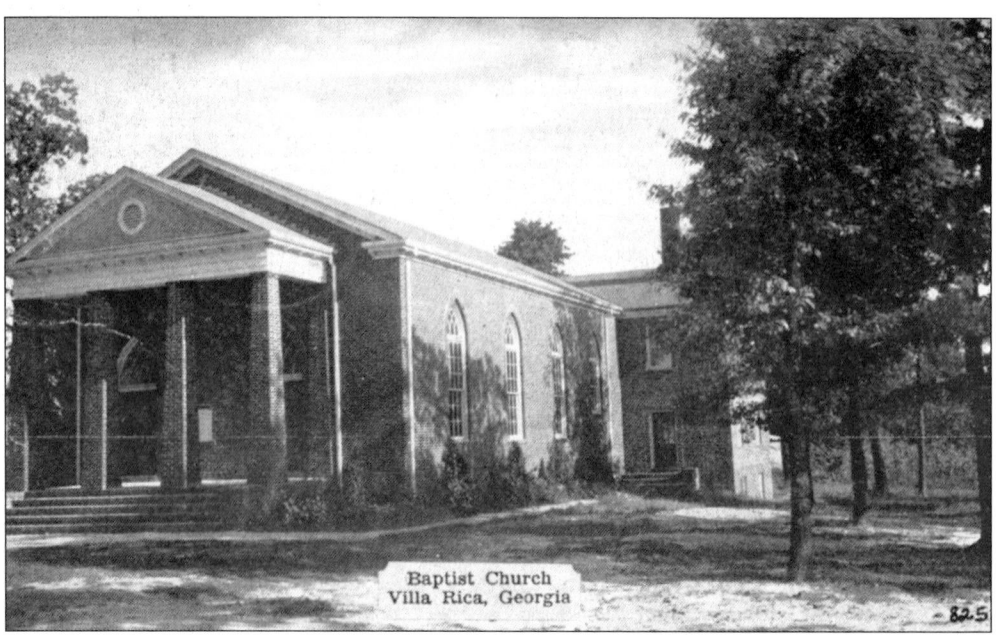

This card was postmarked October 26, 1940, and shows the new brick Baptist church that was erected in 1935 on the site of the church shown above. The Rev. A.J. Bonner was the pastor.

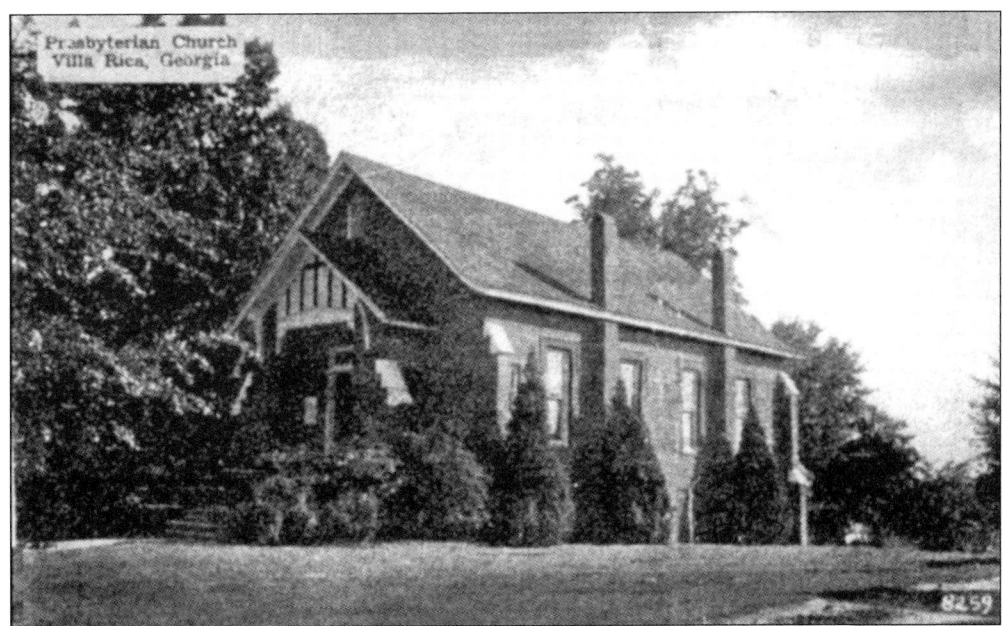

This card features the Presbyterian Church of Villa Rica. In 1930, a brick structure with a large auditorium and Sunday school rooms was built to replace a frame building that had been used since 1886. The lot on which the building and manse are located was the former home of Mr. and Mrs. W.B. Candler Sr. The land was given to the church by their children in their honor. (Courtesy of Ruth Holder.)

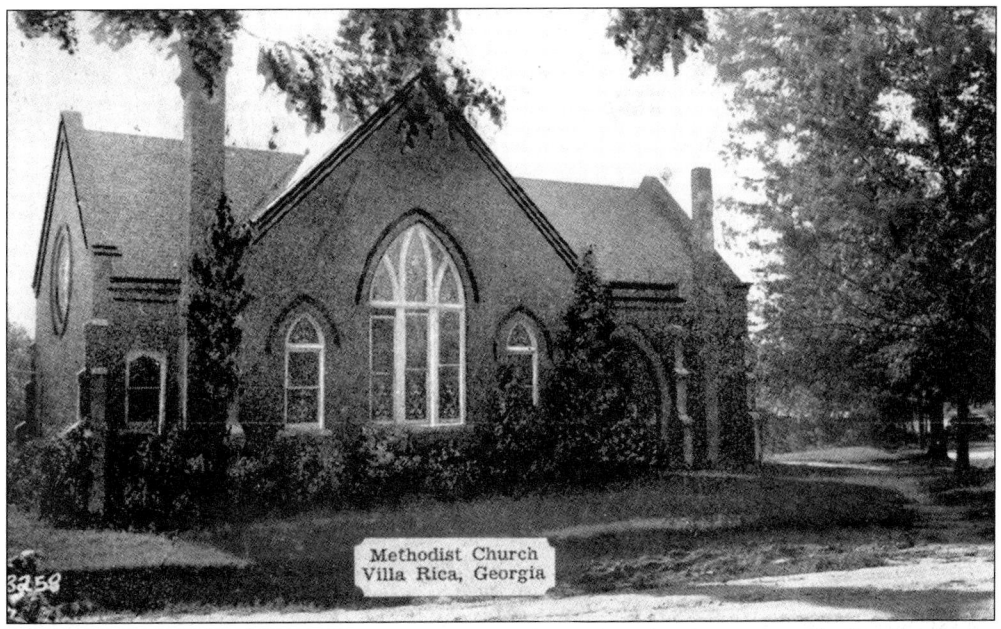

In 1905–1906, a modern brick church building with Sunday school rooms was built to house the Villa Ric Methodist Church. Rev. Loy Warwick was pastor. Prior to this building, services had been held in a wooden church at the same spot. The card was postmarked in August 1942.

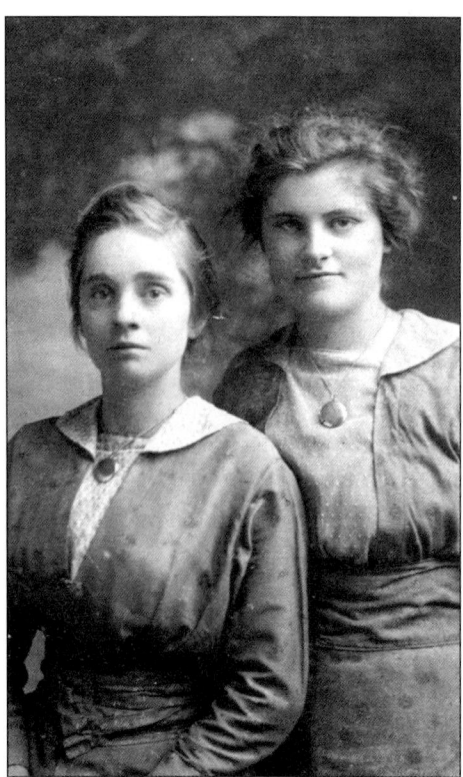

This real photo card from *c.* 1916 features sisters Nora (1898) and Olive Janet Marlow (1899–1997) of Carroll County wearing identical necklaces. Olive married Leon Franklin Lee in 1919. She helped her husband in stores and at one time operated the bus station in Villa Rica. (Courtesy of Doyce Lee.)

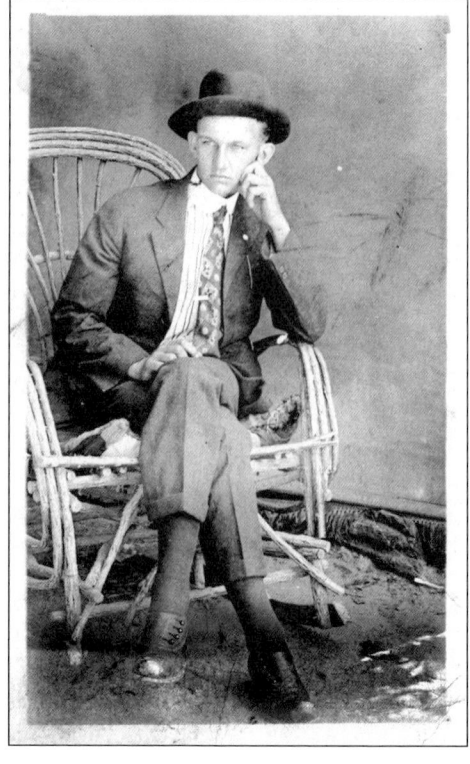

This photo on this card was taken around 1918 and features Leon Franklin Zachariah Lee (1898–1968) prior to his marriage to Olive Janet Marlow. Leon was a county farmer and grocery-store owner in the Temple and Villa Rica areas. For many years, Leon and his family owned the property on which Buckhorn Tavern was located. (Courtesy of Doyce Lee.)

Six
WHITESBURG

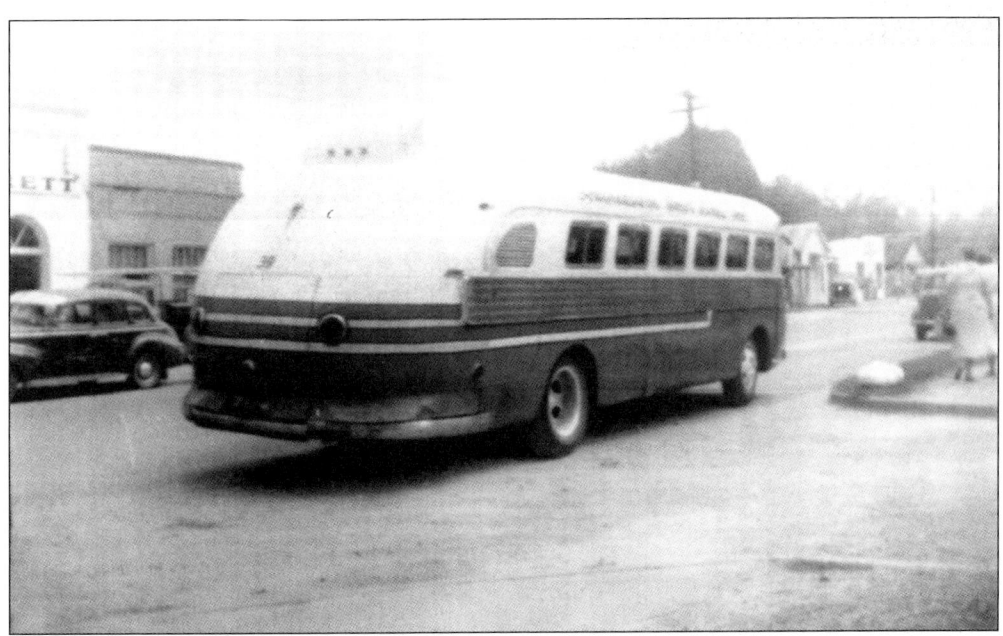

Whitesburg was first settled in 1872 when Mr. J.A. McMullen built the first storehouse. However, the coming of the Savannah, Griffin, and North Alabama Railroad in 1872–1873 resulted in the town finally becoming viable. The town was incorporated in 1874. This 1940s photo shows the Southeastern Motor Line bus in downtown Whitesburg. The bus line made three trips north and three trips south daily. The white building in the background was the Brock-Garrett business, and next to it was Virginia's Grill. (Courtesy of City of Whitesburg.)

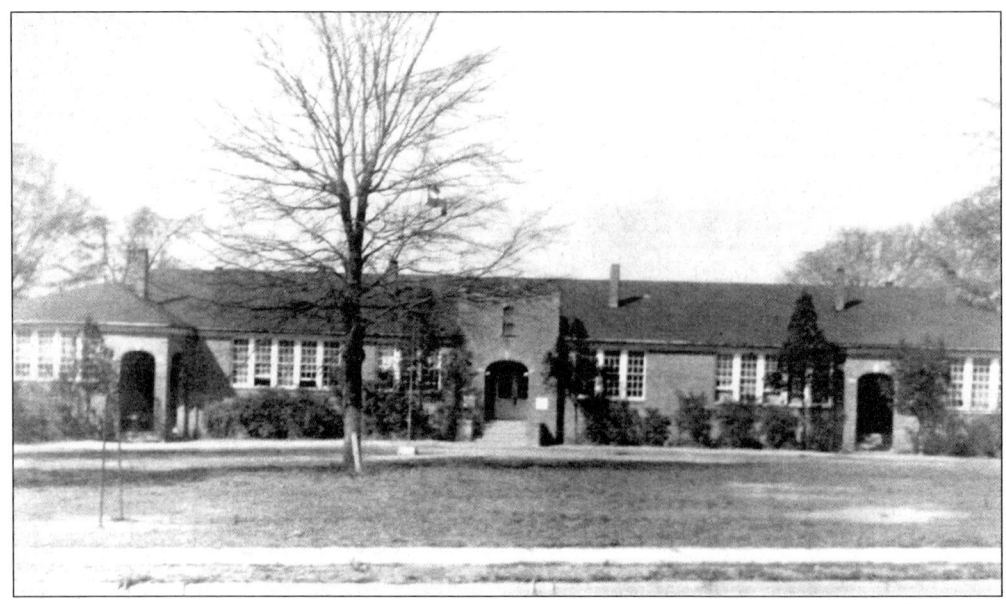

This photo features the old Whitesburg High School, which is no longer in existence. The school ceased serving as a high school in the late 1950s when the consolidation of Roopville and Whitesburg High Schools created Central High School. Whitesburg was named for Andrew J. White, the president of the railroad company. (Courtesy of City of Whitesburg.)

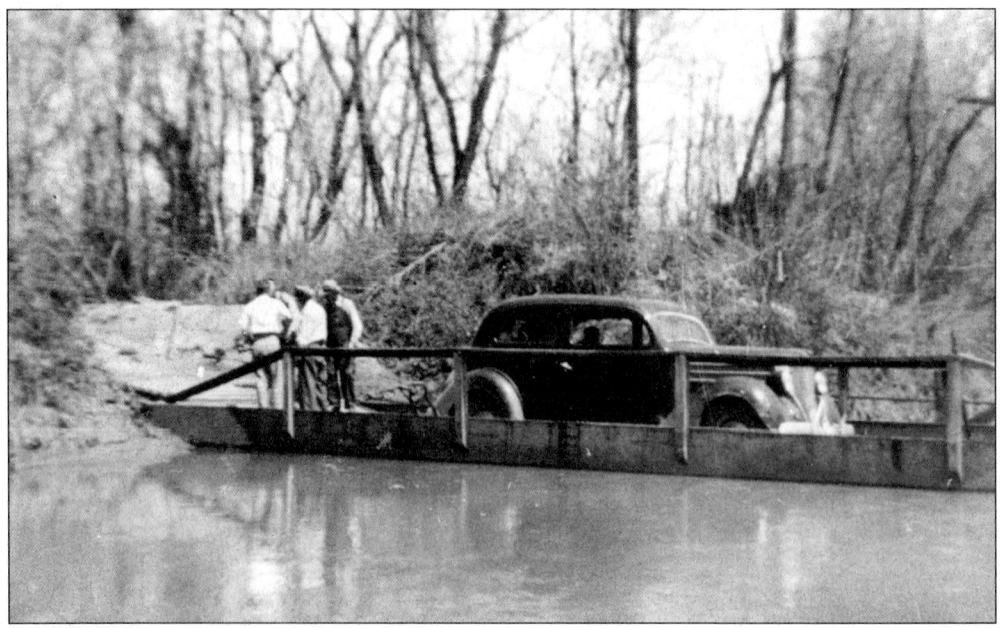

This real photo features the Hutcheson's Ferry near Whitesburg. For many years, the only way for a vehicle to easily get across the Chattahoochee River without driving great distances was by way of the ferry. Many stories are told by the "old timers" concerning the ferry, and include tales about vehicles that fell off the ferry into the river as well as not being able to wake the ferryman up on the other side, which sometimes resulted in overnight stays. (Courtesy of Imogene Carnes Harris.)

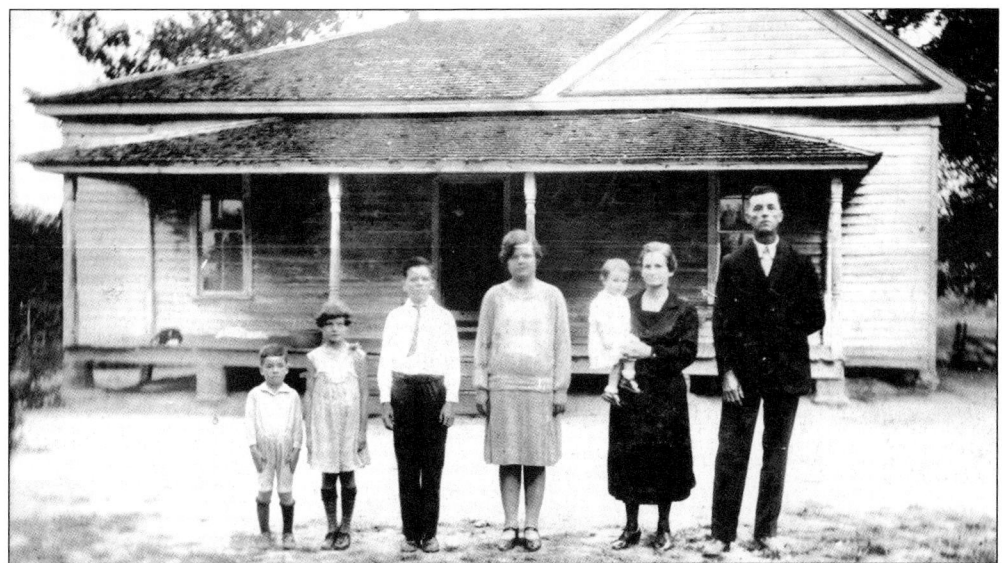
Taken *c.* 1928, this photo features the John Knight Pate Sr. family. From left to right are John Knight Jr., Mabel Irene, Lamar, Dorothy, Maddie (holding Joyce), and John Sr., standing in front of their home on Hutcheson Ferry Road in Whitesburg. John Sr. died of blood poisoning shortly after this picture was taken. (Courtesy of John Pate family.)

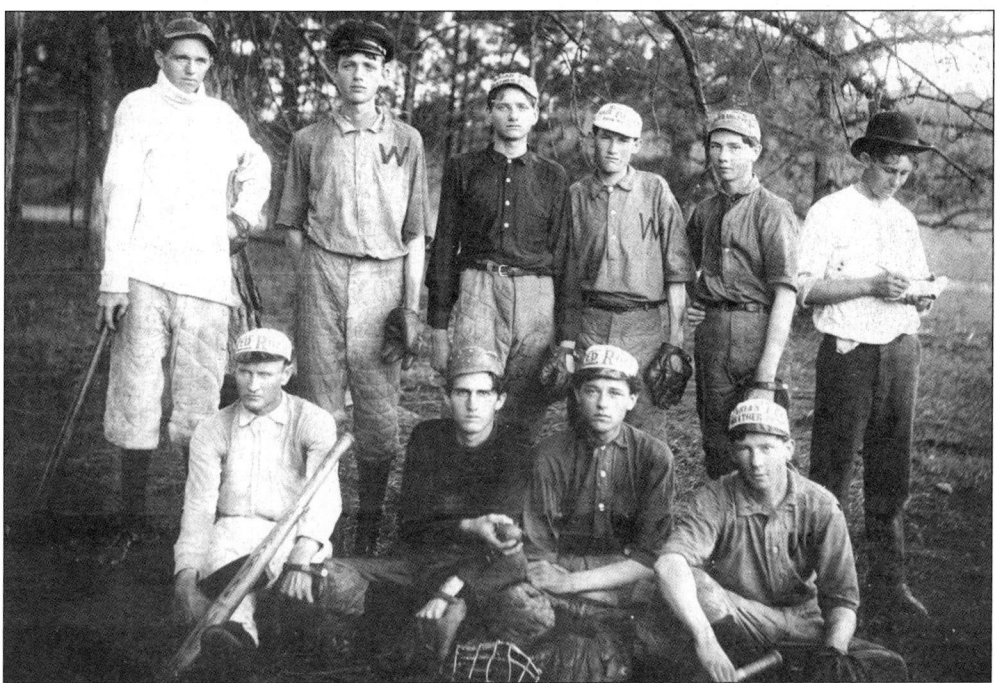
This is an early view of a Whitesburg baseball team. Although the players are unidentified, one is believed to be Horry Pate. The condition of the equipment (bats, gloves, ball, and catcher's glove) indicates a very old picture and players that truly loved the game. The hats are a hodge-podge of advertisement hats, some of which are for Red Rock, while others are for a hair treatment product. (Courtesy of John Pate family.)

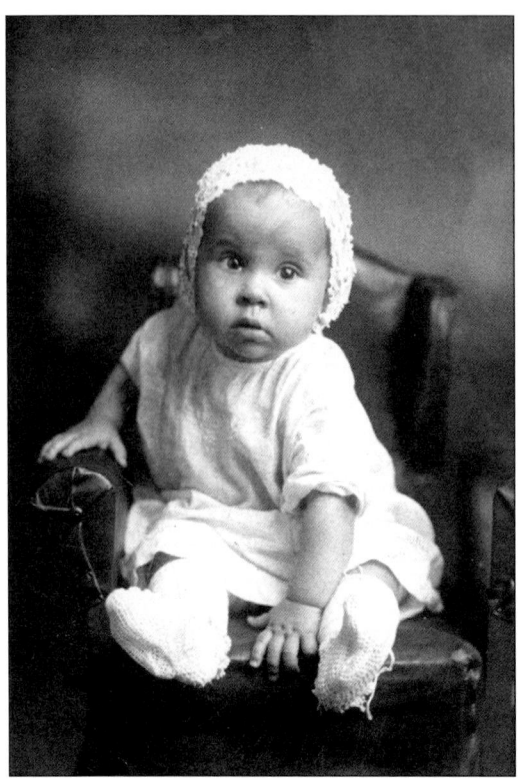

Madelene Carnes Pate is pictured at about eight months old in a dress that her mother had made by hand. Madelene has lived in the Byers Crossroads (Whitesburg) area for over 65 years. She is known for her constant generosity and has always helped the people of her community by providing food and clothing. An outstanding cook, she is best known for her biscuits, tea cakes, and homemade bread. (Courtesy of the John Pate family.)

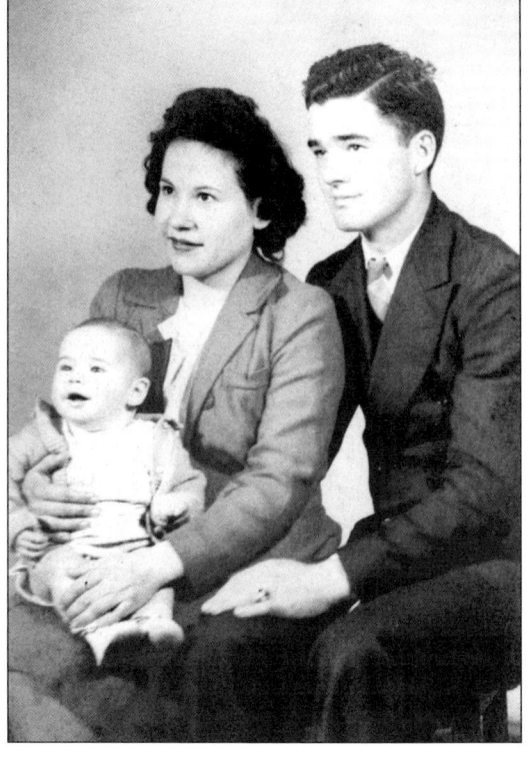

Wilson Knight Pate (1944), Madelene Carnes Pate (1923), and John Knight Pate Jr. (1923–2002) pose for a family photo card in early 1945. John was a farmer and was drafted in the United States Navy on February 1, 1945. During basic training in Michigan, John would wash other servicemen's clothing when off-duty and on weekends to earn extra money to help support his wife and infant son. (Courtesy of the John Pate family.)

Seven
BREMEN

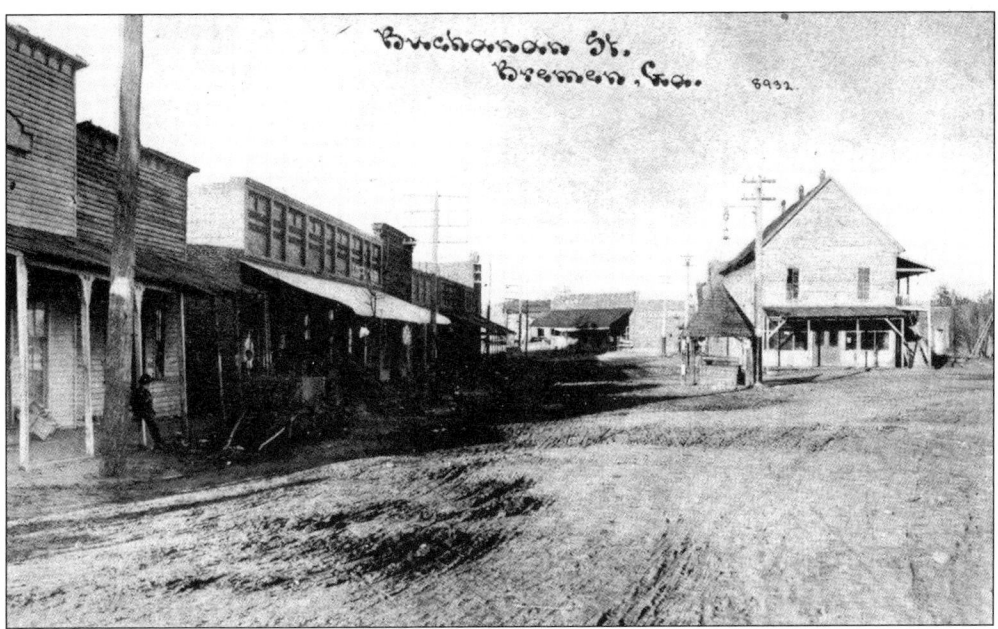

Bremen was incorporated as a city on September 5, 1883, following the building of the Georgia Pacific Railroad through the area in 1882. This is a view of Buchanan Street in Bremen, c. 1910. One of several town wells can be seen in the middle of the street. Like many of the early street scenes, a public well is prominent. Townspeople got drinking water from these public wells, while animals drank from large troughs.

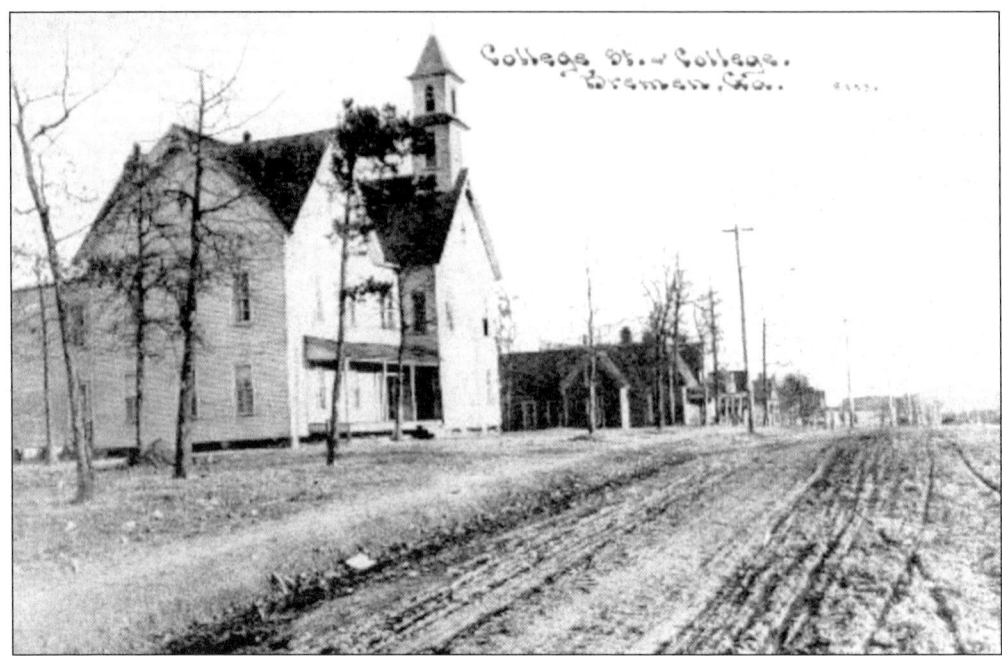

This is an early street scene in Bremen. One of the first schools in Bremen was located in the home of one of the leading citizens of the day, George Reid Hamilton. As a local benefactor, he also gave land for the Methodist, Baptist, and Presbyterian churches. In 1893, he gave land for what became known as Hamilton College in his honor. It was torn down in 1910.

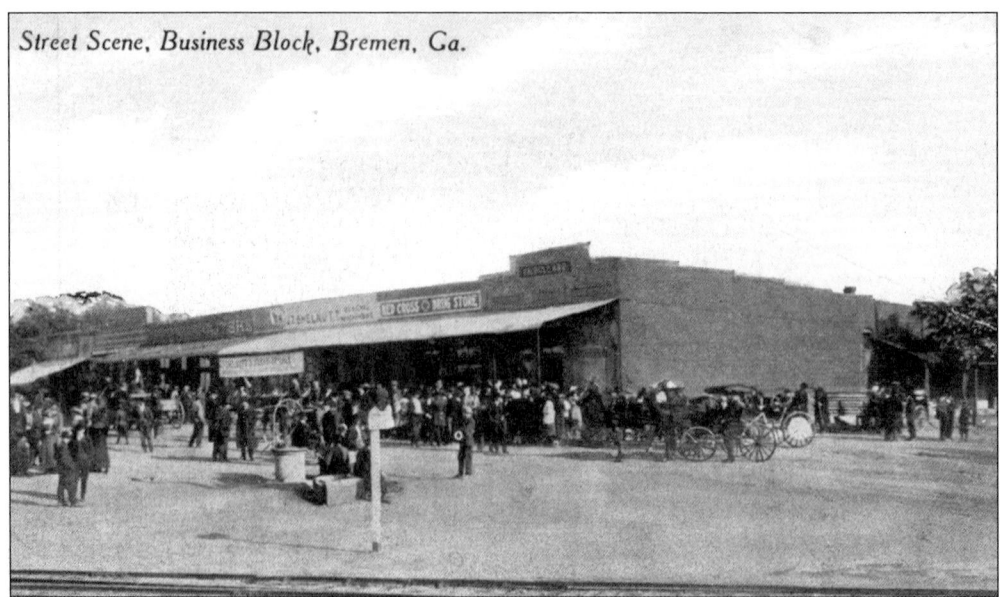

This is an early 1900s street scene of the business block in Bremen, Georgia, published by Gilbert Post Card Company of Chicago. Originally known as Wolf Pen and then Kramer (in honor of a German immigrant who lived in the area), the town was incorporated in 1883 and the name was changed to Bremen. A city well and trough can be seen in the foreground, and in the background are J.T. Shelnutt, Red Cross Drug Store, and Bullards. (Courtesy of Gary Doster.)

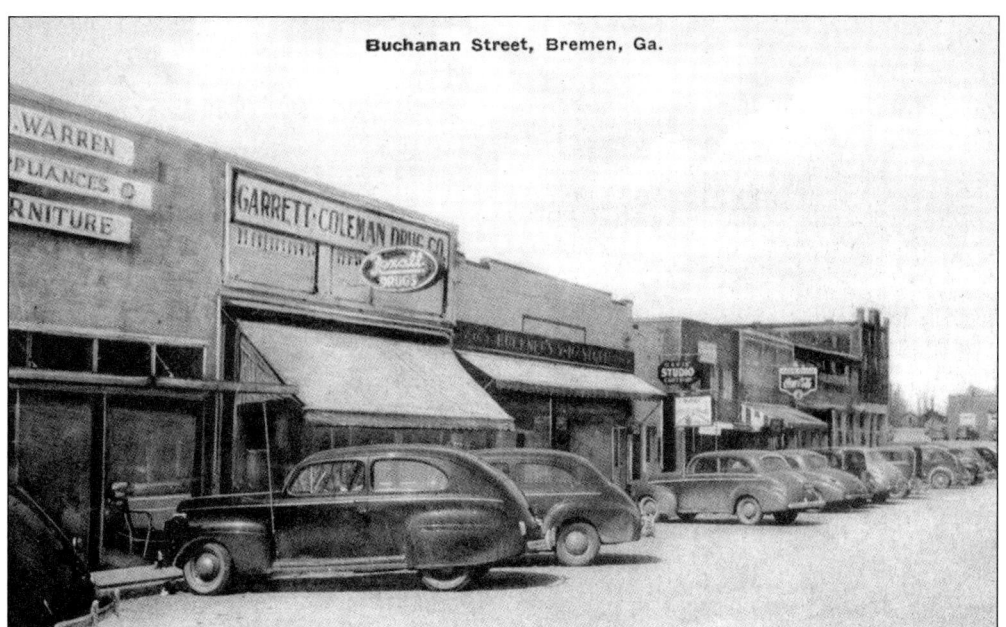

This 1940s view of Buchanan Street in Bremen features businesses that include the Warren Store, the Garrett-Coleman Drug Store, Buckner's 5–10¢ Store, Davis Studio and Gift Shop, and a café. A sign with what appears to be the name "Goldstein's" can be seen under magnification. The card was published exclusively for Garrett-Coleman Drug Co. of Bremen.

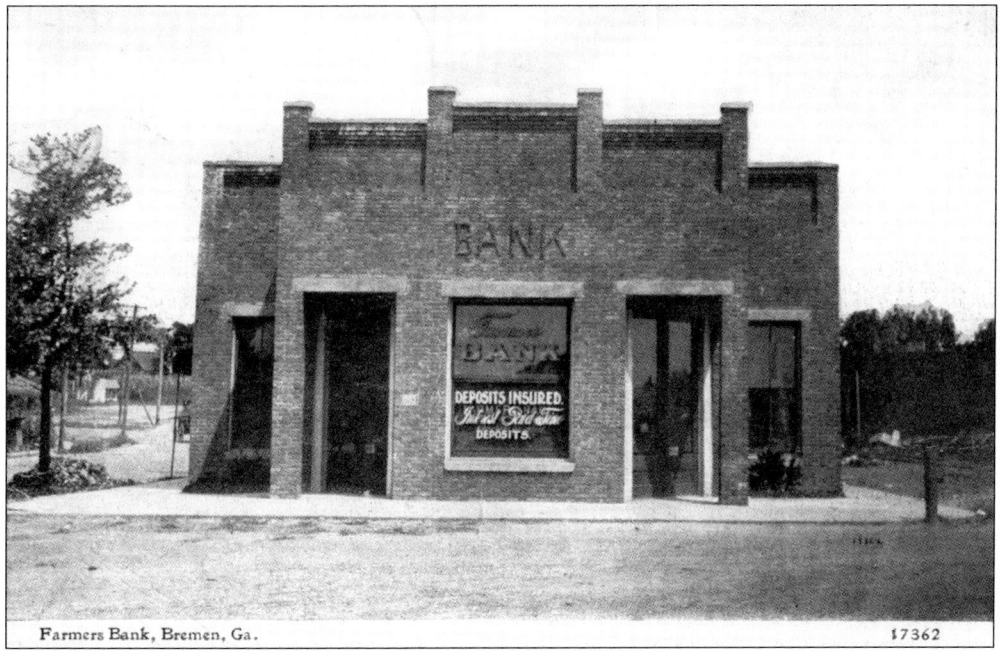

"The Farmers Bank of Bremen, Ga." is the subject of this postcard. The writing in the window indicates, "Deposits Insured, Time and Interest, Deposits."

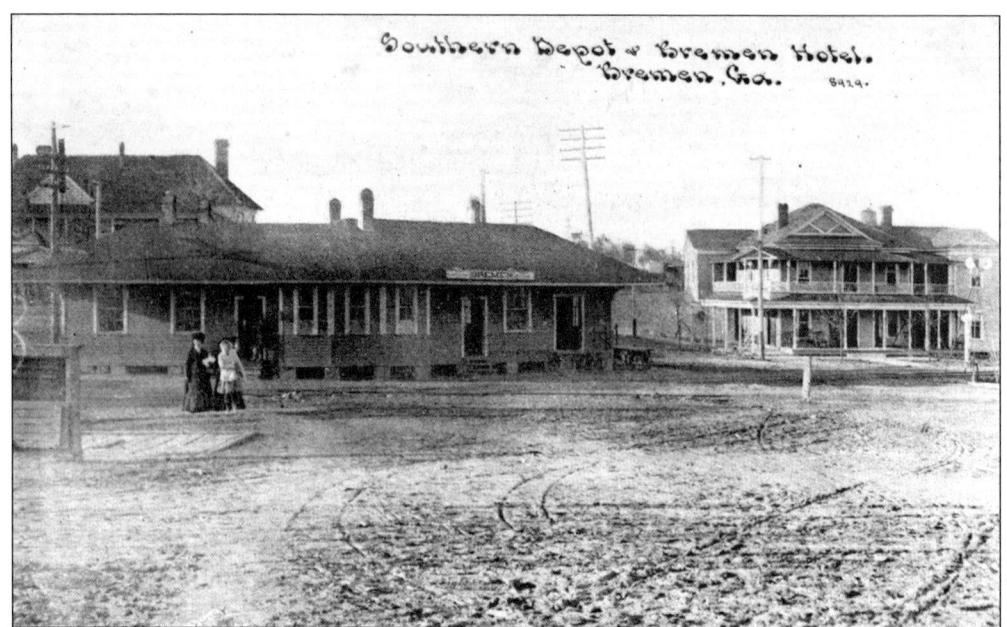

A picture of the early Southern Depot and the Bremen Hotel are seen in this postcard, *c.* 1910. This depot was torn down by 1914 and replaced with a new one. The roof in the background is the Boatright Hotel.

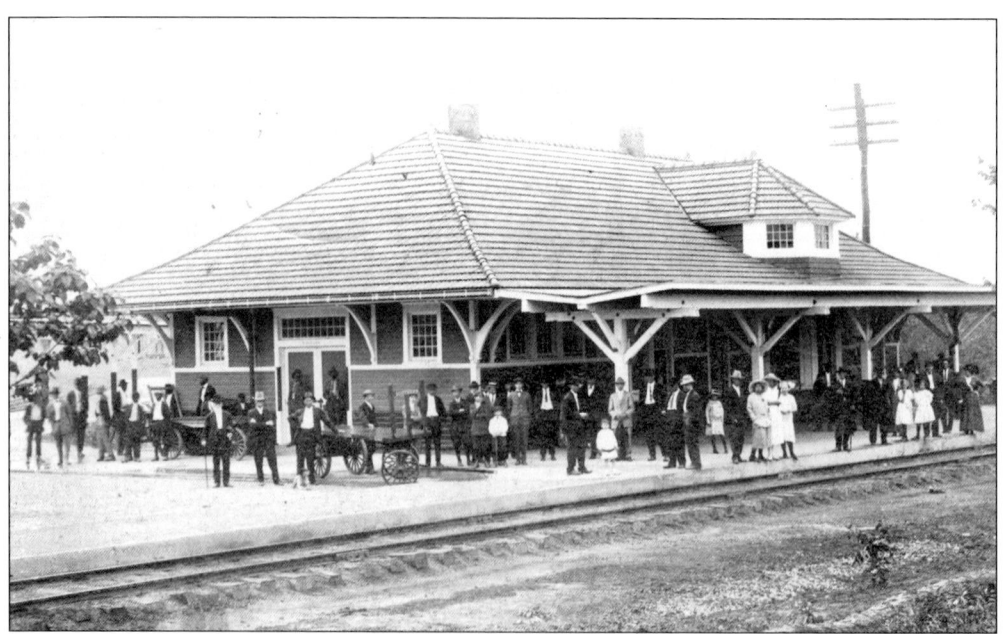

This is a rare photo card of the Bremen Depot, built in 1914, and features a large number of passengers, workers, a dog, and a cow under a tree. Over the years, the depot has gone by the names New Union Depot and the Southern Depot. The depot served as a junction of the Central of Georgia Railway and the Southern Railway. This railroad junction was responsible for much growth and commercialism in the early days of Bremen.

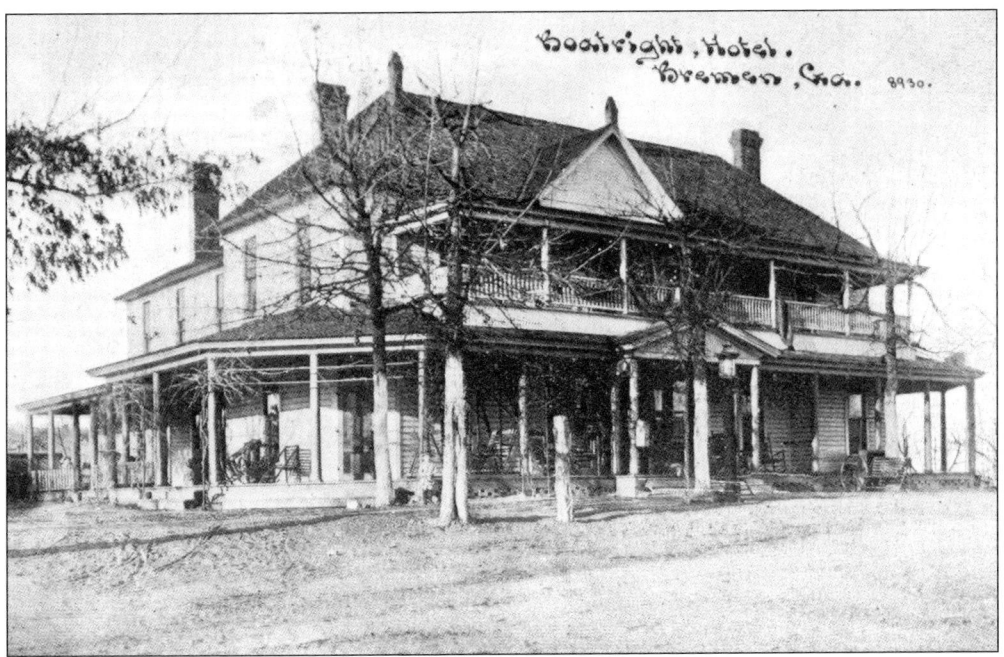

The Boatright Hotel is featured in this photo card. It is an early view of one of several large hotels that were built around the depot in the early 1900s. (Courtesy of Gary Doster.)

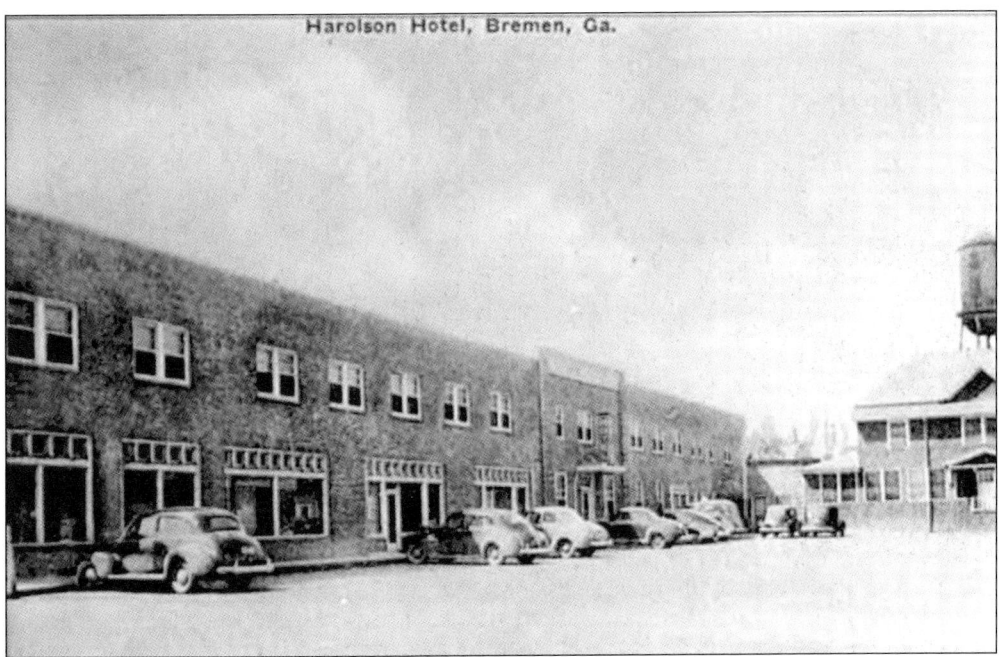

The Haralson Hotel in downtown Bremen is featured in this *c.* 1940 card. Note the water tower in the background.

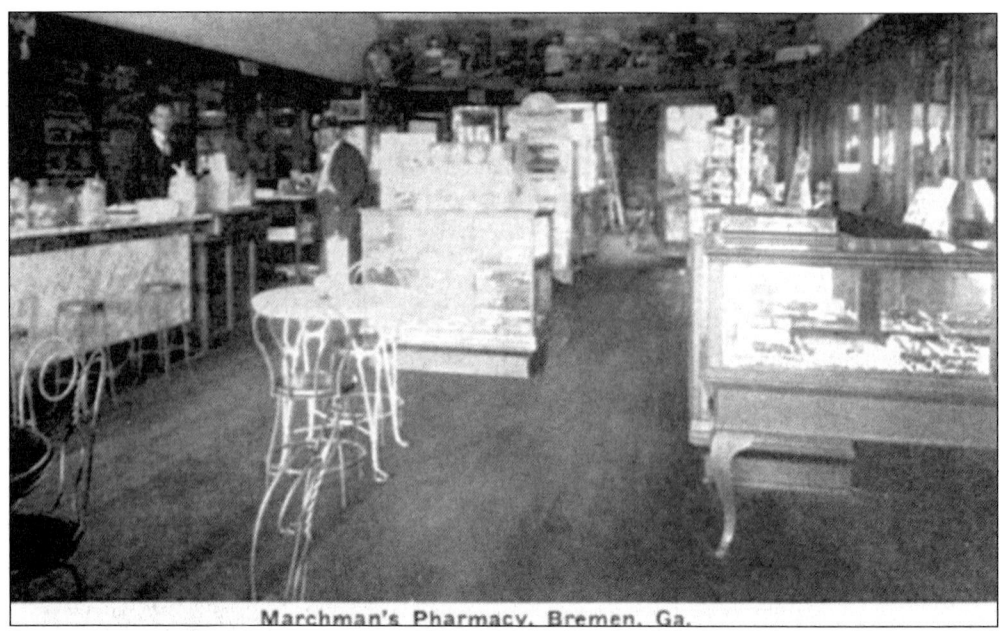

This is a view of the interior of Marchman's Pharmacy, one of Bremen's early pharmacies. The Marchman brothers had stores in Bremen, Villa Rica, and Douglasville. The pharmacy once sold gasoline in front. A vacant lot between Marchman's and the Hotel Haralson was at one time converted to a tennis court.

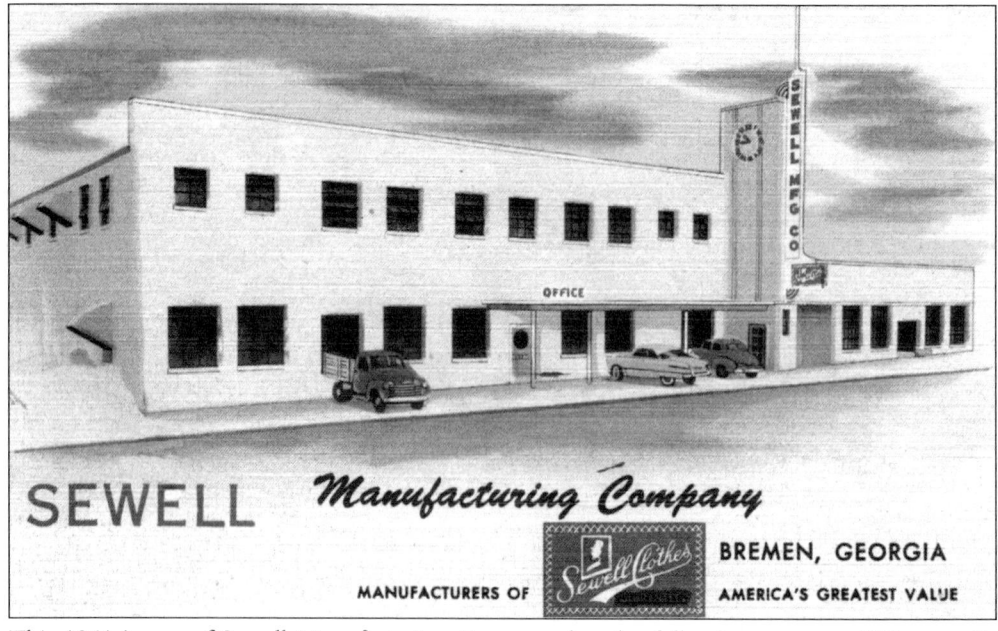

This 1961 image of Sewell Manufacturing Company has the following message: "We proudly present the home of Sewell Clothes which has been in continuous operation by the same families of skilled craftsmen for thirty-three years. Sewell Clothes are styled and priced right. Sewell clothes are guaranteed to give entire satisfaction. When you think of clothing—think of Sewell." The Sewell M. Company was started in 1928 by brothers Roy and Warren Sewell.

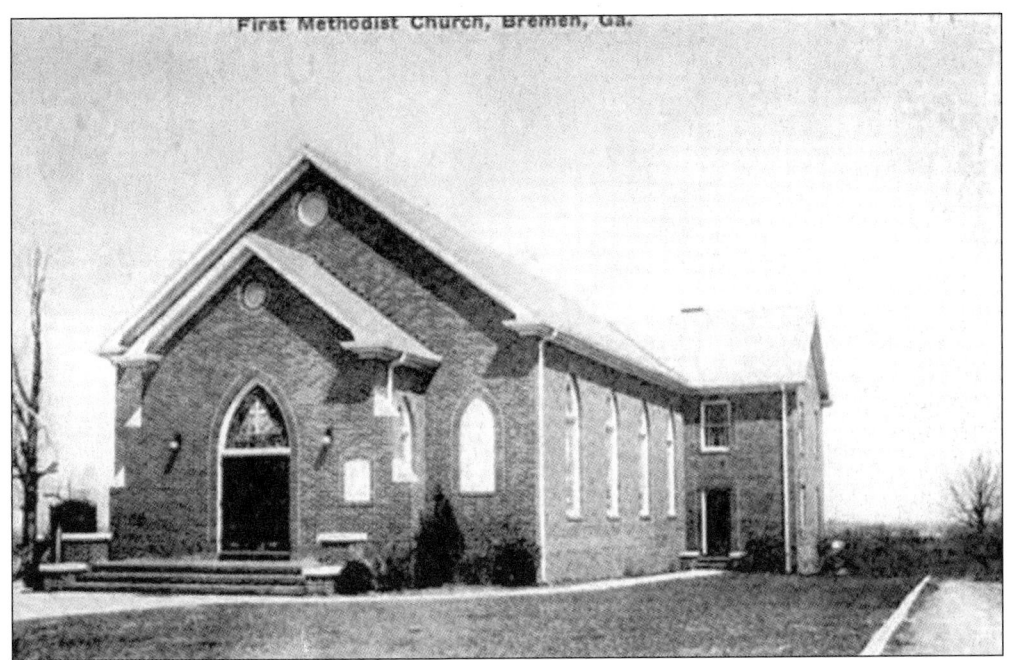

This is a postcard of the First Methodist Church of Bremen, Georgia. Ground was broken for this building on March 31, 1938, and the first service in the church was held later that same year with W.L. Brackman serving as pastor. The church got its start in 1881 with three members, W.F. Cash, Nancy June Cash, and R. Field.

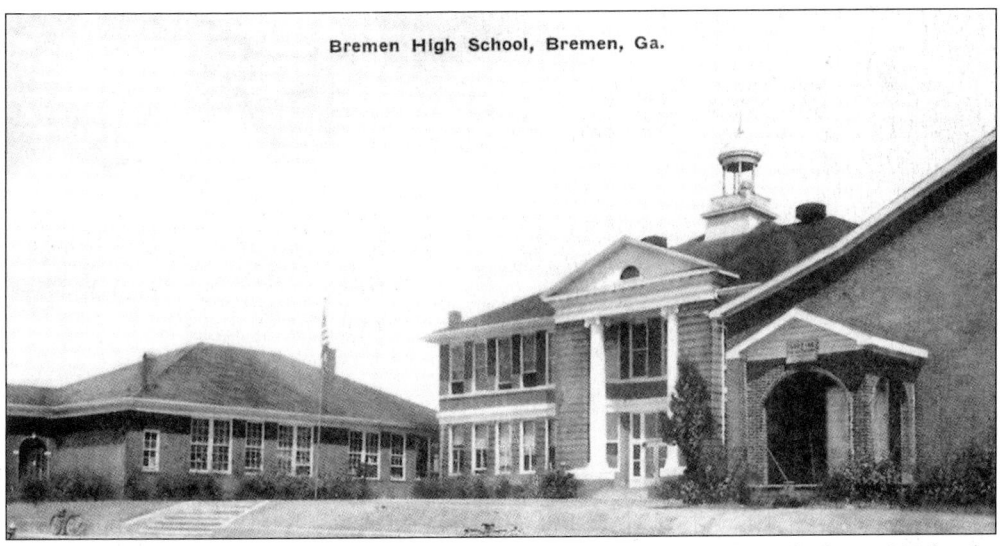

Erected on the site of the old Hamilton College, Bremen High School was built in 1910 by the Bullard Lumber Company. Previously a part of the Haralson County School System, the Bremen School System reverted to the terms of its charter and became an independent school system in 1946. The new high school, pictured above, was built in the 1950s and was occupied in the fall of 1956. (Courtesy of Michael Miller.)

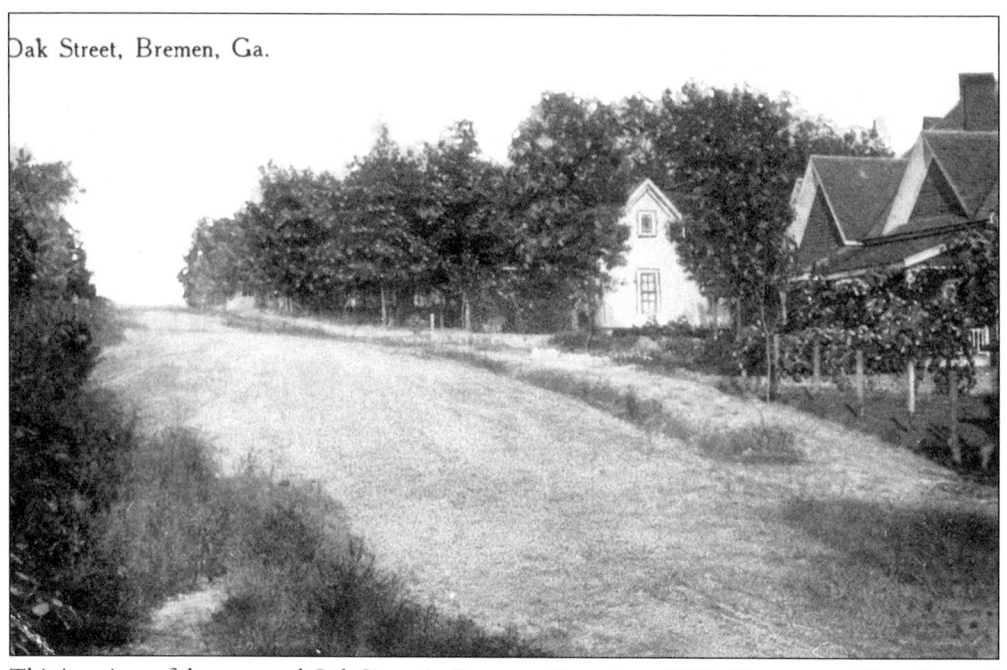

This is a view of the unpaved Oak Street in Bremen, Georgia, c. 1910. (Courtesy of Gary Doster.)

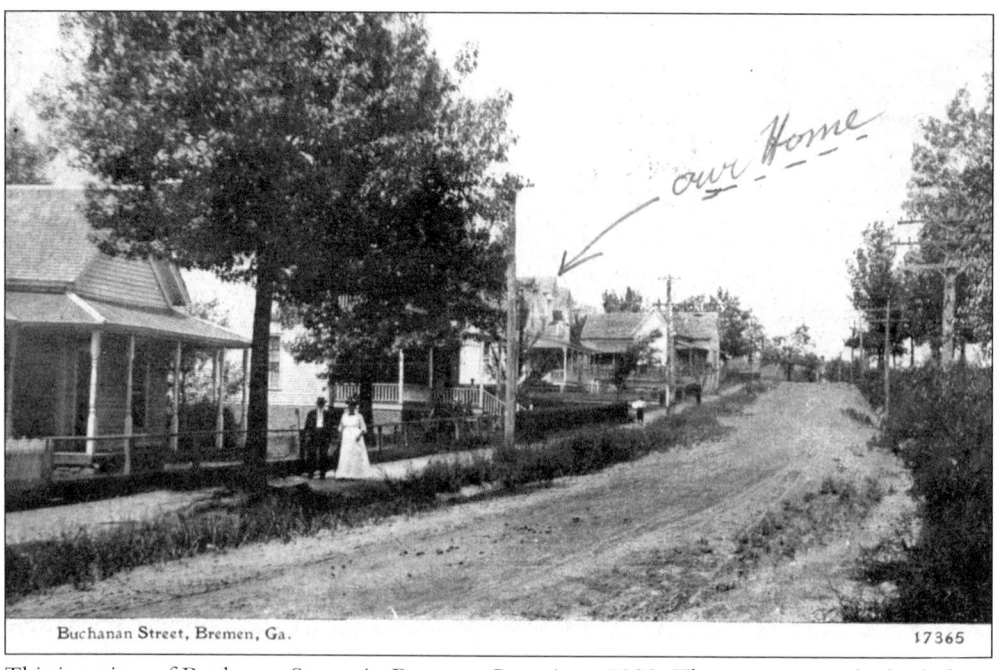

This is a view of Buchanan Street, in Bremen, Georgia, c. 1920. The message on the back from Nellie reads, "Did you ever see this house. There are four Atlanta girls here with me. We go riding every night so I do not have time to get lonesome." Note the arrow on the card that points to "our home." (Courtesy of Gary Doster.)

Eight
BUCHANAN

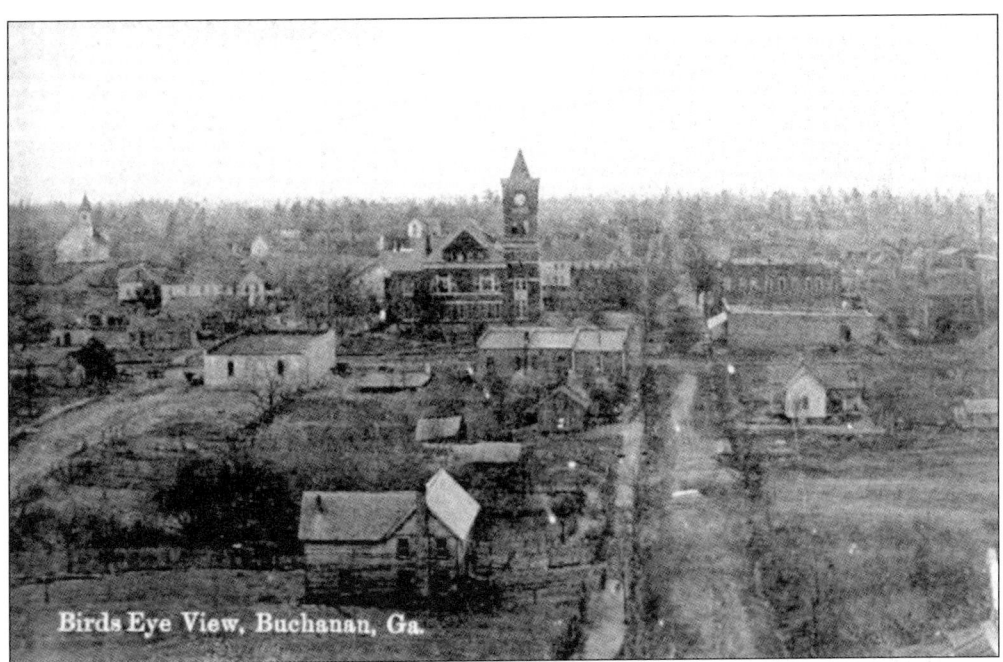

Originally, Buchanan was to be named Pierceville in honor of President Franklin Pierce; however, it was renamed for President James Buchanan when it was discovered that another town with a post office by the name of Pierceville existed. The chapter of incorporation was granted on December 22, 1857, and in 1902, it was re-chartered and incorporated as a city. This bird's-eye view of Buchanan shows the courthouse in the middle of the square, *c.* 1910.

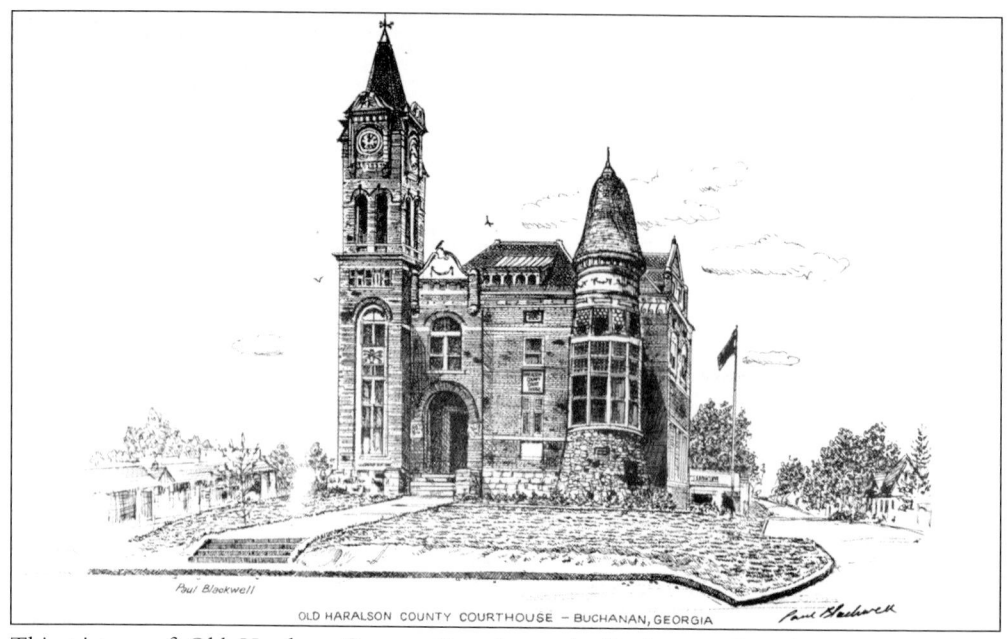

This picture of Old Haralson County Courthouse in Buchanan, Georgia is a pen-and-ink drawing postcard by Paul Blackwell. The back of the card reads, "Built 1981–92. Designed in the Queen Anne style by noted Atlanta architects, C. Bruce and Thomas Morgan, it rates architecturally with the best Victorian courthouses in Georgia. It is being restored by the Haralson County Historical Society and is on the National Register of Historic Places." (Courtesy of Haralson County Historical Society.)

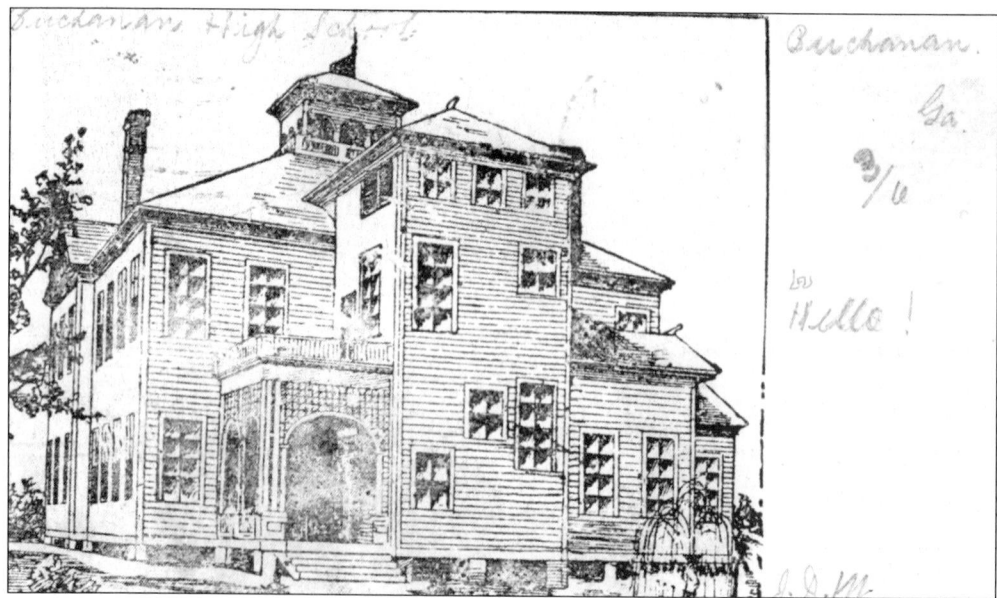

This rare image of the old wooden Buchanan High School is postmarked March 1907. On October 3, 1895, the city of Buchanan voted to issue school bonds to construct a new school. This building officially opened in August 1896 with C.T. Kellog serving as principal. The building burned and was replaced in the 1920s by a brick building that also burned down.

Nine
TALLAPOOSA

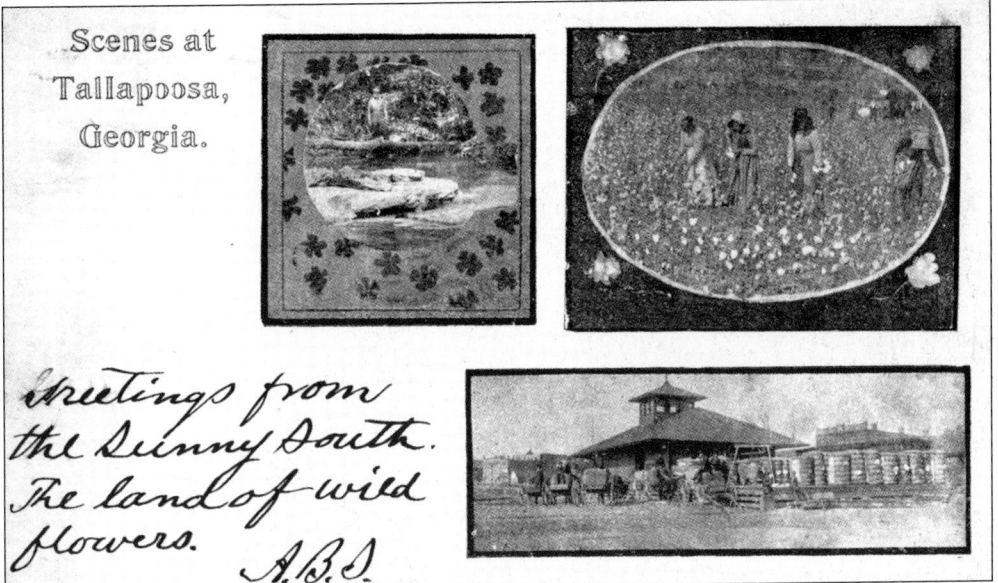

The message on this card, postmarked May 23, 1904, reads, "Greetings from the Sunny South. The land of wild flowers. A.B.D." Three early scenes of Tallapoosa include a man on the Tallapoosa River, ladies picking cotton, and the loading of cotton bales at the railroad depot. In the 1830s, the settlement of Possum Snout was established. Later known as Old Town, the citizens decided on the name Tallapoosa, a Creek word meaning "golden water," at the time of incorporation.

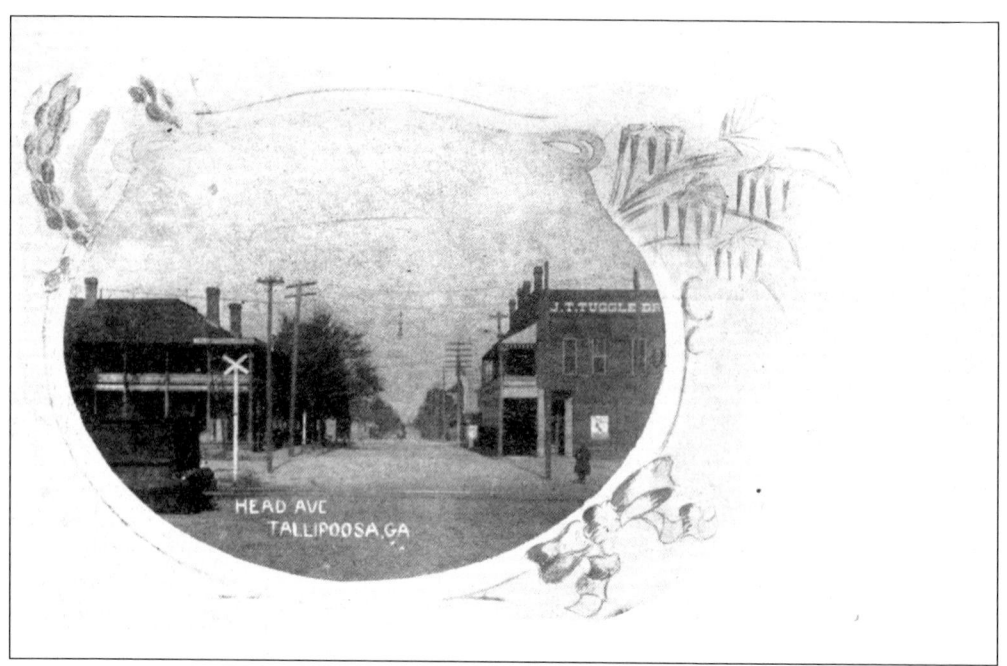

A very early view of Head Avenue in Tallapoosa is featured in this card, postmarked December 1908. J.T. Tuggle Dry Goods store can be seen on the right, and behind the railroad car on the left is the Tallapoosa Hotel. (Courtesy of Gary Doster.)

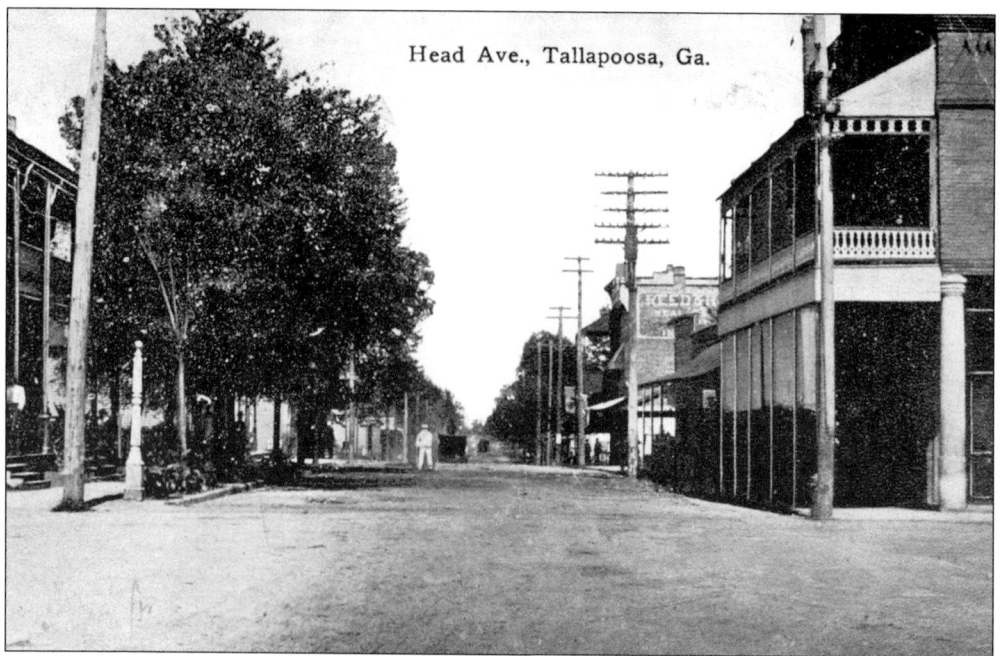

Postmarked September 18, 1916, from Tallapoosa, this card features a view looking down Head Avenue. The J.T. Tuggle Dry Goods store is on the right. Two buildings down, on the same side of the road, is a partially hidden sign on the two-story building that reads "Reed & H___." Across the street is the Tallapoosa Hotel and other stores. (Courtesy of Gary Doster.)

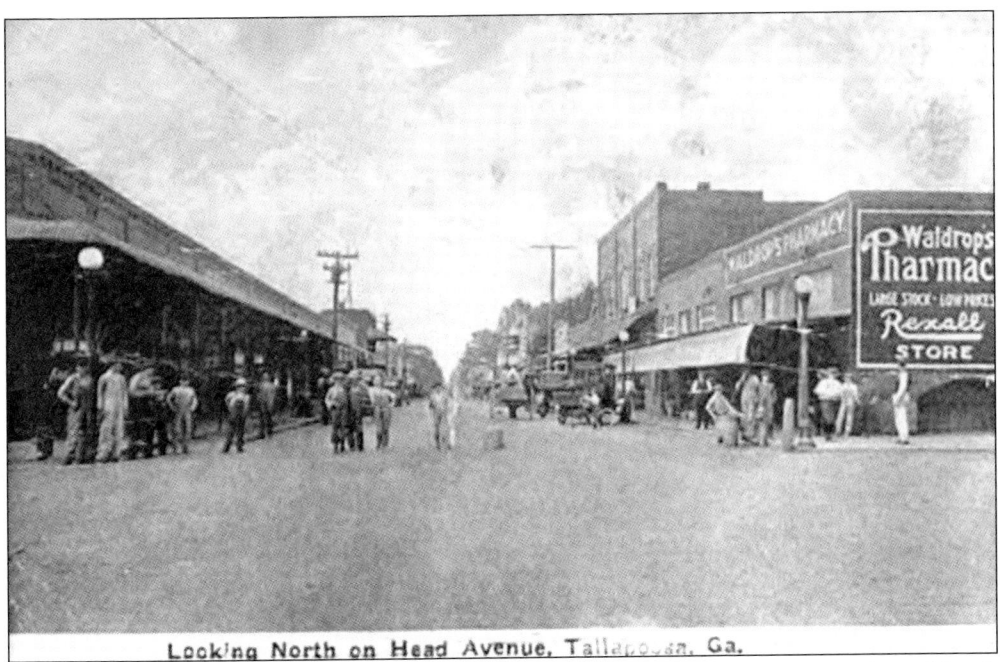

"Looking North on Head Avenue, Tallapoosa, Ga." is the caption of this card. Waldrop's Pharmacy, the "Rexall Store with Large Stock and Low Prices," can be seen on the right. On the left is Hildebrand's Pharmacy. The building housing the Hildebrand's Pharmacy was constructed in 1919 after the Tallapoosa Hotel had burned down.

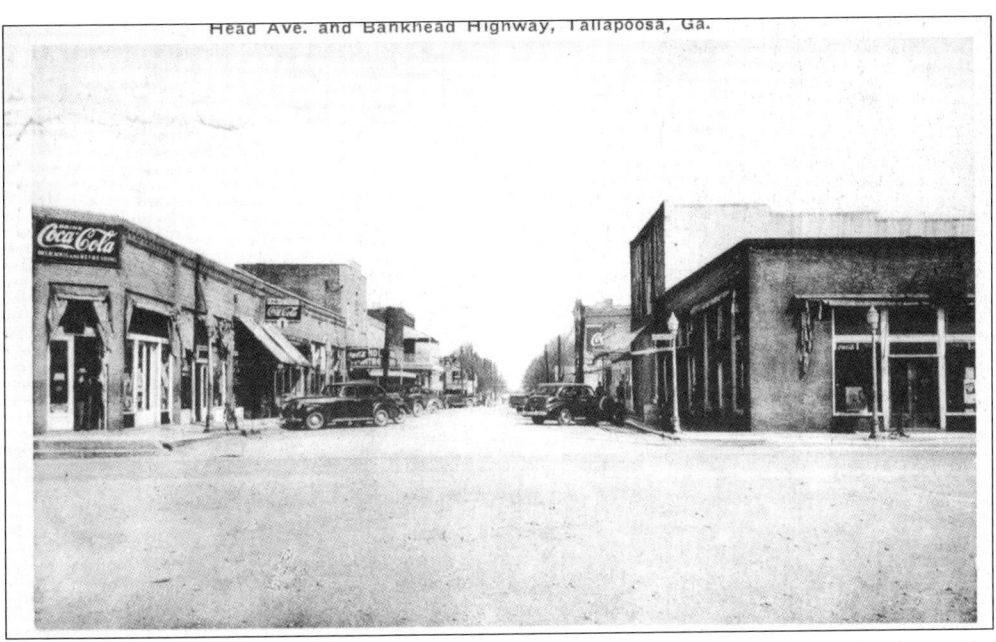

Published for Waldrop's Pharmacy of Tallapoosa, this postcard was postmarked in the 1940s. Coca-Cola signs can be seen on both sides of the street. The Grand Theatre can be seen on the left.

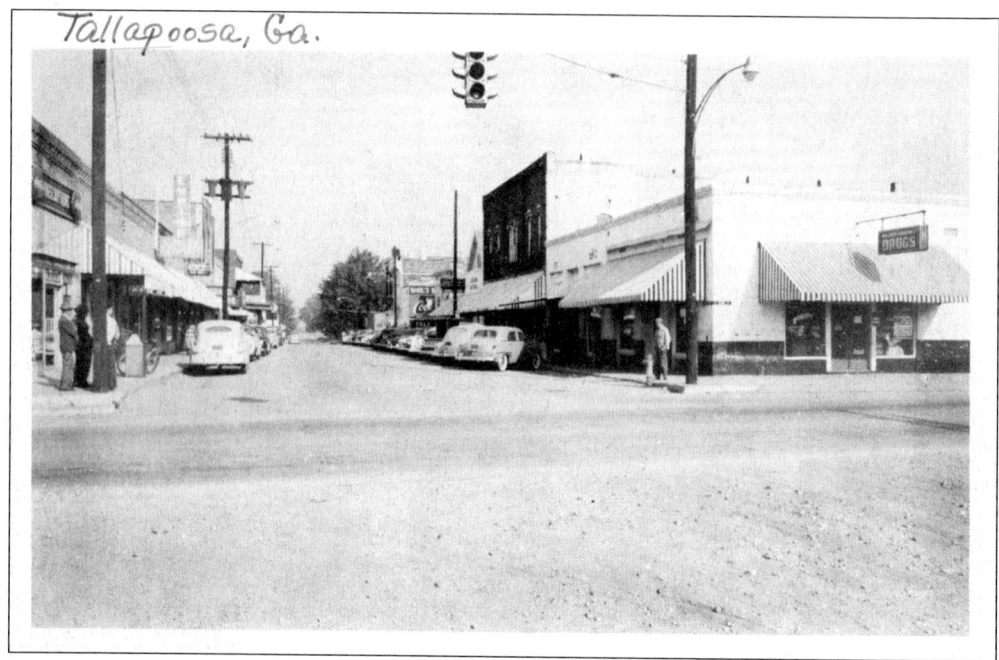

Another Head Avenue Street scene from *c.* 1950 shows how the avenue has changed over the years from the previous few cards. Waldrop's Pharmacy is located on the right side. The Empire 5 & 10¢ Store and the Grand Theatre are on the left.

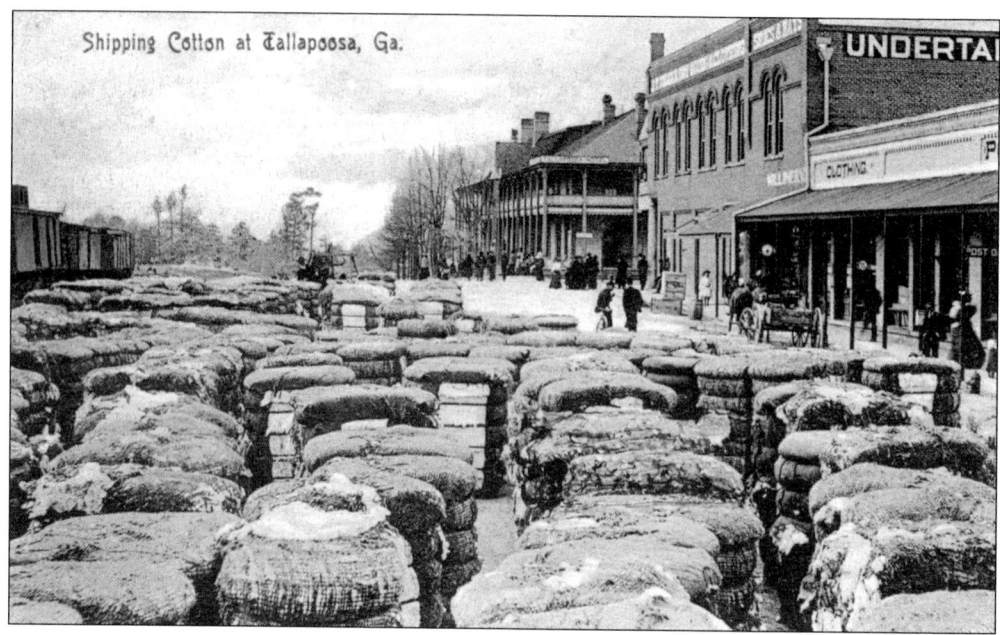

Cotton fills the street in this 1910 view of the railroad and business district. On the right, closest to the viewer, are the post office and J.T. Tuggle Dry Goods Store, which has signs for clothing, shoes, hats, millinery, and undertaking. Across Head Avenue is the Tallapoosa Hotel.

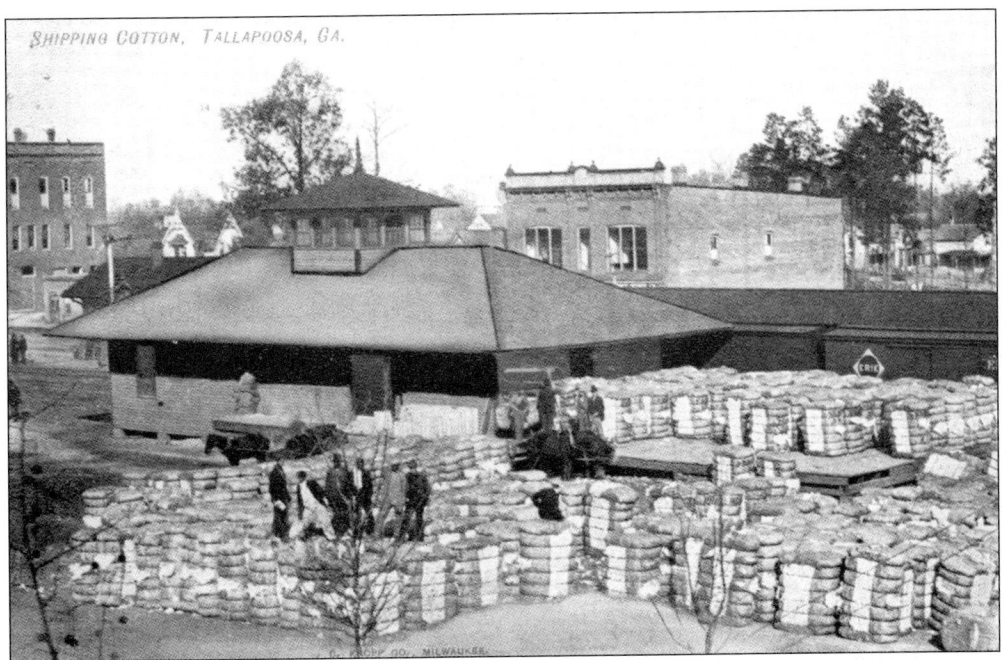

E. Murphy writes the following to Miss Myrtle Morton in New Jersey: "Thought perhaps you would like to have a postal from away down south in Dixie. Hope this will find you well and progressing in your studies." Published by the Knoop Co. of Milwaukee, the card was postmarked on March 13, 1908, in Buchanan, Georgia, and shows an overflow of cotton bales at the depot.

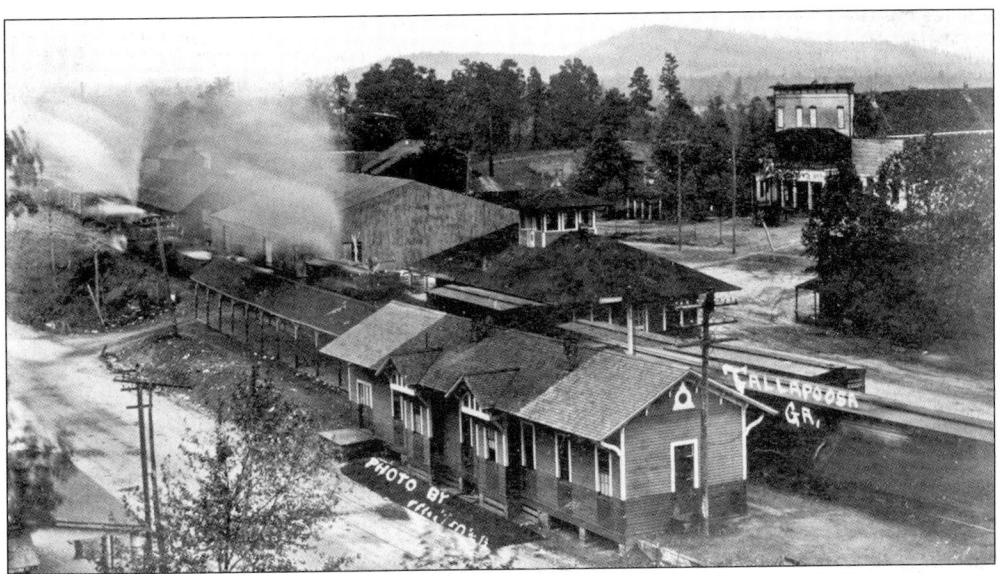

Featured here is a very rare view of locomotives in motion on the tracks at the Tallapoosa Depot, c. 1910. Because quick-speed film was not available at this time, photographers stayed away from photos that had motion. The writing on many of these earliest cards was actually scratched on the negatives and often was uneven or not legible, which is the case with the photographer's name here.

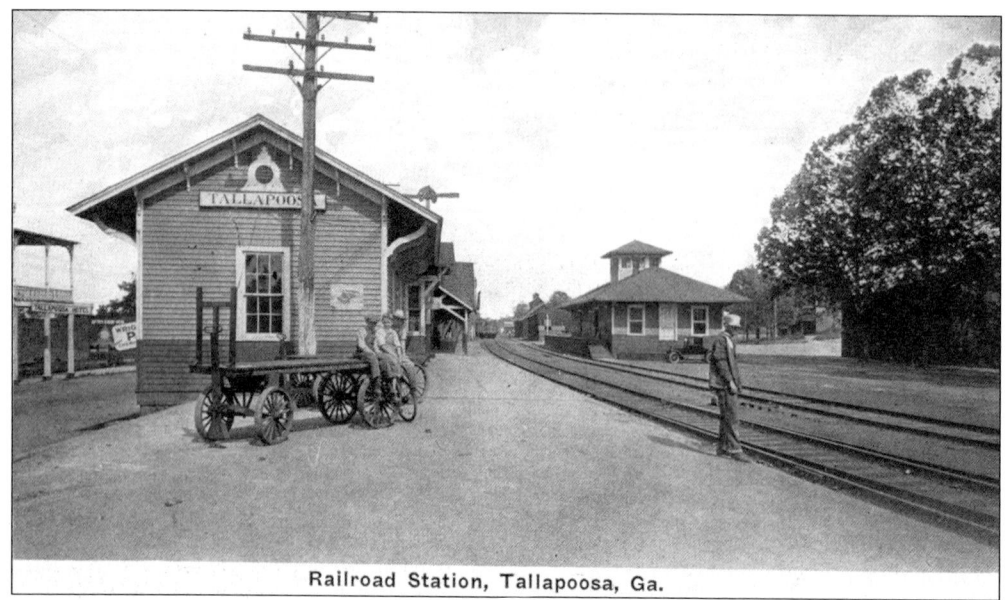

Railroad Station, Tallapoosa, Ga.

The Georgia Pacific Railroad came to Tallapoosa in 1882. The railroad sparked major growth in population and industry. This view, from prior to 1919, shows a railroad man looking down the tracks while three youngsters sitting on a baggage cart look on. To the left can be seen the porch of the Tallapoosa Hotel and part of a Wrigley Chewing Gum billboard.

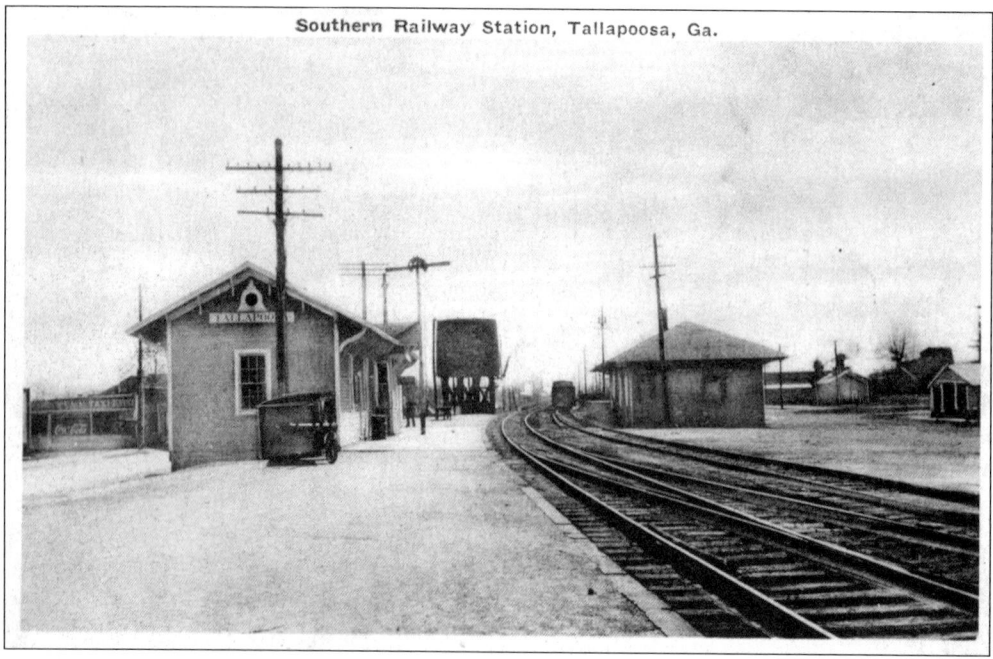

Southern Railway Station, Tallapoosa, Ga.

This is a later view of the Southern Railway Station in Tallapoosa. Note the additional houses on the right side of the card compared to the previous card. Tallapoosa's first boom of growth in the 1890s took place around land investment led by former Union Gen. Benjamin F. Butler. So many people from the North migrated here that the town became known as "The Northern City Under the Southern Sun." (Courtesy of Gary Doster.)

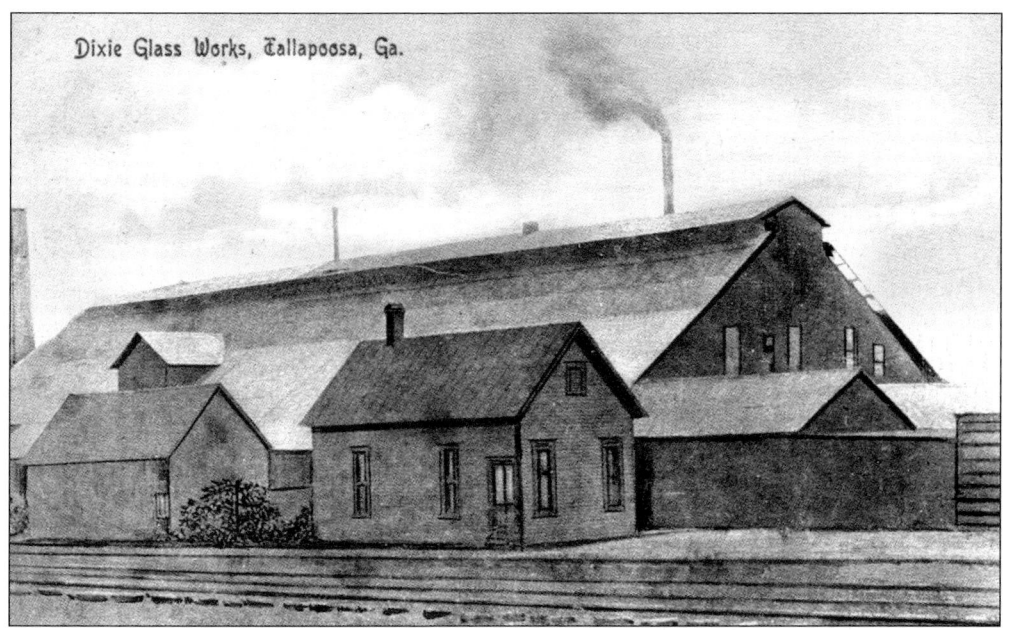

The Tallapoosa community had its second boom of people around grape vineyards starting in the late 1880s. So many grapes were produced that the wine industry was born, and at one time Tallapoosa was recognized as the largest wine center east of the Rocky Mountains. Wine meant bottles, and the Dixie Glass Works was established. They made bottles from one-ounce sizes to one gallon. Prohibition ended the growth boom. The card was postmarked in 1910.

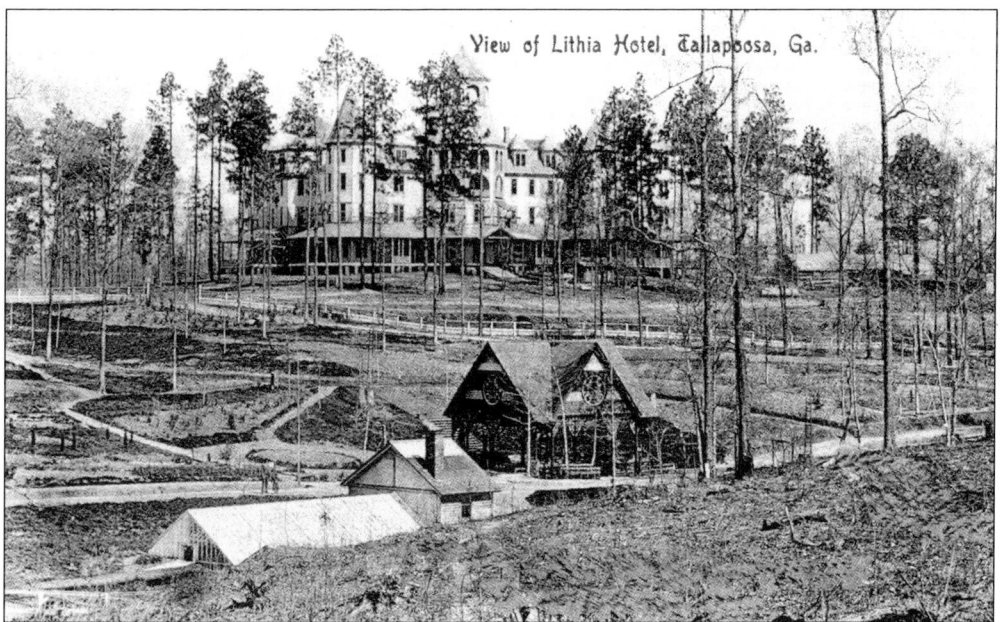

This is an early view of the Lithia Hotel through massive clearings of trees. Mailed January 10, 1910, John writes to his home in Indiana, "This is the sunny south. I hear it is real cold at home but it is nice here."

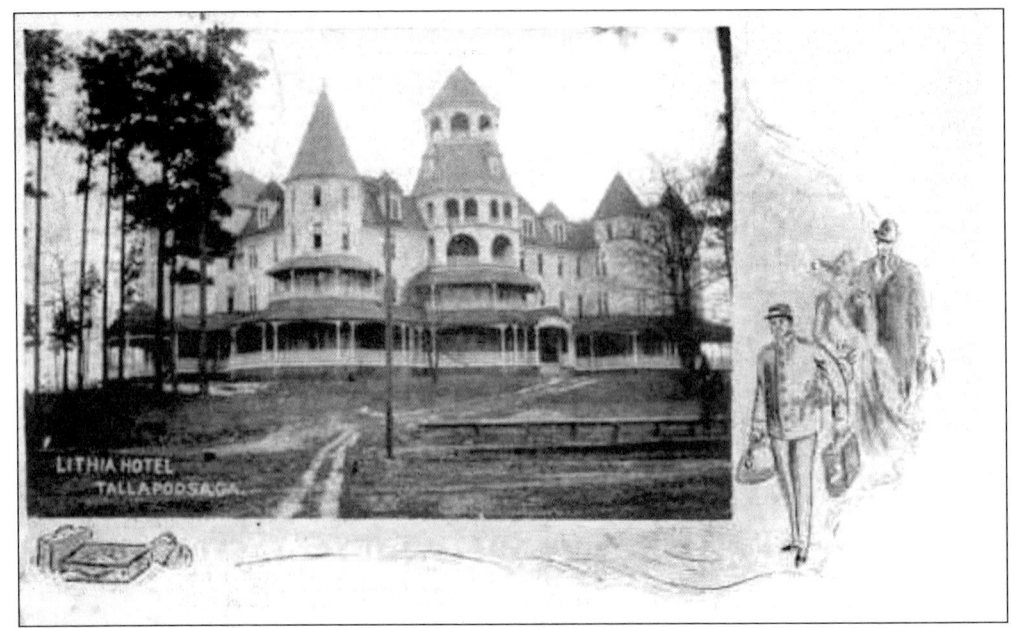

Built in 1892, the Lithia Hotel had 175 rooms and was completed at a cost of $200,000. Located on Boulevard, it had elevators, a ballroom, banquet hall, billiards room, bowling alley, and tennis courts. The "healing" mineral spring waters attracted many travelers to the resort. (Courtesy of Gary Doster.)

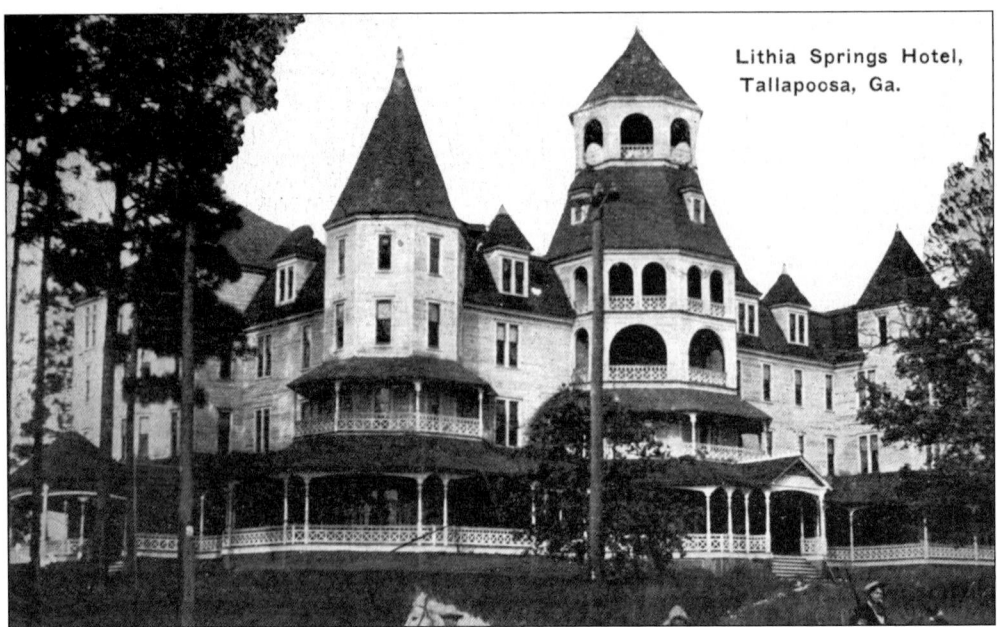

Published by L.C. Waldrop of Tallapoosa, Georgia, and postmarked April 1915, young Virginia writes to her friend, "I am having the nicest time making mud pies and picking violets." By this time the hotel was referred to as the Lithia Springs Hotel.

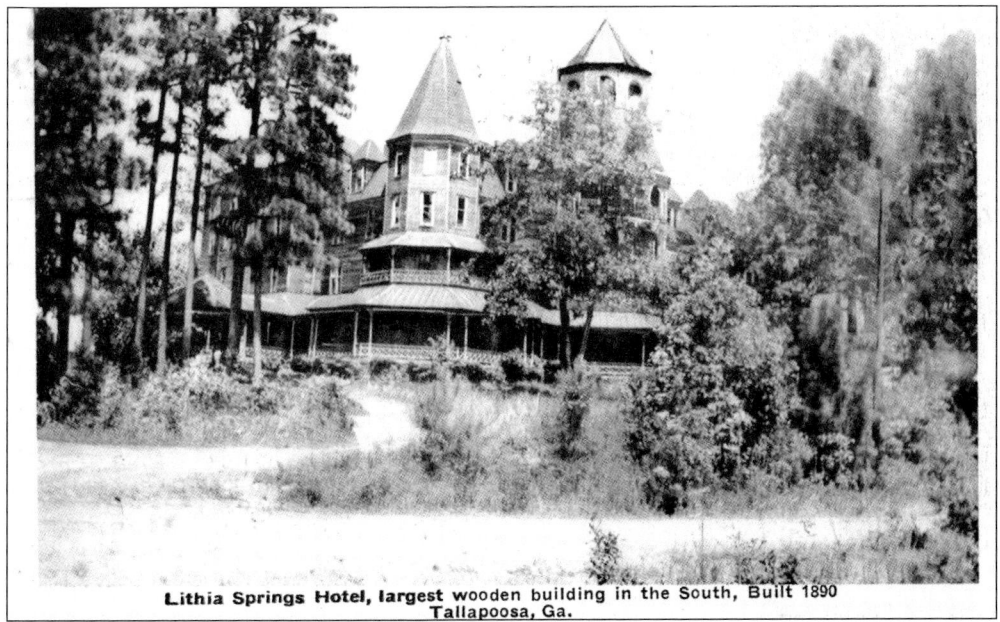

The caption on this card reads, "Lithia Springs Hotel, largest building in the South, built 1890, Tallapoosa, Ga." It was mailed by Elsie Royalty in June of 1942 and was published for Waldrops Pharmacy of Tallapoosa by the Collotype Co. The hotel was disassembled during World War II, and the copper roof went to the United States Navy for the war effort.

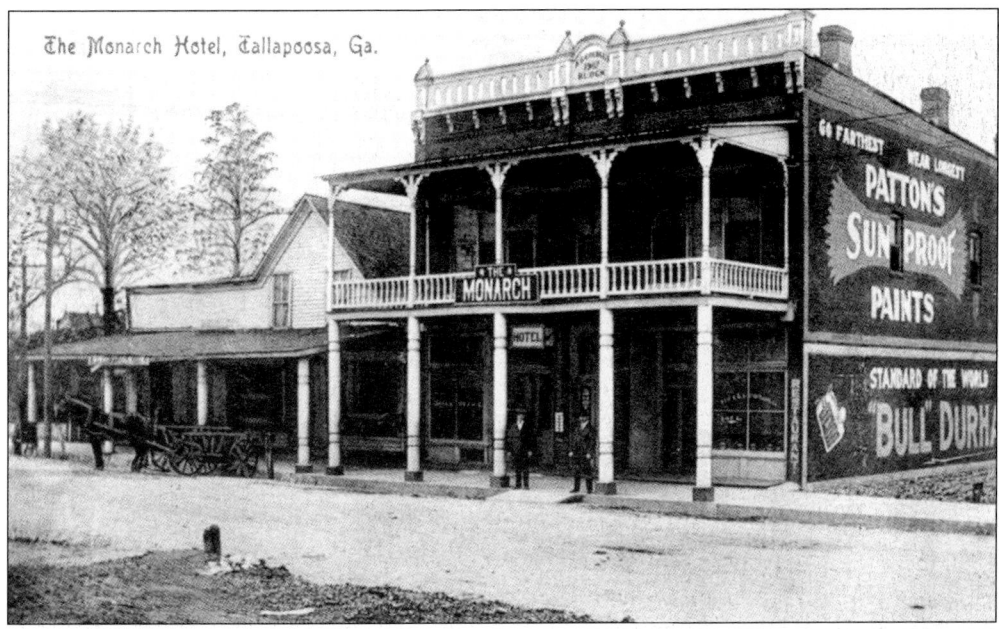

Built around 1900, the Monarch Hotel was located on Head Avenue and had 10 rooms. It was torn down in the 1980s. Note the Patton's Sunproof Paints and Bull Durham signs on the side of the hotel building. Julia writes to a friend in New Jersey on April 19, 1910, "If you would like some chrysanthemum plants let me know and I will send you some."

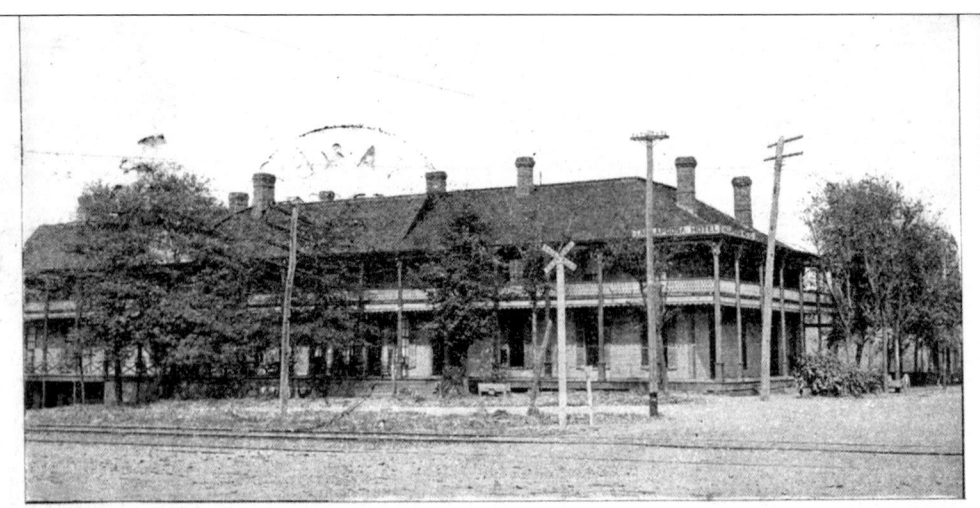

TALLAPOOSA, GEORGIA Is a thriving town of 2500 people, nestled among the foothills of the Blue Ridge Mountains, on the Georgia Pacific Division of the Southern Railway, 63 miles from Atlanta, Ga. and 103 Miles from Birmingham, Ala. The climate is unsurpassed, being far enough south to escape the rigors of the northern winters, and the altitude (1200 feet above sea level) making it cool and delightful in summer. **The Tallapoosa Hotel** Is a modern hostelry of 50 rooms, equipped with accommodations for families, as well as for the traveler who only tarries overnight. It is presided over by a lady, whose every effort is put forth to make her guests feel at home. For rates apply to **Mrs. G. C. Blackmarr**, Tallapoosa, Ga.

The Tallapoosa Hotel was built in the late 1880s on the corner of Head Avenue. It was a large, two-story building with large porches and can be seen in several previously shown cards. Note the interesting description of the hotel on the card, which was mailed in 1910. (Courtesy of Gary Doster.)

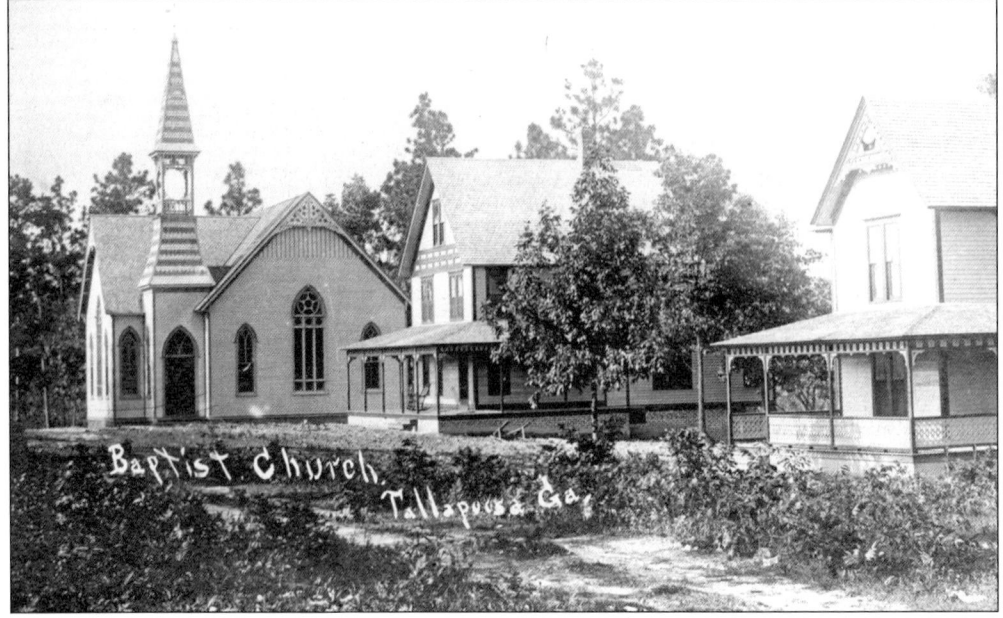

This vintage real picture photo card shows the Tallapoosa Baptist Church and two homes. The first church was organized in 1878 with the first building being destroyed by fire. A new church building was constructed by 1889 and is featured in the image above. The Victorian-style church was located on the corner of Manning and West Mill Streets. (Courtesy of Gary Doster.)

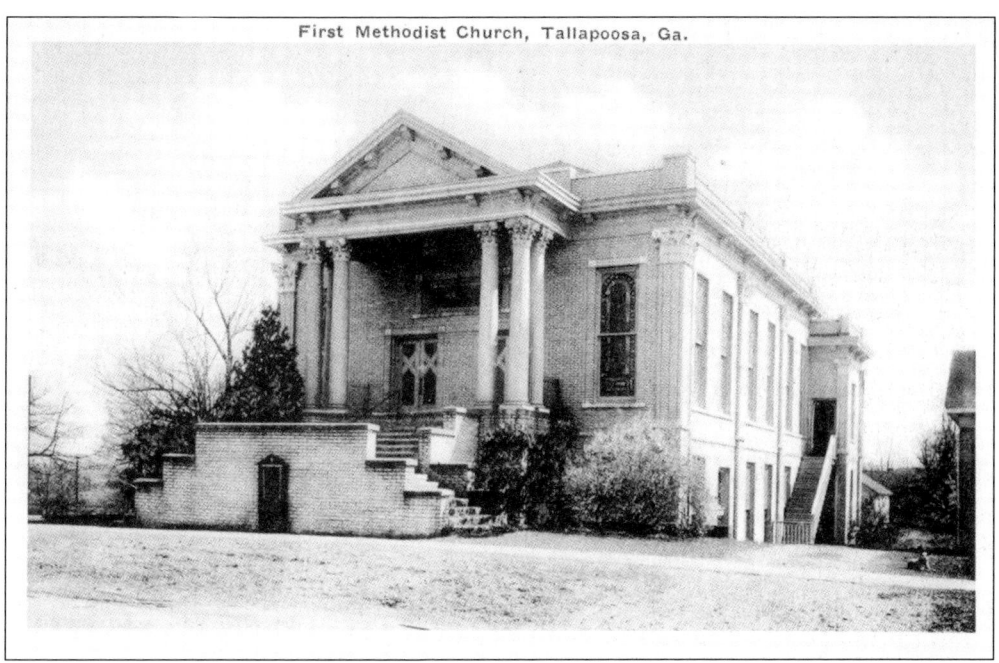

The First Methodist Church was organized in 1882, and a wooden church building was erected soon after. It was the first church constructed in Tallapoosa. Although twice enlarged, the building was razed in 1918, and the brick building pictured was then built. The architect for the project was Dr. Charles M. Lipham. The card was published by Waldrop's Pharmacy of Tallapoosa. (Courtesy of Michael Miller.)

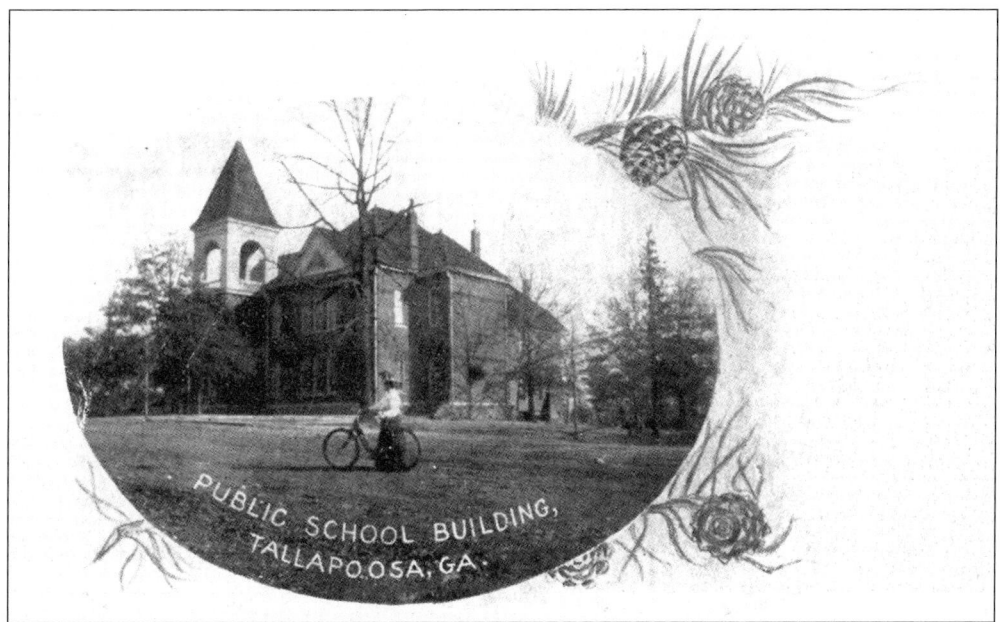

Tallapoosa was authorized by an act of the General Assembly to establish a public school. Organized in 1889 and completed in 1892, it was the first free public school established in Georgia.

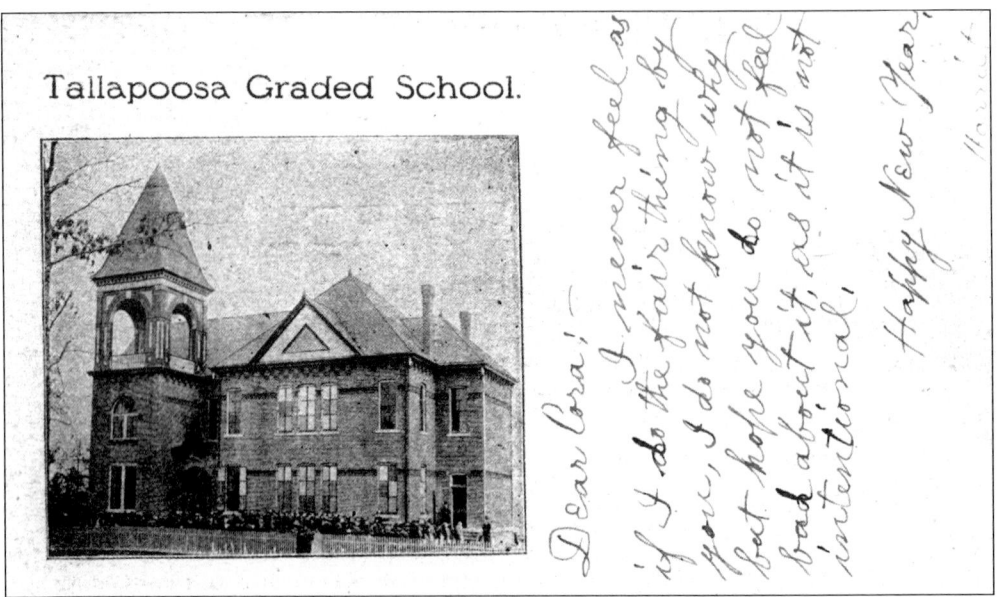

The Tallapoosa Graded School was located at the corner of Taliferro Street and Robertson Avenue. A large number of students can be seen on the school grounds in front of the two-story building. The card features a note from Harriet to Cora and is postmarked 1905. (Courtesy of Gary Doster.)

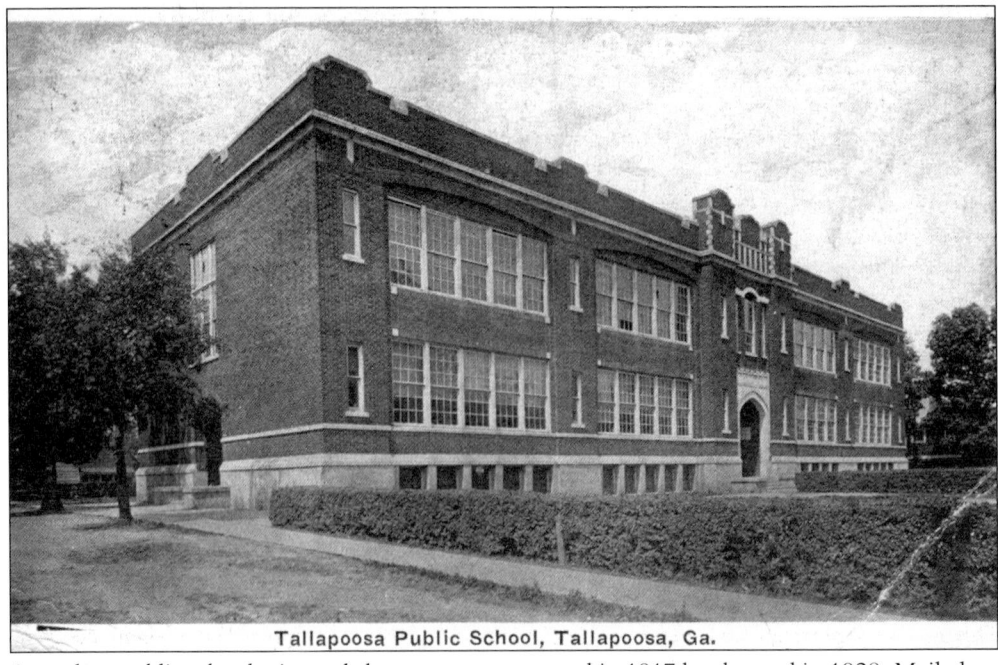

A modern public school, pictured above, was constructed in 1917 but burned in 1928. Mailed on May 3, 1925, D.W. writes, "Dear Grace, Have been grinning like a toothpaste ad ever since I got your letter—was so tickled. Certainly enjoyed the poetic description of the meeting—also the "news." Put this in your post card album."

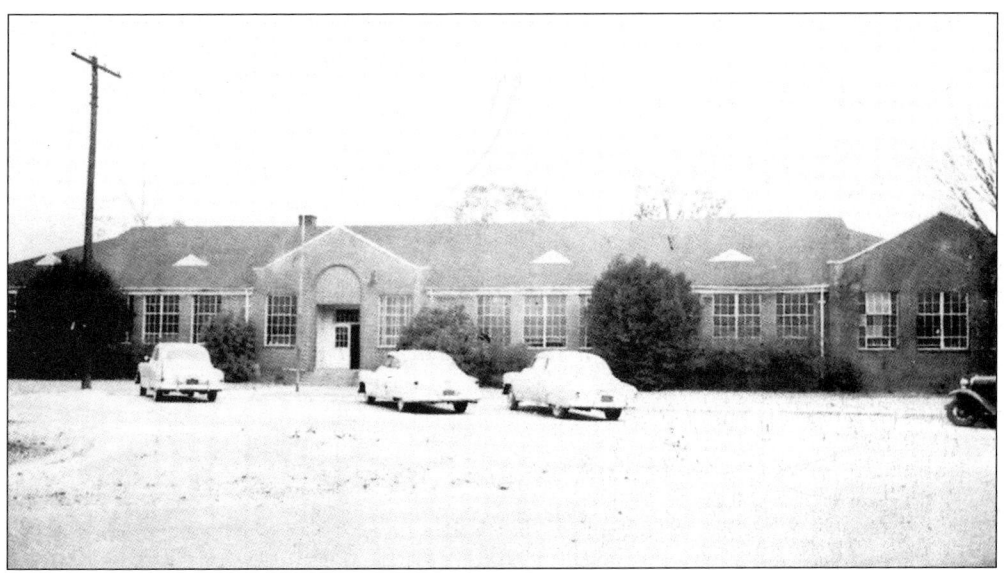

Built in 1936, this 1940s card shows the Tallapoosa High School. It ceased functioning as a high school when the comprehensive Haralson County High School was built. (Courtesy of Michael Miller.)

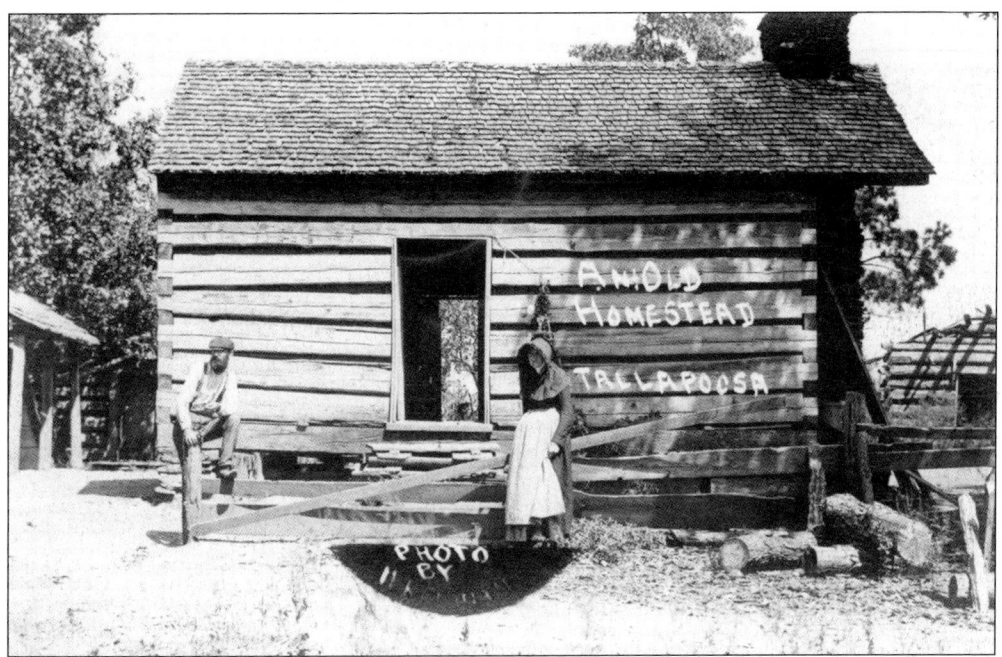

This is a very representative view of the pioneer log cabins that dotted the lands in the 19th century. The card was sent to Mrs. Mitschke of New York City from Elizabeth Schneider and was mailed from Tallapoosa in March 1910. It appears to be written in German. A large European population had moved to the Tallapoosa area during the heyday of the land speculations and vineyards.

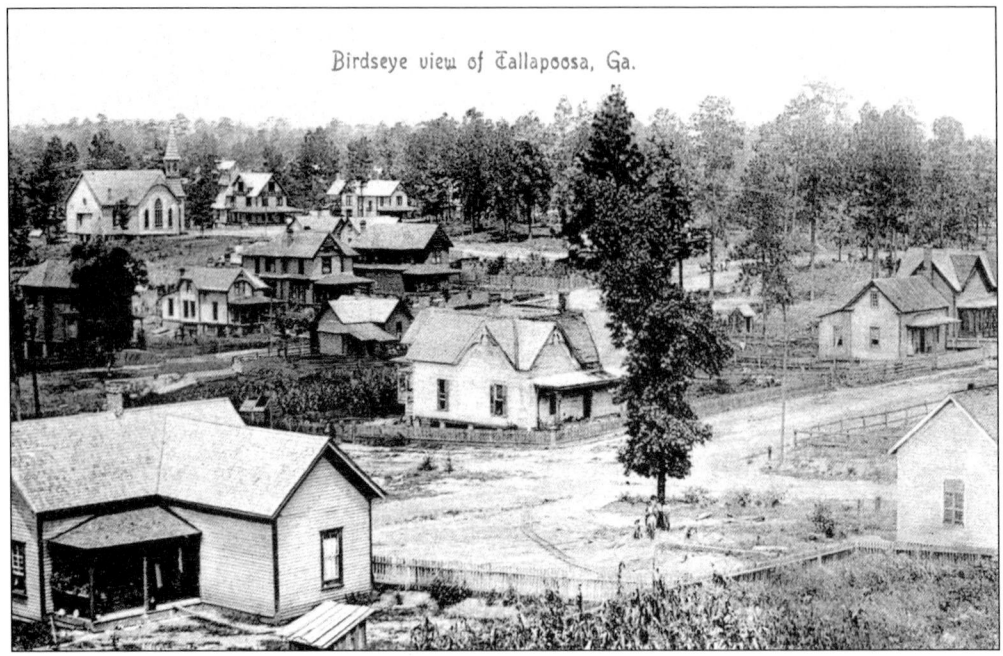

This is an early bird's-eye view of Tallapoosa, Georgia. The vintage view shows many homes around 1910 along with what appears to be the Baptist church in the upper left corner.

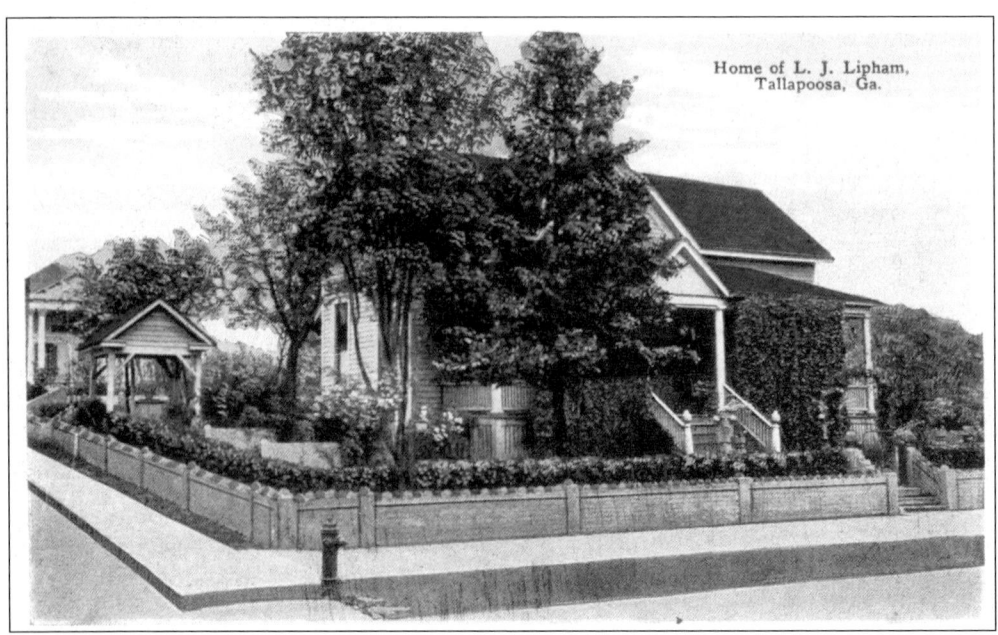

This is a view of the home of L.J. Lipham of Tallapoosa.

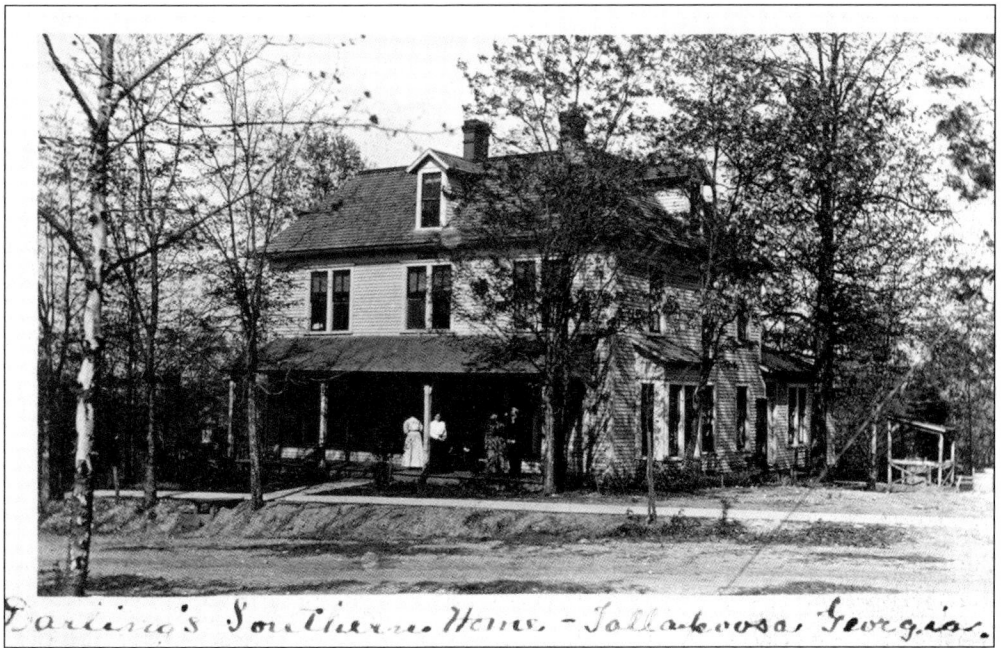

The caption on this card reads, "Darling's Southern Home—Tallapoosa, Georgia." Family members are enjoying the front porch. Note the covered well to the right of the house. (Courtesy of Gary Doster.)

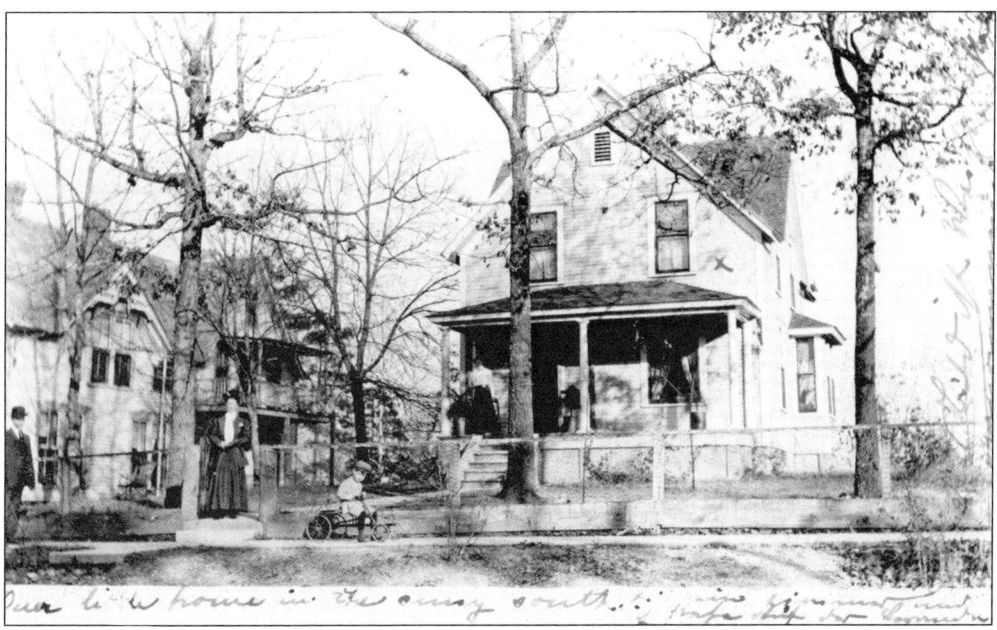

"Our little home in the sunny south" is the caption of this card. The image features very properly dressed individuals with a child on his tricycle. The card was mailed in February 1910 to Mrs. Mitschke of New York City from Elizabeth Schneider. The back of the card appears to be written in German.

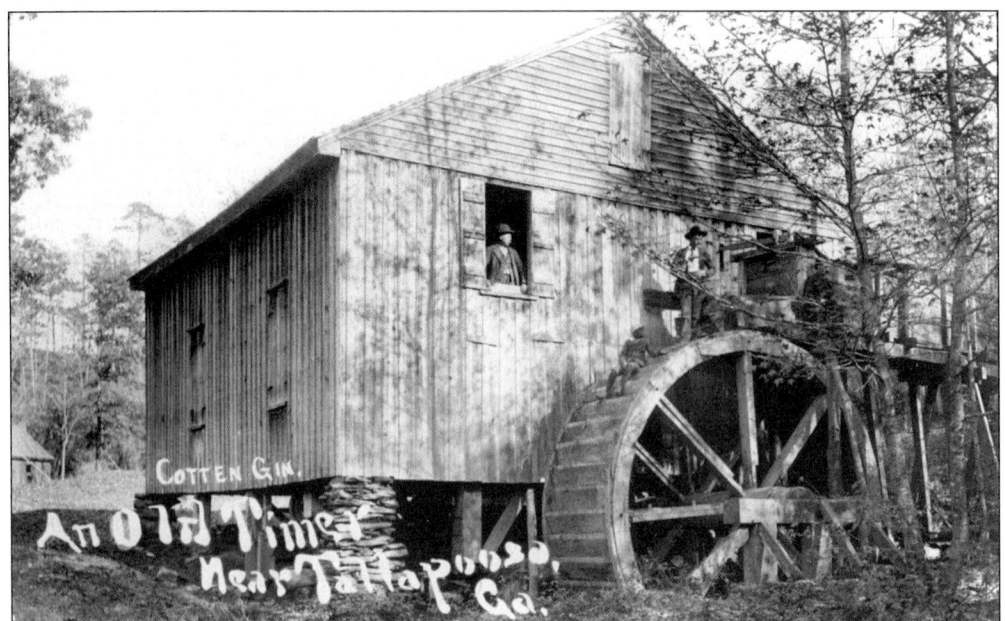

"Cotton Gin, An Old Timer Near Tallapoosa, Ga." was scratched on the negative of this old postcard from c. 1910. (Courtesy of Gary Doster.)

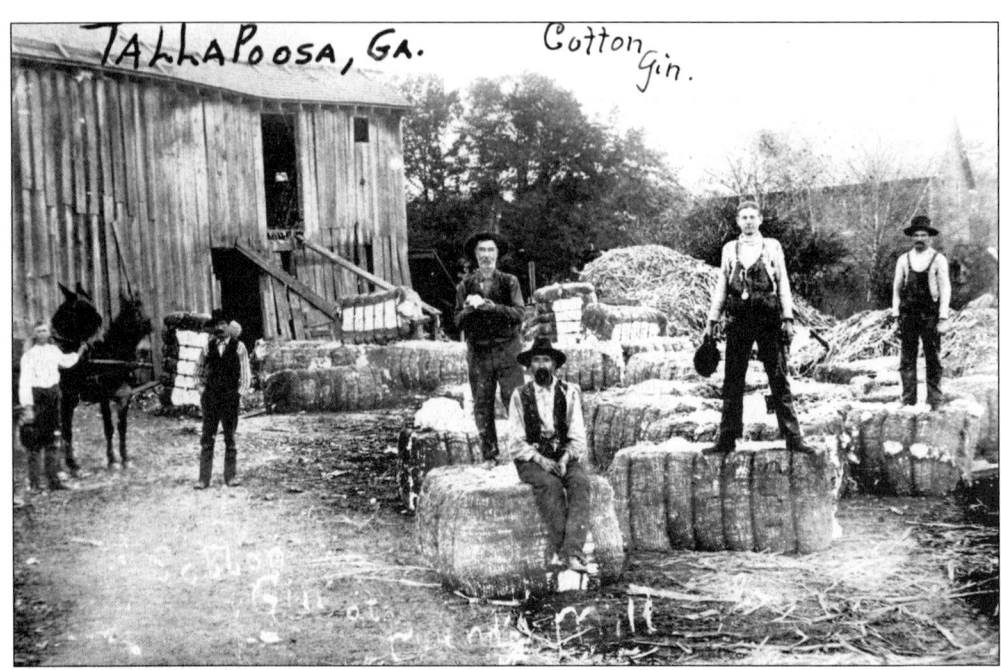

A note on the back of this card, which was sent in October 1909, reads, "All have bad colds but otherwise feeling fine. Leave here next Tuesday. Simpson." The writing at the top of the card appears to have been written much later; however, scratched and barely legible at the bottom of the card are the words, "Cotton Gin at - Mill."

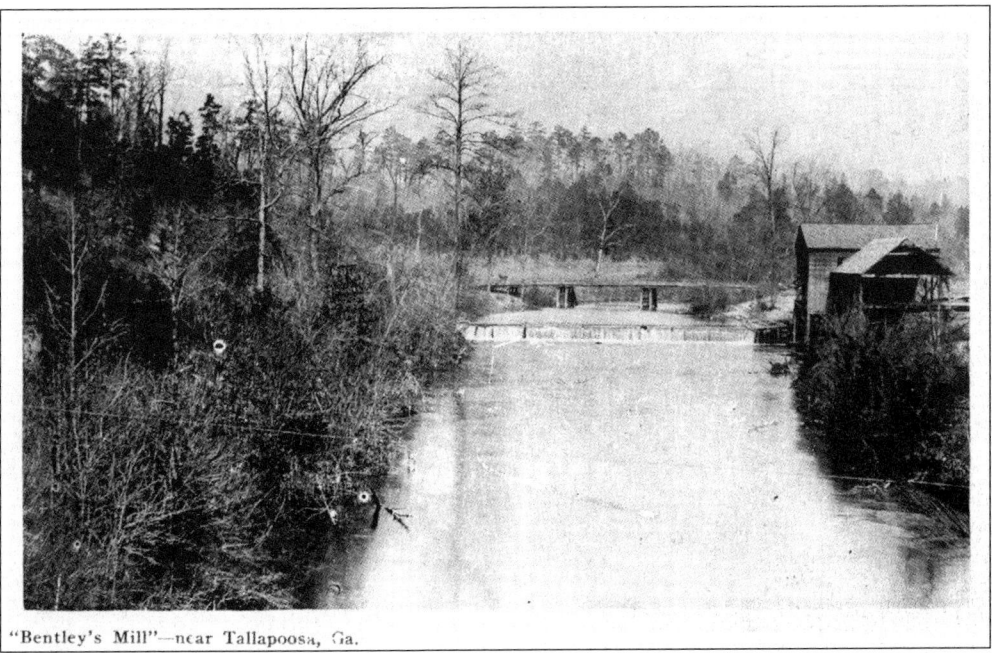

"Bentley's Mill"—near Tallapoosa, Ga.

Mailed in the 1910s, from Tallapoosa, this is a vintage image of Bentley's Mill. A wooden bridge can be seen beyond the spillway. J.M. Hooper built the mill in the 1880s, and the area around the mill became known as Hooper. John W. Bentley later owned the mill.

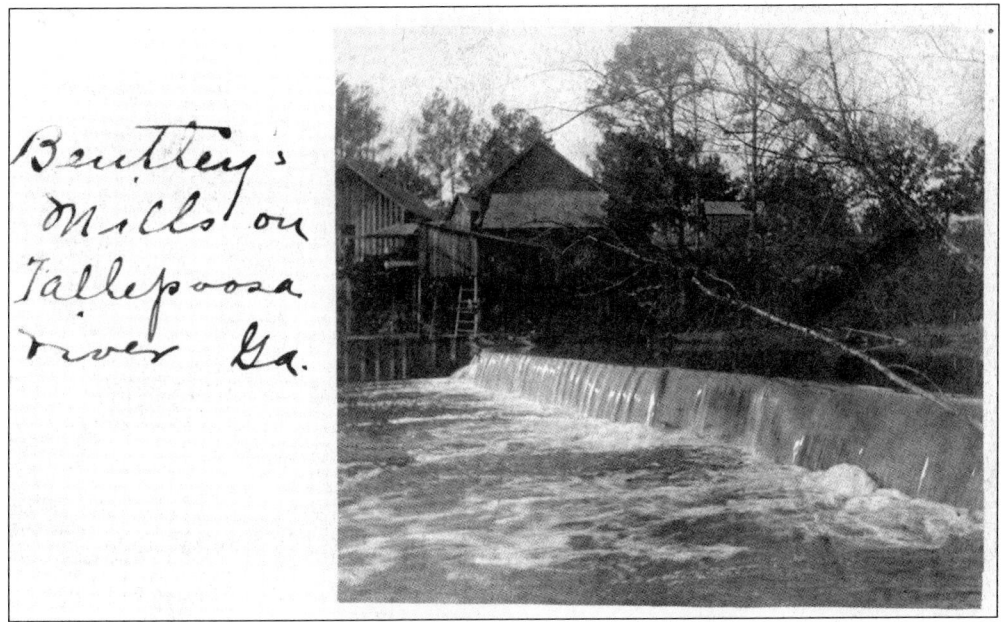

Looking across the spillway at Bentley's Mill on the Tallapoosa River is the subject of this card. The mill ground corn and wheat and was a local meeting area for family gatherings.

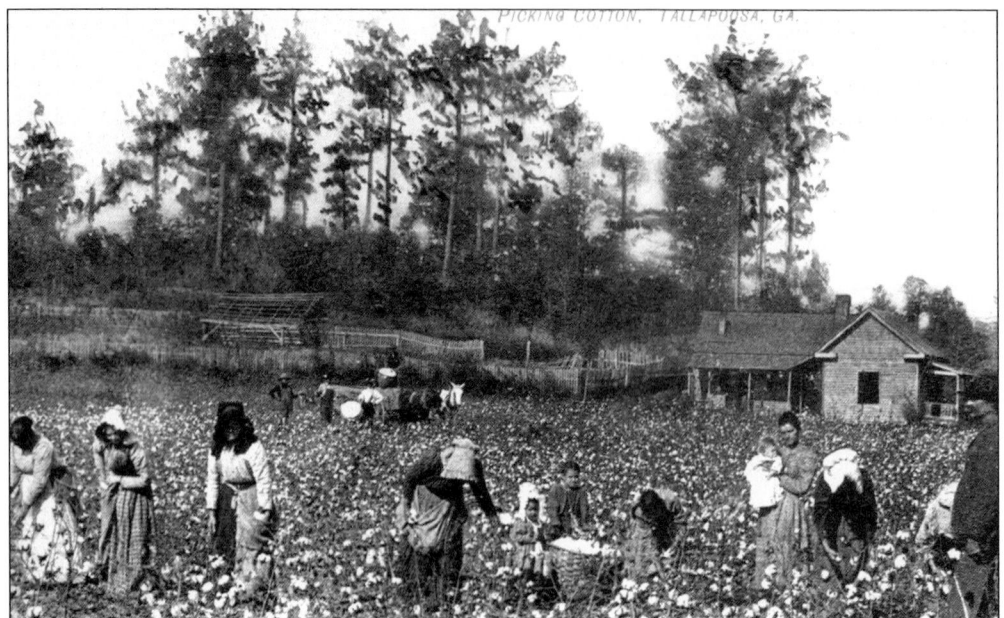

This vintage image predates 1904 and features a number of women and children picking cotton. Note the large cotton bags the women carry to collect the cotton, and the bonnets they wore to help keep the sun out of their eyes. The men in the wagons in the background appear to be gathering the cotton from the fields.

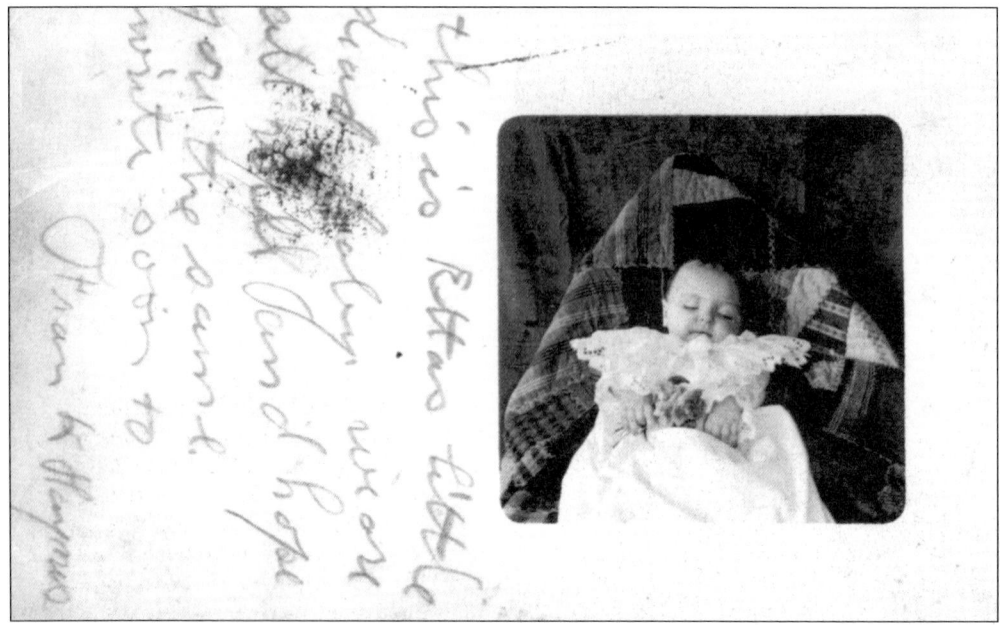

Known today among collectors as a "death card," family members often sent images of dead loved ones. Although not a practice seen today, when one remembers what was available to people of the time, it is understandable that loved ones wanted to share news, good or bad. The card was written by Frank Haynes, the youngest brother of the baby's mother, Etta Haynes, and was sent to the great aunt of the baby, Cora Etta Allen of Tallapoosa. (Courtesy of Donald Allen.)

Addressed to Miss Alice Trimble in 1908, this note is from E.C.G. The photo by Gersbeck is of three African-American children on a donkey in Tallapoosa. (Courtesy of Gary Doster.)

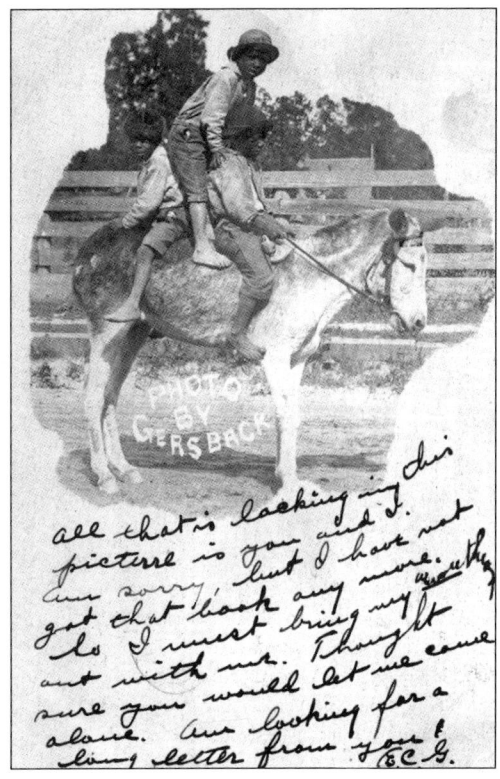

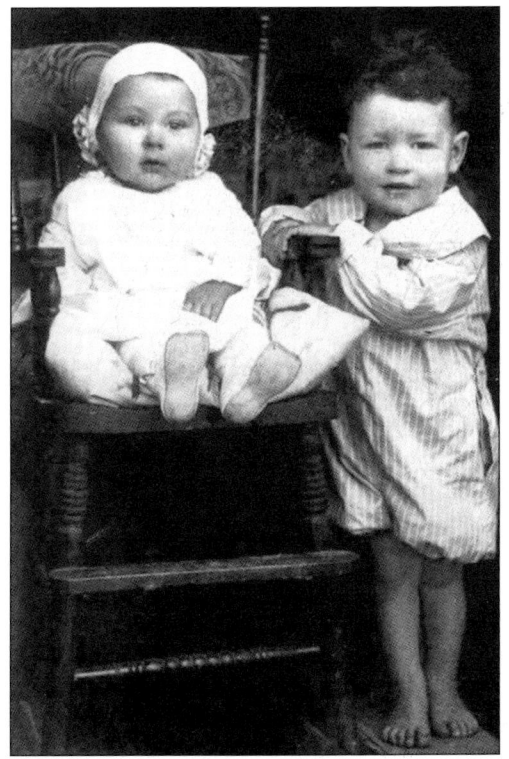

Kenneth L. Carroll (left), born on July 30, 1920, in Haralson County, and Warren Opal Carroll (right), born on December 27, 1918, in Carroll County, were the first two sons of McAllister Carroll and Ollie M. Warren. They were the grandsons of James Moses Blackburn and Minnie Lee McBurnett, and William Gabriel Warren and Drewry Melvina Silvey. The picture was taken about 1920, and the Carroll and Warren families were long-time residents of the Jake-Buncombe and Smithfield area. (Courtesy of Betty Jo Parsons.)

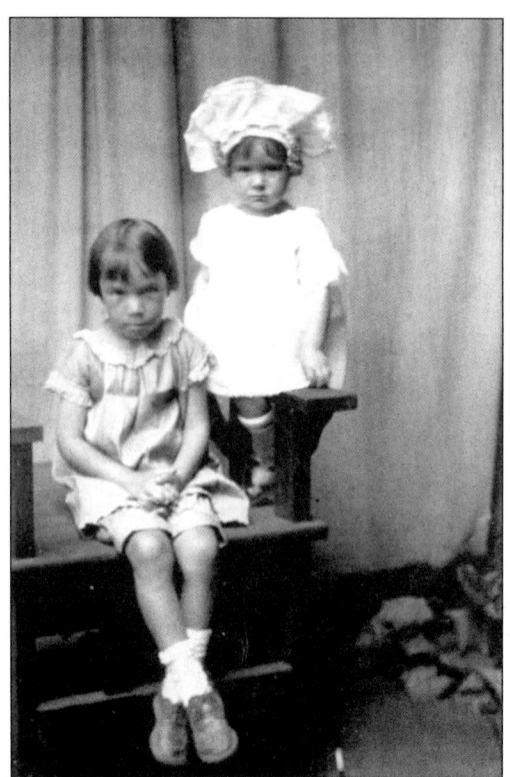

Pictured are Henry Lawton Carroll and Lallie Morris's daughters, Clarice (left) and Gladys Carroll (right). The girls' grandparents were James Moses Blackburn Carroll and Minnie Lee McBurnett. Clarice was born on May 19, 1920, and married Ralph L. Peacock on December 16, 1939. Gladys was born on July 22, 1923, and married Clarence N. Daniell on September 16, 1940. The J.M.B. Carroll family was a long-time resident of the Jake-Buncombe area. (Courtesy of Betty Jo Parsons.)

Pictured are Eucleod McAllister Carroll and Ollie Melvina Warren's daughters, Betty Jo Carroll (left) and Hilda Melvina Carroll (right). Their grandparents were James Moses Blackburn Carroll and Minnie Lee McBurnett, and William Gabriel Warren and Drewry Melvina Silvey, all of Carroll and Haralson Counties. Betty Jo was born in 1933 in Tallapoosa, and Hilda, with her bright red curls, was born in 1925 in Newnan. (Courtesy of Betty Jo Parsons.)

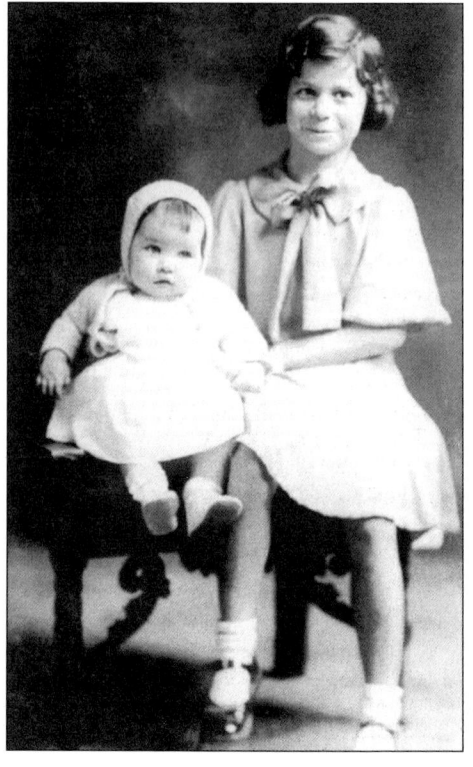

INDEX

Not meant as an inclusive index, it is hoped that this index will assist the reader in finding the major card subjects. Most surnames found in the work are not listed in the index.

A & M School 51-53
Adamson, Charles 14,26
Adamson Hal 14
Alden Courts 85
Armstrong, Lance 128
Baptist Church, Bowdon 16
Baptist Church, Tallapoosa 16,120
Baptist Church, Temple 83
Baptist Church, Villa Rica 90
Barnes family 74,75
Baskin & Baskin 45
Bell Store 80
Bentley's Mil 123
Boatright Hote 100-101
Bonner House 51
Book Dedication 8
Bowdon College 13,14
Bowdon High School 14,15
Bowdon Inn 17
Bremen High School 103
Bremen Hote 100
Buchanan High School 106
Buchanan Street 104
Carroll Café 46
Carroll County Courthouse 25,31-34
Carroll County Jail 36
Carroll family 125,126
Carroll Mote 68
Carrollton Band 71
Carrollton City Hall 34,35
Carrollton Fire Department 31,35
Carrollton Furniture & Under 44
Carrollton High School 50

Carrollton Public School 49,50
Carrollton Pumping Station 69
Citizens Bank, Carrollton 38,39
Community Hospital 89
Confederate Monument 27-30
Copeland family 19
Depot, Bremen 100
Depot, Carrollton 36
Depot, Tallapoosa 107
Depot, Temple 82
Depot, Villa Rica 88
Dixie Glass Works 113
Dixie Street 62,63
Dixie Mote 67
Farmers Bank 99
First Baptist Church, Carrollton 55
First Christian Church, Carrollton 59
First Methodist, Bremen 102
First Methodist, Tallapoosa 117
First National Bank, Carrollton 40-42
Folds Motor Company 45
Halycon Club 42
Hamilton College 98
Haralson County Courthouse 105,106
Haralson Hote 101
Haynes family 124
Hayward, Susan 76
Hotel Carrollton 66
Hotel Clifton 65,66
Hutcheson's Ferry 94
J. R. Holt Drug Company 46
Kennedy Chape 59
Kline Court 67

Lee family 92
Lithia Springs Hotel 113-115
Lovvorn House 17
Mandeville Mills 47
Maple Street 61
Maple Street School 48
Marchman's Pharmacy 102
Masons 43,44
M. E. Church, Bowdon 15
M. E. Church, Carrollton 27,56,57
McIntosh, Chief William 2,7
Methodist Church, Villa Rica 91
Monarch Hote 115
Newnan Street 60
Oak Street 104
Pate family 95,96
Peoples Bank 38,39
Presbyterian Church, Carrollton 58
Presbyterian Church, Villa Rica 91
Price family 18,23,24
Rome Street 61
Roopville Baptist Church 79
Roopville Hardware 79
Roopville Trading Post 78
Round Barn 86
Rowell family 20
Sewell Manufacturing 102
Shirey's Mote 68
Southland Hote 64,65
Sunset Hills 70
Tabernacle Church 56
Tallapoosa Hote 108,111,112,116
Tallapoosa Public School 117-119
Tanner Memorial Hospital 64
Temple Model School 84,85
Tyus 24
U.S. Post Office, Carrollton 37
U.S. Post Office, Roopville 78
Villa Rica Cotton Oil Company 89
Walker family 75
Walker Hote 83
Wessinger family 21,22
West Georgia College 54
West Georgia Regional Library 4,54
Whitesburg High School 94

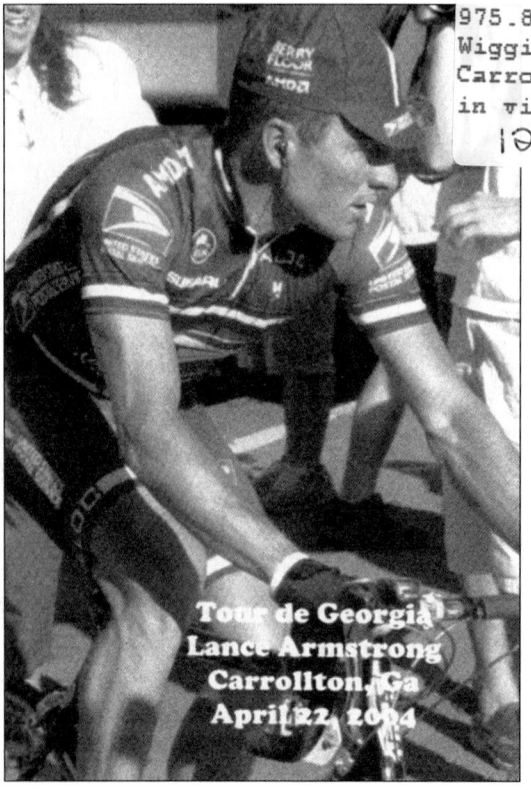

A homemade modern-day postcard features Lance Armstrong, six-time Tour de France Champion, during the Tour de Georgia Bike Race. On April 22, 2004, he and other bicyclists started at the State University of West Georgia and rode through Carroll and Haralson Counties on the way to Rome, Georgia. This one-of-a-kind postcard illustrates how a digital camera, a computer, a printer, a little know-how, and a 23¢ stamp can result in your own card.